Published by
ACADEMIC FOUNDATION
in association with

Institute of Public Enterprise

Revolutionising Corporate Social Responsibility

Towards a Sustainable Tomorrow

Editors

R.K. Mishra

Shulagna Sarkar

Punam Singh

ACADEMIC FOUNDATION

NEW DELHI

www.academicfoundation.org

First published in 2015
by

ACADEMIC FOUNDATION
4772-73 / 23 Bharat Ram Road, (23 Ansari Road),
Darya Ganj, New Delhi - 110 002 (India).
Phones : 23245001 / 02 / 03 / 04.
Fax : +91-11-23245005.
E-mail : books@academicfoundation.com
www.academicfoundation.com

in association with
Institute of Public Enterprise, Hyderabad.

Disclaimer:
The findings/views/opinions expressed in this book are solely those of the authors and do not necessarily reflect the views of the publisher.

Cataloging in Publication Data--DK
Courtesy: D.K. Agencies (P) Ltd. <docinfo@dkagencies.com>

Revolutionising corporate social responsibility : towards a sustainable tomorrow / editors, R.K. Mishra, Shulagna Sarkar, Punam Singh.
pages cm
Contributed articles.
ISBN 9789332701816

1. Social responsibility of business. 2. Social responsibility of business--India. 3. Sustainable development. 4. Sustainable development--India. 5. Industrial laws and legislation. 6. Industrial laws and legislation--India. I. Mishra, R. K., 1948-, editor. II. Sarkar, Shulagna, editor. III. Singh, Punam, editor. IV. Institute of Public Enterprise (Hyderabad, India)issuing body.

DDC 658.408 23

Typeset by Italics India, New Delhi.

Printed and bound by The Book Mint, New Delhi.
www.thebookmint.in

CONTENTS

List of Tables and Figures

Tables

Figures

About the Editors/Contributors

Editors:

R.K. Mishra, Senior Professor and Director, Institute of Public Enterprise (IPE), Hyderabad, is a graduate of International Management Programme, SDA Boccioni, Milan, Italy, and has been a fellow of British Council and Commonwealth Secretariat. He is a member of the UN Task Force on International Taskforce on Standards of Excellence in Public Administration and Education and associated with the United Nations Development Programme (UNDP) project on macroeconomics of poverty reduction carried out by the Reserve Bank of India's (RBI) Indira Gandhi Institute of Development Banking and Research. He has handled assignments for the Ministry of Finance, Ministry of Power, Ministry of Trade and Commerce, Ministry of Heavy Industry and Public Enterprises and Ministry of Disinvestment. He has supervised doctoral research for several universities in management, economics, commerce and public administration. His current interests include: economic reforms, privatisation and restructuring, finance, poverty management and good governance.

Shulagna Sarkar, Assistant Professor, IPE, has completed her PhD from Rashtrasant Tukadoji Maharaj Nagpur University (RTMNU) and MBA (HR) from Kavikulguru Institute of Technology and Science (KITS), Ramtek. She is also a law graduate. She is the Jt. Coordinator for the Centre for Corporate Social Responsibility at IPE. She has published a book in the area of training needs based on competency mapping. She has presented papers at national and international conferences. She is involved in teaching, research activities, training and consultancy at the institute. Her areas of interest include: corporate social responsibility and sustainable development, competency management, and training and development.

Punam Singh, Assistant Professor, IPE, is MBA from Indian School of Mines, Dhanbad. She is currently pursuing her PhD from Jawaharlal Technological University (JNTU), Hyderabad, in the area of Compensation Management. She is the Coordinator for the Centre for Corporate Social Responsibility at IPE. She has presented papers at national and international conferences. She is involved in teaching, research activities, training and consultancy at the institute. Her current interests include: corporate social responsibility, compensation and performance management, and training and development.

Contributors:

A. Sridhar Raj, IPE, Hyderabad.

Anupam Anand, Hindustan Copper Limited, Kolkata.

Arun Kumar Rath, Centre for Corporate Governance & Social Responsibility, International Management Institute, New Delhi.

Bibhu Prasad Mohanty, Independent Corporate Social Responsibility Consultant, Bhubaneswar, Odisha.

Dharmesh Pushpa Dhawankar, Department of Mass Communication, RTM Nagpur University.

Dhirendra K. Vajpeyi, Department of Political Science, University of Northern Iowa, Iowa, USA.

Dillip Kumar Kar, GMR Foundation, Hyderabad.

H. Urdhin, University of Technology, Mauritius.

Jibitesh Rath, NMDC Limited, Hyderabad.

K. Padachi, University of Technology, Mauritius.

K. Seetah, University of Technology, Mauritius.

Kirti Chawla, Eden Information Services (S) Pte. Ltd, Singapore.

Krithika Ram, Icreon Communications Ltd., Noida.

M. Jothi, Faculty of Science and Humanities, SRM University, Kattankulathur, Tamil Nadu.

Manosmita Mahapatra, Department of Sociology, Pondicherry University, Puducherry.

P. Shyam, NMDC Ltd., Hyderabad.

Rajender Singh Sajwan, Hindustan Copper Limited, Kolkata.

Roopinder Oberoi, Department of Political Science, Kirori Mal College, University of Delhi.

Subhransu Panda, Rural Lending, Axis Bank, Bangalore.

Sweta Saurabh, Symbiosis Law School, Noida.

Tulsi Jayakumar, S.P. Jain Institute of Management & Research, Mumbai.

Preface

> We need business to understand its social responsibility, that the main task and objective for a business is not to generate extra income and to become rich and transfer the money abroad, but to look and evaluate what a businessman has done for the country, for the people, on whose account he or she has become so rich.
>
> —Vladimir Putin

Issues relating to corporate social responsibility (CSR) have taken a centre stage in modern societies as organisations worldwide have realised the importance of CSR as a strategic tool for a sustainable business. CSR is an organisation's obligation to consider the interests of their customers, employees, shareholders, communities and the ecology, and to consider the social and environmental consequences of their business activities. By integrating CSR into core business processes and stakeholder management, organisations can achieve the ultimate goal of creating both social value and corporate value.

In the 21st century marketplace, businesses are increasingly showing signs of becoming conscious of ethics and human rights as well as being economically, environmentally and socially active and responsible. Social responsibility has become one of the most talked areas in today's world. With the growing concern for the triple bottom line approach and introduction of CSR as a part of Companies Act, 2013, in India, the world awaits a serious discussion in the area of social responsibility to identify the areas of intervention for developing community, environment and business at large.

The book presents an understanding of international perspective on CSR by discussing legislations applicable to various countries. It also discusses the highlights of Companies Act, 2013, and its applicability to Indian industries. The editors have pulled different strings of CSR from approaches to CSR and sustainable business, legal implications relating to CSR, social audit and reporting, and best practices in public and private sector. Considering the strategic importance of CSR that permeates into the society through various business processes of companies and the potential implication, this volume focuses on the dynamics of CSR as a strategic tool for sustainable business. It discusses the need for concern and needed initiatives towards social responsibility. The book will be of interest to academics, researchers, practitioners, consultants, corporate managers, governments, non-governmental organisations (NGOs) and international organisations with special interest in issues relating to corporate responsibility and sustainable business.

We take this opportunity to thank the contributors and our Conference Advisory Committee including Shri S.K. Acharya, Director-HR, Neyvelli Lignite Corporation, Neyvelli India, Shri Anupam Anand, Director-HR, Hindustan Copper Ltd., Kolkata, Prof P.D. Jose, Associate Professor, Indian Institute of Management (IIM)-Bangalore, Dr Stuart Locke, Professor, Waikato Management School, New Zealand, Dr Geeta Duppati, Senior Lecturer, Waikato Management School, New Zealand, Shri Shankar Rajagopalan, Regional Head EHS&S, Hospira Healthcare, Chennai, Dr Arun Kumar Rath, Professor & Chairman, Centre for Corporate Governence and Social Responsibility, International Management Institute (IMI), New Delhi. We also acknowledge the effort of Paper Review Committee in bringing out this edition. We hope that this book will provide greater insights and pave way in linking CSR to sustainable business.

— R.K. Mishra, Shulagna Sarkar and Punam Singh

SECTION I

Corporate Social Responsibility and Legislations

1

R.K. MISHRA • SHULAGNA SARKAR
PUNAM SINGH

Decoding Corporate Social Responsibility

The Global Perspective

Introduction

Corporate social responsibility (CSR) as an agenda has matured rapidly, driven by demand for greater accountability by corporate to society. CSR began with focus on how business leaders manage their organisations to benefit the society and how they return to the local communities. Global organisations by the nature and its vast expanse are now expected to take up CSR activities in its areas of operation irrespective of the boundaries. CSR has been interpreted differently in various nations. It has been observed that CSR initiatives in developing countries are addressing more on social issues like poverty reduction, employment generation, education, health and environment. However, the rest of the world considers CSR more as conservation of nature-based initiatives. There is a large difference in the nature of initiatives considered under CSR in developed *versus* developing countries.

Irrespective of the acceptance and presence of CSR across the world, Levitt (1958) set up a base for the debate about the social responsibility of business where it is emphasised that 'government's job is not business, and business's job is not government'. Friedman (1970) expressed the same sentiment and added that the mere existence of CSR was a signal of an agency problem within the firm. Countries have debated that whether CSR should be mandated by introducing it as a part of legislation or not. CSR by its definition is interpreted to remain voluntary and market-driven.

Reich (1998) argues that the government should act as arbiter of business responsibility in society. This view of government as arbiter of business responsibilities to society is reinforced by another argument that sees government as helping business to achieve corporate social responsibility through regulation, control and enforcement. This view is driven from experience in Scandinavian countries (Broberg, 1996). The model of non-shareholder interests' representatives is also extensively used in Scandinavia with particular emphasis on employee representation. This model is also imposed by state regulation and necessitates the representation of employees, the local community, consumers and the environment, in the firm's meetings (Broberg, 1996).

The concern of CSR being mandated may lead some individuals and interest groups being in a favourable position whereas others may not. The idea of legislating on company's CSR activities grabs away the essence of CSR and its successful implementation. There is a less possibility of raising standards through standardisation, as this would remove the competitive incentive driving forward CSR activity and would also place an unmanageable burden on organisations. There is large possibility of CSR processes and practices leading to more corruption in such scenario.

Believing in the voluntary nature of CSR, a large number of countries have made reporting mandatory. The support extended from government or legislations in various countries are distinctly different. Irrespective of the arguments by number of researches, the fact cannot be changed that the role of government is more of an enabling entity to more structured CSR implementation.

The paper aims at identifying the interpretations of CSR across various developing and developed countries. The paper explains the need for international indexes and compares few of them. The paper also shares a model for enhancing the role of government in enabling CSR and making a difference to the people, society and world at large.

Methodology: The paper is based on secondary data collected on legislation documents of eight countries. These documents have been majorly studied to identify the thrust areas emphasised by the legislation. CSR initiatives of companies, sustainability reporting of companies, CSR policy document and sustainability policy document were studied in details. The findings have been tabulated in Table 1.1.

CSR: Global Perspectives

Comparative studies of CSR are relatively rare, certainly as contrasted with other related fields, such as comparative corporate governance or comparative corporate law. This is to be expected in a field, CSR, that is still 'emergent' (McWilliams *et al.*, 2006). Literature review talks about the lack of constituent definition of CSR. This lack of consistency of CSR definitions across studies makes it difficult to evaluate and compare the findings from different studies because they usually refer to different dimensions of CSR. In the backdrop of the above concern, an attempt has been made to study CSR in an international perspective and try to understand the approach to CSR adopted across the world.

History reveals the journey of legislations supporting social agendas. During the 1970s, most social issues became public policy matters and legislations were passed to address health and safety at work, environmental protection and consumer protection rights. Since the earlier 20th century, European member states had developed legislations to control the relationship between employee and the firm, health and safety at work, issues of environmental interest, discrimination and equal opportunities at workplace. Across Europe, state-owned companies were created to pursue commercial and social objectives, whereas private sector companies were allowed to pursue their commercial objectives almost exclusively. Legislation, regulation and taxation have been the favourable tools employed by government to promote and protect social objectives.

In Britain and the United States (US), new laws were introduced and new agencies were created like the Department of Environment and Environmental Protection Agency respectively. Corporations responded positively to the new legislation realising, first that environmental policy could not be formulated without their expertise, and secondly, that a uniform set of national regulations would provide 'a level playing field' for business (Carroll, 1991).

In the UK, the first real law of CSR is based on 'Disclose.' Section 172 of the Companies Act, 2006 emphasises on environmental, social and economical sustainability by redefining the duties of the director. Even though the act does not make spending or implementing CSR activities mandatory, the duties of director to promote the success of the company are based on Triple Bottom Line.

> Duty to promote the success of the company (Section 172 of the Companies Act, 2006):
>
> A director of a company must act in the way he considers, in good faith, would be most likely to promote the success of the company for the benefit of its members as a whole, and in doing so have regard (amongst other matters) to:
>
> - the likely consequences of any decision in the long term,
> - the interests of the company's employees,
> - the need to foster the company's business relationships with suppliers, customers and others,
> - the impact of the company's operations on the community and the environment,
> - the desirability of the company maintaining a reputation for high standards of business conduct, and
> - the need to act fairly as between members of the company.

Sweden is viewed as a pioneer in the field of CSR. In Sweden, there are no specific regulation systems in place concerning CSR conducted by companies in the country. There are however accounting practices that affect CSR to some extent. Irrespective of any specific regulation concerning CSR, in 2013 Sweden topped the RobecoSAM Country Sustainability Ranking. Sweden became the first country to demand sustainability reports from state-owned enterprises. The reports have to comply with guidelines from the Global Reporting Initiative (GRI). About half of all the private companies that report on sustainability use GRI as a way of communicating CSR-efforts (PWC, 2010).

Emerging markets such as Brazil, China and South Africa have become forerunners in CSR reporting in the developing world in terms of their involvement in CSR-related activities in order to promote the listed companies' credibility, transparency and endurance. The Johannesburg Stock Exchange was the first emerging market stock exchange to create a socially responsible investing (SRI) index in 2004.

China's policy vision during mid-2000s was building 'a harmonious society' which was adopted as a policy mandate by the Central Committee of the Communist Party in 2006. This policy focused on harmonious and scientific development and motivated the enactment of new labour and environmental legislation and the incorporation of CSR into the 2006 revision to Chinas' Company Law. Although its meaning is much debated, Article 5 of the Company Law now provides that mainland Chinese companies shall comply with the laws and administrative regulations, social morality and business morality and bear social responsibilities. (Gongsifa, 2005). China has also encouraged CSR reporting in guidelines released through the Shanghai and Shenzhen Stock Exchange.

A number of studies have compared the CSR practices and have come up with very significant difference in their approach to CSR. Matten and Moon (2004) have compared CSR in Europe *versus* in the US, and have proposed a conceptual framework of 'explicit' *versus* 'implicit' CSR. They defined explicit CSR as that seen in the US, where companies volunteer to address important social and economic issues through their CSR policies, in significant part because of less stringent legal requirements than in Europe for issues such as health care provision, employee's rights and environmental protection. In contrast, in Europe and the UK, responsibility for these issues is undertaken as part of a company's legal responsibilities, and thus CSR is 'implicit' in the way the company does business. Studies consistently find that reporting rates are highest in Europe, followed by Japan, and with the US showing the lowest rates of reporting among comparable companies (Kolk, 2003; KPMG, 2005).

Maignan and Ralston (2002) also show variance across these four industrialised Organisation for Economic Co-operation and Development (OECD) countries in the principal motivations for CSR, whether these were mostly performance driven, as in the UK, an extension of their core company values, as in the US, or a combination of performance-driven, values-driven, and stakeholder-driven such as was in the case of Dutch and French firms. Lastly, stakeholders' pressure on companies to address CSR issues also differed across countries. Maignan and Ralston (2002) show that communities and consumers were the primary stakeholder drivers in the UK while customers and regulators were more salient in France and the Netherlands.

Government in developing countries are beginning to view CSR activities as a means to enhance sustainable development strategies, as a component of their national competitiveness strategies to compete for foreign direct investment and to position their exports globally and to improve poverty-focused delivery of public policy goals. Thus from the literature, we can conclude that CSR practices/initiatives and approaches are influenced by a number of factors such as national and international legislations, non-governmental organisation (NGO) activism, stakeholder influence, national culture and top management team orientation towards responsible business.

According to Dossing (2003), three generations of CSR are generally thought to have evolved. The first focused on short-term corporate interests and motives; the second on long-term success strategies; and the present third generation is aimed at addressing the role of business in matters essentially within the public domain, such as poverty, exclusion and environmental degradation.

Governments are beginning to view CSR and codes of conduct as a cost-effective means to enhance sustainable development strategies, and as a component of their national competitiveness strategies to compete for the 'right' type of foreign direct investment (FDI) inflows and to position their exports globally. It is realised that the emergent 'soft law' and the efforts to make it part of corporate practice have emanated from public international bodies and NGO efforts. Laws on CSR can be categorised as emerging from three sources: public international instruments, NGO guidelines and domestic legislation relating to CSR.

Public International Instruments

The most influential public international CSR instruments are the OECD Guidelines, the UN Global Compact and the 1998 International Labour Organization (ILO) Declaration on Fundamental Principles and Rights at Work. The OECD was a pioneer in developing the concept of CSR which established a set of guidelines for multinational enterprises in 1976. OECD Guidelines for multinational enterprises elaborate on the principles and standards for responsible business conduct for multinational corporations. These guidelines were recently updated in 2011. They cover areas such as employment, human rights, environment, information disclosure, combating bribery, consumer interests, science and technology, competition and taxation. They contain defined standards for socially and environmentally responsible corporate behaviour, and also provide procedures for resolving disputes between corporations and communities or individuals adversely impacted by business activities.

In addition to the OECD's 30-member countries, 11 observer countries have endorsed the guidelines. The 11 observer countries are: Argentina, Brazil, Chile, Egypt, Estonia, Israel, Latvia, Lithuania, Peru, Romania and Slovenia. The involvement of the European Union (EU). with CSR commenced in 1995 with the signing of the European Business Declaration against Social Exclusion between the Commission and a group of business leaders. The publication of the Commission's CSR Green Paper in 2001 resulted in a consultation process with more than 250 organisations and individuals, leading to the release of an official EU strategy document on CSR in July 2002.

NGO Guidelines on CSR

CSR guidelines most often entailing reporting standards, or acting as indicators self-assessment mechanism or are a combination of the both. Social Accountability 8000, Global Sullivan Principles, The Caux "Principles for Business" issued in 1994 by senior business leaders from Europe, Japan and North America "are a worldwide vision for ethical and responsible corporate behavior and serve as a foundation for action for business leaders worldwide." The principal concerns are, among other issues: social impact of business upon local communities, support for multilateral trade agreements that promote 'judicious liberation of trade,' environmental respect, and avoidance of illicit or corrupt practices, the standard to provide information to investors committed to SRI or other stakeholders, and the most widely known self-performance standard is the GRI that focuses on the economic, environmental and social dimensions of corporate activity, products and services.

Regulation of CSR Through Domestic Legislation

In 2007, the Malaysian government passed a regulation to mandate all publicly listed companies to publish their CSR initiatives in their annual reports on a 'comply or explain' basis. Accordingly, all public listed companies (PLCs) in Malaysia have to either publish CSR information or they need to explain why they should be exempted.

In 2009, Denmark mandated CSR reporting, asking all state-owned companies and companies with total assets of more than €19 million, revenues more than €38 million and more than 250 employees, to report their social initiatives in their annual financial reports. France passed a law called Grenelle II which mandates integrated sustainability and financial reporting for all companies listed on the French stock exchanges, including subsidiaries of foreign companies located in France and unlisted companies with sales revenue of more than €400 million and more than 2,000 employees. Although some CSR standards are mandatory, there are others which comprise of both, mandatory and voluntary standards. In 2006, the British Companies Act mandated all companies listed in the UK to include information about their CSR activities in their annual reports; however, a full length CSR reporting was made voluntary.

In India, a number of initiatives have been taken: the National Voluntary Guidelines for Social, Environmental and Economic Responsibilities of Business (NVGs) accompanied by the *Business Responsibility Reports* mandated by the SEBI for the top 100 companies and the CSR clause within the Companies Act, 2013, are two such instances of the steps taken.

CSR: The Indian Way

Central Public Sector Enterprises (CPSEs) have been undertaking a lot of community development initiative as part of their CSR from their very inception but the approach was not systematic and transparent. Introduction of the CSR as a part of the act have paved a new way for CPSEs in undertaking more relevant and need-based CSR activities leading to inclusive growth. CSR definitely is a concept beyond law but it is expected to be implemented in a systematic, integrated, project-based approach with top management accountability and transparency in terms of reporting is a better approach to sustainable CSR.

CSR Scope and Implementation: Post Companies Act 2013

The CSR provisions of the Companies Act, 2013, seek to create an enabling environment by promoting and facilitating far better connect between businesses and communities. It aims at facilitating deeper thought and longer-term strategies for addressing some of our most persistent social, economic and environmental problems; they will assist in synergising partnerships between corporates, governments, civil society organisations, academic institutions and social entrepreneurs. Business resources can be channeled into a diverse array of programmes to address social, economic and environmental problems and to bring about a sustainable future for all.

Table 1.1

Highlights of the Domestic Legislations of Select Countries

Name of the Country	*Legislation/Programmes With Regard to CSR*	*Thrust Areas*	*Essentialities*	*Disclosure*
Australia	The Australian Securities Exchange, 2014	Environment and social sustainability	Listed companies	Mandatory
	Corporate Social Responsibility & Human Rights, 2008	Fair wages, non-discrimination, work conditions, harassment and other employees rights	All companies	Mandatory
	The Australian Sustainable Asset Management(SAM) Index, 2005	To assess the corporate CSR voluntary activities	All industries	Voluntary
Canada	The Environmental Protection Act,1999	"An Act respecting pollution prevention and the protection of the environment and human health in order to contribute to sustainable development."	All companies	Voluntary
	Social Venture Connexion, 2013	Connect capital seeking social enterprise (socially responsible investment) and accredited investors	Social companies	Voluntary
	GOC announced its intention to make CSR reporting mandatory from 2015.	Transparency of payments they make to government	Mining industry	Mandatory
US	Morningstar Socially Responsible Investment Index (MS-SRI) 2003	Social responsibility	All listed companies	Mandatory
	1986 Emergency Planning and Community Right-to-Know Act (EPCRA)	to inform citizens of toxic chemical releases and waste management activities in their areas	All manufacturing companies	Mandatory
	Regional Greenhouse Gas Initiative, 2008	Greenhouse Gas emissions (energy Conservation and Renewable energy)	Power plants	Voluntary

Contd...

.contd...

Argentina	National Labour Law No. 25.877, regarding Social Balance, 2004	Social impact	More than 300 workers	Mandatory
	Glacier Law, 2010	Environment	Mining companies	Mandatory
	Environment & Climate Change Law 2014	Sustainable Development	All companies	Obligatory
China	Shenzhen Stock Exchange Social Responsibility Guidelines for Listed Companies, 2006	Social responsibility	All listed companies in SZSE 100 index (100 companies)	Mandatory
	Shanghai Stock Exchange, 2008	Protection of employee health and safety, quality control of the company products, and promoting a sustainable environment and ecosystem	Companies listed in both domestic and overseas markets, financial companies	Mandatory
	The State-owned Assets Supervision and Administration Commission of the State Council (SASAC) guidelines 2008	Social and environmental aspects of enterprises	State-owned enterprises directly under the central government	Mandatory
	Consultation Conclusions on Environmental, Social and Governance Reporting Guide, 2012	Social and environment: workplace quality, environmental protection, operating practices, and community involvement	Listed	Comply or explain' basis of reporting from 2011
Myanmar	The Environmental Conservation Law 2012	Environment	All especially oil and gas	Voluntary
Maldives	The Nasheed Administration, in 2010	Leasing islands for tourism and other developments	Tourism sector	Mandatory
	The UN Anticorruption Convention, 2005	Anti corruption	All	
Bhutan	New industrial emission standards set up by the National Environmental Commission, 2013	Environment/ climate change/ community health	Factory	Mandatory

Source: Prepared by Authors.

The latest Companies Act, 2013, reflects on the importance of CSR as part of a firm's business strategy. Section 135 contains 5 sub-section on CSR. Schedule VII of the Companies Act, 2013, lists out the CSR activities. Section 135 (5)–CSR Expenditure states that the board of every company referred to in sub-section (1) shall ensure that the company spends, in every financial year, at least two per cent of the average net profits of the company, made during the three immediately preceding financial years, in pursuance of its CSR Policy, provided that the company shall give preference to the local area and areas around it where it operates, for spending the amount earmarked for CSR activities. Provided further that if the company fails to spend such amount, the board shall, in its report made under clause (o) of sub-section (3) of Section 134, specify the reasons for not spending the amount. Corporates are now required to adopt the 'Project Mode' to execute their CSR programmes. An activity will qualify as a project when it includes the following:

Table 1.2

Decoding Section 135 of Companies Act, 2013

Challenges: Interpretation and Implementation of the Section 135 of the Act.	*Opportunities: The Way Ahead*
Framing of a CSR Policy	A reference document to guide structured CSR implementation in organisation, linking CSR with business strategy.
Board Level CSR committee	Strategic focus to CSR by incorporating CSR as a part of the structure.
Defining the responsibility of Board	Top management accountability for CSR implementation
Schedule VII	Activities in line with societal and environmental needs.
Mandatory Reporting	Informing the stakeholders the reasons for not spending CSR amount. A way to ensure responsible and continuous CSR spending.
Sustainability Reporting	A way to showcase responsible business practices to stakeholders, transparency in spending, knowing the impact of company's activities.
Implementing Partners	Need for capacity building initiatives at all levels: corporate, NGOs, government and academic institutions.

Source: Same as Table 1.1.

- Duration of Project.
- Amount allocated to the project.
- Start Date/End Date.
- Monitoring and Documentation.
- Objective Evaluation.
- Impact Assessment.

International Indexes: The Need

As businesses today are not bounded by boundaries, it is essential that companies are recognised for the act that they initiate. Companies are operating in different nations and are thus governed by the local act and based on which their CSR initiatives vary. It is important to have indexes which evaluates or ranks the companies at a global platform. It is also required that all stakeholders become aware about the company's rank in doing good to the society, environment and to investors. This helps investors and other stakeholders to cautiously think and invest in the company. International indexes makes or breaks an image of the company. An attempt has been made to identify the various indexes across world and also share the parameters for assessing under each of the indexes.

Enabling Role of Legislations

Government is expected to play an enabling role in initiating CSR activities in the country. Government interests in bringing out CSR-focused legislation should be solely for societal development. Areas where government can focus while framing legislations are:

- CSR spending.
- Reporting.
- Monitoring.
- Impact evaluation and assessment.
- Collaborations.
- Tax benefits.

Table 1.3

International Indexes

Index Names	*Process*	*Parameters*
Dow Jones Sustainability	Based on analysis of companies' performance in business ethics, the environment and social issues	Analysis of corporate economic, environmental and social performance, assessing issues such as • Corporate governance, • Risk management, branding, • Climate change mitigation, • Supply chain standards and labour practices.
RobecoSAM Country Sustainability Ranking	Ranks 59 countries (21 from developed and 38 from emerging markets)	Based on 17 environmental, social and governance indicators. Economic dimension: Corporate governance, risk and crisis management, innovation and customer relationships. Environmental dimension: Company's climate strategy, product stewardship or environmental management systems. Social dimension: Human resources development, occupational health and safety, and stakeholder engagement.
FTSE4 Good Index Series (London Stock Exchange subsidiary)	Focus on the environmental, social and governance aspects of the companies	Parameters of the study include: • Human rights, • Relationship with stakeholders, • Environmentally sustainable, • Good labour standards for the company and for supply chain, • Fights bribery and corruption.
Corporate Knights	Global 100 study focuses companies' environmental, social and governance performance	Parameters of the study include: • Carbon dioxide emissions, • Leadership diversity • Taxes paid
Global Cleantech Innovation Index	Based on average between inputs to innovation and outputs of innovation, determined by equally weighted four pillars built from a total of 15 indicators	• General innovation inputs • Entrepreneurial Culture • Government policies • Public R&D spending • Access to private finance • Infrastructure for renewables • Cleantech industry Organisations • Early-stage private investment

contd...

...contd...

		• High impact companies • Environmental Patents • Company revenues • Renewable energy consumption • Late-stage investment and exits • Listed cleantech companies • Employees
Global Reporting Initiative	The GRI guidelines set standards for companies' sustainability reporting. indicators includes Economic, Environmental and Social	Indicators in details include: a) Economic • Results • Market presence b) Environmental • Materials • Energy • Emissions—air and water • Waste c) Social • Work methods and processes • Human rights • Society • Product liability

Source: Same as Table 1.1.

Role of Indian Government in Enabling CSR

In a developing country like India, the CSR provisions of the Companies Act, 2013, seek to create an enabling environment by promoting and facilitating far better connect between businesses and communities. It aims at facilitating deeper thought and long-term strategies for addressing some of our most persistent social, economic and environmental problems. The act also aims to synergise partnerships between corporates, governments, civil society organisations, academic institutions and social entrepreneurs. Even though the act has only been in existence from 2013 applicable from April 2014, there is no valid evidence which clarifies that the regulation has brought in positive changes to the society. Also discussions reveal that as the Companies Act, 2013, makes CSR mandatory, there is a possibility of higher corruption with the large pool of money as CSR expenditure. An estimated 14,358 companies fall into this 'Mandatory' CSR reporting category. CSR activities in the first year would be between ₹20,000 crore plus spent in social welfare (Companies Act, 2013). There is a possibility to measure the impact of the mandatory nature of CSR regulation in another years span.

Role of Government, Corporate and Civil Societies

The crisis at the ground level has made people look for new ways to develop collective action to deal with social demands that cannot be met by the government alone. This has led to the appearance of partnership projects, with governments, companies and civil society organisations working together. CSR has oiled the wheels of these new partnerships, and the CSR literature reflects the clear link between CSR and social partnership (Nelson and Zadek, 2000, Gribben *et al.*, 2001; Kjaergaard and Westphalen, 2001). The challenge for governments is to find a way to design and implement public policy that will generate leadership and partnership-based innovation, seeking to maximise the benefits of these innovations by ensuring their systematic acceptance and application among the wider business community.

Figure 1.1

Role of Government, Corporate and Civil Societies

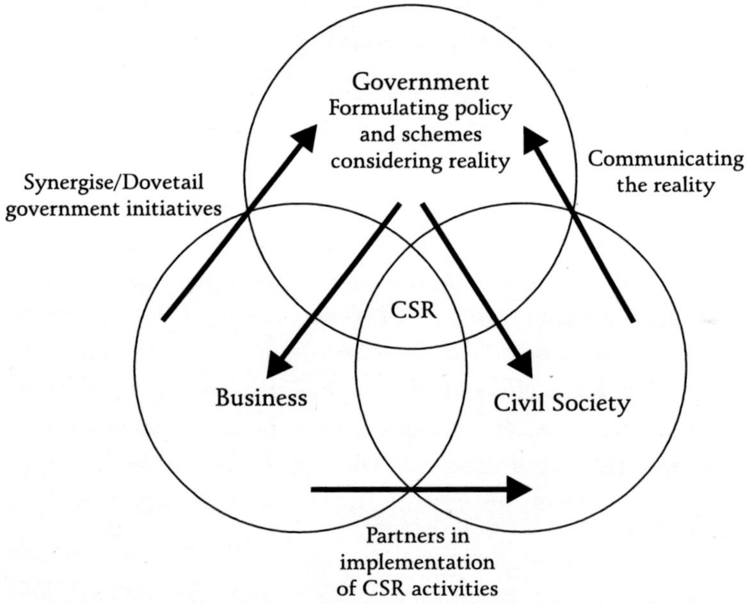

Role of Government

The two main roles played by the government agency in CSR project by the corporation to the community are the role of a supporting agency and as a leader in the community. These roles have assisted in the implementation of the CSR project with the objectives to develop the community involved. At the macro level discussion, government sector is expected to play the roles as the driver of CSR initiatives by the corporation for the benefit of the society (Moon, 2004; Fox *et al.*, 2002).

However, at the micro level the roles are reflected in the implementation strategy which is known among others as public-private partnership (PPP) CSR strategy. The aims of the partnership are to share resources, knowledge and capability between business corporations and the government agency. The government sectors are expected to provide enabling environment to assist and encourage the business corporation to undertake CSR effort as one of the business strategy in the country. The enabling role played by the government sector would refer to four key roles that are mandating, facilitating, partnering and endorsing (Fox *et al.*, 2002).

The role of government in the development of CSR is centred on its role as mediator, facilitator and partner. Government has a critical role to play in strengthening innovation in ensuring an inclusive growth for which it must enforce on CSR policy formulation based on a reality check.

Role of Corporate

With the prolific number of both public and private sector companies in India, there is a huge fund in flow which needs to be channelised appropriately to make a reach to the grass-roots level. The role of corporate is to ensure support to the civil society organisations (CSOs) and also extended an arm to the government for fulfilment of the vision of developed India. The corporate are required to envision CSR as a tool for inclusive society and for sustainable tomorrow. This requires them to formulate a CSR policy in line with their organisational strategy. Corporates need to design CSR projects by understanding the real need of the community and to synergise/dovetail the initiatives of the government towards a sustainable inclusive growth. They have to partner with the CSOs to understand the ground realities and with their help develop a successful implementation model with the involvement of the local government.

Role of Civil Society

The term civil society organisations (CSO) may be wider in scope and include an array of organisations, including NGOs and not-for-profit organisations. Among others, CSOs include trade unions, religious institutions, academic institutions, ethnic tribal groups as well as different charitable organisations and foundation. Civil society has a crucial role to play in strengthening of local institutions and in bringing innovation into government programmes. Government must strongly encourage partnerships with civil society including not only NGOs, but also academic institutions, professional associations and universities. The precise institutional arrangements could vary, depending on the requirement and context, but the need for such partnership needs to be emphasised in the design of programmes. They could be either in-sourcing or out-sourcing types of relationships, so that the synergy of the government and civil society can truly be harnessed.

The role of CSO includes awakening of all stakeholders. CSOs have played a critical role in pushing for CSR globally. Campaigning groups have been key drivers of inter-governmental negotiations, ranging from the regulation of hazardous wastes to a global ban on child labour and the elimination of slavery. The CSOs are also expected to be implementers of CSR initiatives of companies in different spheres, particularly related to community issues. CSOs have a critical role in influencing public policy and opinion, and corporate CSR decisions through advocacy, networking, lobbying and public campaigns, shaping and delivering CSR programmes. Grass-roots CSOs usually are required to have deep knowledge about communities and their needs to enable stakeholder engagement and dialogues.

Conclusion

CSR has gained prominence globally and has been discussed as one of the tools for the corporate sector to contribute to the process of developing the community. Opinion in the CSR world is just as diverse, some countries favouring a legal framework for CSR and others fearing it would destroy the existence. In various countries, governments have adopted CSR only in a reactive way, for example, in response to requirements in export markets. A more proactive stance is appropriate to the overall development of the nation. Where companies do not appear ready to engage with CSR, government needs to take a lead. Government needs to ensure effective governance and a business environment that encourages CSR by providing a functioning legal and regulatory structure, and effective delivery mechanisms for companies to adopt more development-based CSR. This suggests that if there were legislation around CSR, then companies will deliver what the law requires and not more. The most common reason given for why new legislation would set CSR back is the lowest common denominator argument.

At the moment, voluntary CSR is experiencing higher contributions and legislation would wither ethical motivation to its root. In many parts of the world where legal norms are not embedded to CSR, ethical performance is centrally concerned with whether or not the laws which do exist are actually observed in practice. Government should adopt a carrot-led rather than a stick-driven approach to CSR. Legislation in CSR area would simply constrain business activity and reduce CSR to a lowest common denominator.

Discussion about corporates' responsibility to societal cause has grabbed more attention in the context of the Companies Act, 2013, which has made CSR mandatory reporting for Indian corporate. It cannot be denied that in spite of numerous initiatives of government, there is a huge gap between what is being done and what needs to be done? In the backdrop of the Companies Act, 2013, CSR in a collaborative form can make a significant impact on addressing the social sector issues in India. Inspite of the effort, the Indian government is leading development though a corporate-based focus of CSR activities. The world eagerly awaits the impact of the implementation of CSR legislation in India.

References

Broberg, M.P. (1996). "Corporate Social Responsibility in the European Communities: The Scandinavian View", *Journal of Business Ethics* 15: 615-22.

Carroll, B. (1991). "The Pyramid of Corporate Social Responsibility: Towards the Moral Management of Organisational Stakeholders", *Business Horizons*, July- August.

Dossing, H. (2003). "The Business Case for CSR", in *International Chamber of Commerce (ICC) UK, Guide to Global Corporate Social Responsibility* 34.

Friedman, M. (2002). "The Social Responsibility of Business is to Increase its Profits", in L.P. Hartman (ed.), *Perspectives in Business Ethics* (2nd ed.) New York: The McGraw-Hill Companies. (Original work published 1970). pp. 260-640.

Fox, T., H. Ward and B. Howard (2002). *Public Sector Roles in Strengthening Corporate Social Responsibility: A Baseline Study*. Washington, DC: World Bank.

Gribben, C., K. Pinnington and A. Wilson (2001). *Governments as Partners: The Role of the Central Government in Developing New Social Partnerships*. Copenhagen: The Copenhagen Centre.

Kjaergaard, C. and S. Westphalen (2001). *From Collective Bargaining to Social Partnerships: New Roles of the Social Partners in Europe*. Copenhagen: The Copenhagen Centre.

Kolk, A. (2003). "Trends in Sustainability Reporting by the Fortune Global 250". *Business Strategy and the Environment* 12: 279-91.

———. (Forthcoming). "Sustainability, Accountability and Corporate Governance: Exploring Multinationals' Reporting Practices". *Business Strategy and the Environment*.

KPMG (2005). *KPMG International Survey of Corporate Responsibility Reporting 2005*. Amsterdam, the Netherlands: KPMG Global Sustainability Services.

Levitt, T. (1979). "The Dangers of Social Responsibility", in T.L. Beauchamp and N.E. Bowie (eds.) (1979), *Ethical Theory and Business* (pp. 138-41). Englewood Cliffs, NJ: Prentice-Hall. (Original work published 1958).

McWilliams, A., D. Siegel and P. Wright (2006). "Corporate Social Responsibility: Strategic Implications", *Journal of Management Studies* 43: 1-18.

Matten, D. and J. Moon (2004). ""Implicit" and "Explicit" CSR: A Conceptual Framework for Understanding CSR in Europe", in A. Habisch, J. Jonker, M. Wegner and R. Schmidpeter (eds.) (2004), *CSR across Europe* (pp. 335-56). Berlin, Germany: Springer-Verlag.

Maignan, I. and D. Ralston (2002). "Corporate Social Responsibility in Europe and the U.S.: Insights from Businesses' Self-presentations", *Journal of International Business Studies*, 33: 497-514.

Moon, J. (2004). "Government as a Driver of Corporate Social Responsibility: The UK in Comparative Perspective", *International Centre for Corporate Social Responsibility Research Paper* No. 20-2004. Nottingham, UK: Nottingham University Business School.

Nelson, J. and S. Zadek (2000). *Partnership Alchemy—New Social Partnerships in Europe*. Copenhagen: The Copenhagen Centre.

PWC (2010). *CSR Trends 2010 Report*. (Available at: *http://www.corresponsables.com/ sites/ default/files/csr-trends-pwc-2010.pdf*).

Reich, R.B. (1998). "The New Meaning of Corporate Social Responsibility", *California Management Review* 40(2): 8-17.

Documents:

Companies Act, 2013 (India)—Sec 134, Sec 135.

Companies Act, 2006 (UK)—Sec 172.

Gongsifa [Company Law] (promulgated by the Standing Comm. Nat'l People's Cong., 27 October 2005, effective 1 July 1994, amended 1 January 2006), accessed from *http://www. lawinfochina.com*

MCA CSR Guidelines, Retrieved on 18th Feb, 2013 from *http://www.mca.gov.in.* National Voluntary Guidelines.

2

DHIRENDRA K. VAJPEYI
ROOPINDER OBEROI

Embedding Corporate Social Accountability Through Ruggie's Framework (2011)

An Initiative to Plug-in the Corporate Human Rights Contravention

Plugging-in the Loopholes in Responsibility Architecture

The question of whether businesses are purely profit-seeking or as obligated to respond to societal needs is, essentially, a question which had bogged society as a whole and for quite sometime. Business and human rights are often thought to be adversative. Debates about the social obligations of the corporation are also 'hopelessly circular' because "beliefs about what are proper concerns of the business community are themselves social constructs, and have evolved significantly over time in tandem with broader changes in the social and political environment." With the advent of contemporary economic globalisation, the regulatory milieu in which these enterprises functioned has been drastically altered. Corporates were once imagined being creatures of the states that recognised and regulated their existence; these corporates currently are ever more able to systematise their conduct beyond the regulatory span of any state. This chasm between operational and regulatory capacity has shaped an unrelenting response from all quarter at the national and global levels.

Equally at the national and transnational levels, the concern of corporate accountability in sphere of Human Rights currently carries a strong resonance. At the international level, there has been a striking new strategy in the protection of international human rights: "a shift ... from nearly exclusive attention on the abuses committed by governments to close scrutiny of the activities of business enterprises, in particular multinational corporations" (Steven, 2001). Indeed, it has now become trite to declare that corporations have been complicit in infringement of human rights. This complicity takes place within the context of globalisation, deregulation, and the emergence of transnational business enterprises as the "linchpins of the contemporary world economy" (Held, 1999). Articulating the sweeping influence of these transnational network organisations, many deem that they are effectively operating in "quasi-governmental" positions at the global stage (Rondinelli, 2003). It is this location of authority that gives rise to novel obligations of justice for multinational corporations, that is, obligations that have traditionally been associated exclusively with governments. The notion of the quasi-governmental institution inevitably puts the issue of power and authority in the global political economy on the agenda. This is also being termed as 'the neoliberal paradox' which essentially is the (unintended) implicit politicisation of multinational corporations (MNCs) within the reverse process of a combined depoliticisation of the economy and economisation of politics. Put differently, the political and regulatory vacuity in the global economy has led to a tremendous increase of MNCs' political power, and with it, to the implicit politicisation of virtually all its actions, its decisions and, ultimately, its very nature (Wettstein, 2010). This helps render these power associations more perceptible that have conventionally been enclosed and shorn of by the dominant economic liberal ideology. As power always implies corresponding responsibilities, in this context, it is often unproblematic for commanding agents or those who guard and operate in the interests of multinational corporations to refute the reality of any such power than to deal with the moral contract deriving from it. Consequently, with respect to regulation and responsibility, there is noteworthy divergence in the expectations of corporates and human rights activists. Baxi (2006) remarked that "[t]he suffering of impoverished people is irrelevant to the ruling standards of the global capital, which must measure excellence of economic entrepreneurship by standards other than those provided by endless human rights normativity."

Up till now mainly companies' engagement with human rights responsibilities has been through voluntary codes and initiatives. On the contrary, transnational corporations (TNCs) suppose all-pervasive deregulation and appeal for regulation only in those areas where deregulation hampers their capacity to maximise profit. Human rights activists, in contrast, insist extensive regulation in matters affecting public interest, including human rights. They suppose that only states can provide some form of level playing field to the otherwise asymmetrical bargaining positions of TNCs (used interchangeably with MNCs) and the general public, whether they be employees, consumers or otherwise. This discrepancy in positions acquires new bearing with the proposition that states (at least in terms of their sovereignty) are loosing some ground in an era of hyper globalisation.

The present controversy surrounding globalisation takes us back to the work of Karl Polanyi, particularly in *The Great Transformation* (1957). Polanyi believed the historical evidence indicates that self-regulating markets are not sustainable and that markets must be embedded in the social and political order to survive. In a post-modern world system, however, the appropriate social and political order in which markets are to be re-embedded is, as of now, problematic. Barnett and Muller (1974) identified several problems regarding corporate behaviour particularly in the developing world. These problems among others include the now familiar manipulative accounting practices so as to reduce local tax burdens for corporations while leveraging (through political bribery and payoffs) huge investment incentives from local governments and communities (e.g., free land, major infrastructure installations, and assistance and guarantees of a quiescent work force). TNCs as a dominant actor on the global stage extensively affect the enjoyment of human rights. Yet, the existing international human rights regime remains largely state-centric and fails to adequately account for business entities. Human rights abuses in the extractive, security, apparel, finance, natural resource and other sectors in developing countries—with the direct and indirect participation of TNCs—reveal that corporate impunity is an international legal problem Therefore, the debate over the human rights obligations of

MNCs is part of a larger discourse on the role of corporates in the modern era of globalisation.

Unwieldy Ascendancy of Corporates Power in the Era of Globalisation

We are observing the shift where earlier national governments were the overriding and indeed the only players on the international political parquet to a transnational or even global system characterised by an institutional pluralism based on shared and overlapping power and a "fragmentation of political authority" (Kobrin, 2008). While the state certainly remains a significant actor, the system is no longer state centric: non-governmental organisations (NGOs), multinational corporations and international organisations such as the World Trade Organization (WTO) have surfaced as noteworthy transnational actors in world politics (Kobrin, 2008). Peter Drucker in his book *Concept of the Corporation* (1993) portrays the big American corporation as the institution "around which crystallise our social problems and to which we look for their solutions."

Berle and Means (1967) observed that any vacuum in human organisation is invariably filled by power, consequently, the global regulatory vacuum that has opened up between a partial "retreat of the state" (Strange, 1996) and the lack of an adequate institutional response at the global level shift is power to new players entering the political carousel—new "geographic or functional entities," as Mathews *et al.* (1985) puts it, "that might grow up alongside the state, taking over some of its powers and emotional resonance." Neoliberalism innately also deviates from its classical ancestor in one vital aspect and its novelty lies in its explicit acknowledgement of the active role of the state as a facilitator and guarantor of the undistorted working of the "free" market (Ulrich, 2008). In other words, neoliberalism does not intend at the depoliticisation of the economy but rather the economisation of politics. What is depicted as an essential and even curative process by neoliberal ideologues is, in fact, the most enhanced and persistent form of economism: the "displacement of politics by the market." However, MNCs' growing control over our lives is not limited to the contractual relationships of employment. The ongoing economisation of politics and civil society supports the penetration of the public sphere by the undemocratic power structures of the market. Therefore, "we are inescapably surrounded by their (corporate) culture, iconography, and ideology" (Bakan, 2004). The key to almost universal acceptance and recognition of corporate authority lies in what Derber (1998) termed the "corporate mystique." The corporate mystique is a "set of cherished beliefs and illusions" that dictates how we imagine the character and value not only of corporations but also of government, markets, and democracy, as well as the good life and just cohabitation in general. It is at its core "an ideology" that, according to Derber, has effectively disguised the steadily growing power of corporations for decades.

Where 50 years ago, the majority of the corporation operated within a single country, today, we live in a world of some 77,000 transnational companies, with approximately 770,000 subsidiaries and millions of suppliers (Ruggie, 2007). An increasingly large share of global trade is now conducted within MNCs and is internalised within their supply chains. The attribute of economic globalisation that is generally discussed is the approach in which businesses have managed risks and rewards by outsourcing activities that conventionally they assumed themselves.

> To understand the system of dominant power in contemporary society, it is necessary to understand the role that TNCs play within it. TNCs are active in the production of goods and services—in practically all spheres of human activity—as well as in speculation in the financial markets. They engage also in illicit activities and in the gray area between legality and illegality. They play a role front and center in the making of decisions by the powerful and dominate the instruments that enable them to dictate human behaviour, ideas, aspirations and habits. This multi-facetted activity is dominated by a fundamental objective: obtaining maximum profit in minimum time, and, to attain it, TNCs, especially those enjoying the greatest power, will use any means at their disposal, assured as they are of the complicity of a majority of national and international political elites and of the services of many of the intellectual elites as well as of civil society's most-in-

view personalities. This prompts reflection on how human beings "born free and equal in dignity and rights" can recover their decision-making power over their destiny within the framework of a democratic and participative society (Alejandro and Özden, 2011).

In 2010, cross-border non-equity business relationships (through which companies coordinate the activities of other companies without owning a stake in them) approximately generated over $2 trillion of sales. These associations are apparent in a wide range of industries and take diverse forms, including contract manufacturing and farming, service outsourcing, franchising and licensing, management contracts, and supply chains. In the same year, roughly 80 per cent of the 18-21 million workers employed through these arrangements were in developing and transition economies. Capital flows across borders, in the form of mergers and acquisitions (M&As), joint ventures (JVs), and foreign direct investment (FDI), have also developed spectacularly. Some 145 cross-border M&As were reported in South Asia alone in 2011, a 131 per cent increase in value over the previous year, as well as 1,045 green field FDI projects involving TNCs. All sectors are caught up in these relationships. JVs are widespread in the oil and gas and mining sectors, but they have also proliferated in the automobile, telecommunications, technology and apparel sectors. Investment is not simply moving from Organisation for Economic Co-operation and Development (OECD) to non-OECD countries. Chinese investment into the European Union (EU) tripled between 2006 and 2009, and tripled again by 2011 to $10 billion (€7.4 billion). In the last decade, South-South trade and investment has also been on an upward trajectory. Political leaders from Association of Southeast Asian Nations (ASEAN) regularly discuss investment and trade links with their peers in Latin America.

The observations on ever-growing power of corporates have since been corroborated by scientists. In a interdisciplinary study of some 43,000 TNCs (according to the criteria of the OECD), three researchers from the Swiss Federal Institute of Technology in Zurich concluded that 737 TNCs, through dense and complex networks woven across the world among all TNCs, control 80 per cent of the value of all TNCs, while 147 of them (which the researchers call "a tightly-knit core of financial institutions" or "super-entity") control 40 per cent. It is against this background that MNCs have increasingly been described as private political authorities (Cutler, 2001; Kobrin, 2008, Wettstein, 2010).

Naomi Klein's *No Logo* (2000) maps out the processes through which large corporate brands are colonising people's lives. Traditional, cultural and political spaces, she claims, are being removed and replaced by neatly packed branded equivalents. Brands sell to individuals a lifestyle. As she suggests "Nike, Microsoft and Starbucks have sought to become the chief communicators of all that is good and cherished in our culture." Similarly McDonald's (McDonaldization) has become a byword for globalisation, uniformity, predictability, calculation and control. The predatory instinct of corporations destroys the culture and indigenous way of living besides causing harm to others—workers, consumers, communities and environment (Klein, 2000). Corporations have an inbuilt compulsion to externalise its costs—every cost they can unload onto someone else is a benefit to itself, a direct route to profit thus making them institutions needing regulation and control referred to as corporate governance. The intense phase of financial capital with multinational enterprises deepening their investment in various countries has its inevitable costs especially when there is no binding regulation adequately making multinational enterprises comply with minimum regulations, human rights, labour and environmental standards. Information about corporate behaviour and global issues is no longer within the purview or interpretive frame of any one individual, group or organisation.

In recent years, TNCs were involved in a number of scandals that shocked the global public. At one extreme, corporate involvement may include paying such forces to suppress opposition to corporate activities. The Enron Corporation, for example, has been accused of collaborating with the Indian police to violently repress local residents opposed to a massive energy project. Royal Dutch Shell has been sued for alleged complicity in the executions of activists protesting the company's environmental and development policies in Nigeria. Human rights groups have also criticised

British Petroleum for contracting with the Colombian armed forces despite reports of military human rights abuses from many sources, including the US State Department. British Petroleum has acknowledged paying millions of dollars to the government to protect oil operations and has been criticised for taking no steps to ensure that human rights will be respected (Beth, 2002).

A hotly contested lawsuit has charged the Unocal Corporation with complicity in human rights violations committed by the Burmese military government. Such issues are also presented in the area of labour rights. Certain core labour rights have been recognised as entitled to international protection, including the rights to organise and to collective bargaining and the prohibitions of forced labour and certain kinds of child labour. TNCs search out inexpensive locations to manufacture their products, often choosing countries with low wages and weak protection of labour rights. These practices often lead to denials of these basic rights. Investigations of working conditions in factories supplying goods to well-known brands such as Disney, Nike and Levi Strauss have drawn attention to abuses including unpaid overtime, child labour, illegally low wages and dangerous working conditions. Several lawsuits illustrate the environmental harm that transnational can inflict when freed from the environmental regulations that apply in their home countries. Texaco in Ecuador, Freeport-McMaron in Indonesia and Shell in Nigeria have all been accused of using devastating practices long banned in Europe and the United States (US). Current economic incentives are insufficient to trigger voluntary compliance with international human rights standards in the areas of physical integrity, labour rights or the environment. The legal system, however, is also at a disadvantage when regulating multinational actors, particularly those with the economic and political clout of multinational corporations (Beth, 2002).

This latest political and extended economic role of multinational corporations along with gross contravention of rights and corporate malpractices has profound impact on the way we must interpret their moral responsibilities. Young (2004) argues that political responsibility is a shared responsibility. It reckons collaboration involving a variety of actors who may not essentially be directly involved in causing a wrongdoing, but who are structurally linked to the process and thus are in a position to work toward the betterment of the situation. Scherer and Palazzo (2007) reflect on political responsibility in the specific context of corporate responsibility. They also characterise it in deliberative terms which "changes the modus of responsibility from the reactive model [...]to a proactive concept of societal involvement." Corporate responsibility, as they claim, is "increasingly displayed in corporate involvement in the political process of solving societal problems, often on a global scale." The claim is that as political actors of considerable power, corporations do not only have an obligation to respect human rights, but also correspondingly have a responsibility to protect human rights against systematic violations committed by third parties in their perceived sphere of influence and authority. One of the most prominent voices in the Business and Human Rights debate, Sir Geoffrey Chandler, has stated his supportive position on the issue very explicitly.

> These companies are vital to the countries they serve. They help to sustain economically regimes of very varied complexions—from democracies to oppressive dictatorships. We ask them and see it as part of their agenda, to speak out in defence of human rights where they are violated in the countries in which they work. This is a wholly legitimate role. It is not interference in domestic politics, an argument that companies have used as an escape route in the past (Chandler, 1999).

Ruggie (2005) described the situation as follows:

> ...history teaches us that markets pose the greatest risks—to society and business itself—when their scope and power far exceed the reach of the institutional underpinnings that allow them to function smoothly and ensure their political sustainability. This is such a time and escalating charges of corporate-related human rights abuses are the canary in the coal mine, signalling that all is not well.

He further noted that:

> The root cause of the business and human rights predicament today lies in the governance gaps created by globalisation —between the scope and impact of economic forces and

actors, and the capacity of societies to manage their adverse consequences. These governance gaps provide the permissive environment for wrongful acts by companies of all kinds without adequate sanctioning or reparation. How to narrow and ultimately bridge the gaps in relation to human rights is our fundamental challenge.

Liability of Transnational Corporations for Human Rights Contravention: A Conceptual Construct and Slippage

Sensitivity of human rights and notion of global capitalism arise also from very dissimilar theoretical and normative frameworks. The fundamentals of human rights are essentially deontological, authorising certain actions (e.g., fair trials, fair working conditions) and barring other actions (e.g., torture, child labour arbitrary detention) on the basis of requirements due to all human being by virtue of their humanity. Human rights law is analysed in the realm of 'public' law, and draw from international legal obligations which legalise government conduct, necessitating governments to take action with regard to these quintessential rights (Harrison, 2010). Global capitalism on the contrary rests on consequentialist premise; this means individuals pursuing their own self-interests can be harnessed to construct a larger public good (Freeman and Velamani 2006). Regulation of the actions of TNCs has chiefly been part of the 'private realm' and governed by the regulations of the market, spotlighting premise and theories as corporate governance and shareholder value. The core dogmas of these normative frameworks and their rendition into scheme of regulation appear to be poles apart. But over the last few decades, there have been progressively escalating calls for TNCs to be subjected to the norms and standards of international human rights law (Harrison, 2010).

Amidst this morally ambivalent vista, concerns for human rights emerge as something of a beacon. Human rights have come to essentially signify the moral dimension of globalisation: the affirmation of a need for universal values which can be looked for regulation for the humanisation of capitalism, the revitalisation of democratic control and the protection of the values that give meaning and importance to human life. Additionally, in their assertion of the equal worth and supreme value of every human being, human rights can set the stricture for legitimate human organisation. It consequently appears apposite to perceive human rights as an underpinning idea for seminal normative ordering of global capitalism and its governmental construction. The continuous honing of this concept has meant that the link between corporate responsibility and human rights law has become more than just tangential (Campbell, 2007). Conceptually, however, this link remains fragile from an operational point of view, as well as tenuous from the point of view of legal consistency. This fragility is illustrated by various waves of initiatives attempting, one after the other, to 'harden' what would otherwise remain on the 'soft' side of normativity, that is on the ethical ground rather than on the legal normative ground, often referred to as 'hard law' (Aurora, 2009). The human rights approach is arguably the most substantive and promising approach to making sense of the moral responsibilities of MNCs. It grants first priority to those urgent claims for which corporations have an obligation of justice rather than to the ones that are a mere matter of benevolence (Wettstein, 2010). Regardless of the expanding body of literature and interest in this topic (Morrison and Vermijs, 2011), many corporate leaders remain uncertain about the implications for their companies of this emerging paradigm and the means by which human rights considerations can be incorporated into their sphere of influence. This is important because, aside from the legal costs of rights abuses on individuals and communities, corporate executives' possible failure to understand their legal and moral obligations to respect human rights may have significant ramifications for their company's bottom line and the success of their operations.

Human rights have been a concern for some companies since the anti-apartheid divestment campaigns of the 1980s, but there has been no broad-based uptake of human rights as a business discipline. Relatively few companies have human rights in their corporate vocabulary. Several of the merchandise products wholesaled by some of the most prestigious retailers in the US, Canada, the United Kingdom (UK), Japan and Germany are prepared in petite factories far-flung in the Philippines, Bangladesh, Sri Lanka, Guatemala and other countries whose governments offer tax and other incentives to foreign investors. Others are manufactured in small production facilities in the US employing immigrants (Young, 2004). The American or Japanese brand name companies hardly ever manage the factories themselves, but rather position extremely specific orders with other companies, who themselves often contract out the work to local entrepreneurs. It is not a hyperbole to label these factories 'sweatshops.' The 2005 International Labour Organization (ILO) report on forced labour estimates that some 12.3 million people are victims of forced labour worldwide, 9.8 million of whom are exploited by private agents. Furthermore, forced labour is a problem of truly global dimension; it is present on all continents, in almost every country, and in every kind of economy at all stages of development (International Labour Office, 2005). The anti-sweatshop, child labour movements environmental concerns, etc., distinguish the criterion of power or influence by targeting its actions on corporate or regulatory bodies arguably with clout to amend this oppressive structural processes. Charles Beitz and Thomas Pogge also offer elaborate accounts of the foundational assertion for fair practices that people within one nation–state have responsibilities of justice toward many people in other nation–states in the transnational system of interdependence and dense economic interaction, which has systemic cost for the relative privilege and disadvantage that people experience in different parts of the world or within particular locales.

Another example in this category is environmental damage and degradation. Companies in the extracting industries are especially notorious in this regard. Oil companies, for example, cause tremendous environmental damage not only through oil spills and pollution of air and water but also through the extensive infrastructure required for their operations. Environmental degradation caused by oil exploration and production can have a devastating impact on human rights. It may render land unusable for farming, deplete biodiversity, or destroy fishing grounds (Human Rights Watch, 1999[1]), which undermines the local people's right to food, to health or, in cases in which parents are unable to pay school

1. *http://www.hrw.org/reports/1999/nigeria/Nigew991-05.htm*

fees because of their destroyed livelihoods, even to education of their children. Large companies in the water and beverage industry are another example. They dehydrate whole communities and deprive local farmers of their ability to irrigate their lands properly. For example, Coca-Cola, the largest beverage company in the world, uses almost 3 litres of fresh water for the production of one litre of Coca-Cola. According to the India Resource Center, the ratio in India even reaches 4 to 1, which means that 75 per cent of the extracted water is eventually turned into waste water (Srivastava, 2006[2]). Coca-Cola's total water consumption adds up to 283 billion litres a year. These examples unequivocally endorse the view that a globalised economy produces global externalities and augments global inequities.

Samuel Scheffler (1994) suggests that facts of high global interdependence make fundamental features of the conception of responsibility problematic. He also suggests that the prevailing notion of responsibility is extremely restrictive; it aims to delimit a relatively circumscribed sphere of circumstances and persons toward which agents have responsibility. This conception tends to restrict responsibility to what individuals themselves do, as opposed to what they fail to prevent. It also tends to confine responsibility to those persons with whom an agent has special or relatively immediate connection and others with whom one has ongoing interaction (Young, 2004). Young contends that this particular phenomenology of agency triggers this conception. The often cited anti-sweatshop movement well illustrates this challenge to normal structural background conditions for any discourse on justice and rights. He asks consumers, shareholders and other institutions that contract with retailers, brand name apparel companies, and many other agents to reflect morally on the 'normal and hitherto acceptable' market relationships in which they act. It challenges all the agents that are part of the economic chain between the workers who make garments and the people who buy and wear them to bring into question whether 'business as usual,' which hitherto has been understood as within the bounds of moral acceptability, should in fact be thought acceptable (Young, 2004). Pogge (2002) refers to

2. *http://www.indiaresource.org/campaigns/coke/2006/cokewwf.html*

"the design of a global economic order" which is determined by a tiny minority of participants, and finds that a global economic order is being imposed on people in developing countries by Western governments acting in the name of their citizens, which presses many people into grinding poverty and exposes them to domination. Developing country governments in which the TNCs operate ('the host state') are not able to make obligatory human rights norms because these are seen as incompatible with a regulatory regime which will draw FDI. Even a host state which has the desire to implement human rights principles and standards or have ratified international human rights instruments and enacted domestic legislation may not have the apparatus and resources necessary to enforce them. Implicitly such a formulation absolves too many people and institutions, in the South as well as the North, of responsibilities they should take up, if only responsibilities to organise pressure on powerful global actors.

TNCs are therefore increasingly powerful actors in our globalised economy. TNCs have also increased their power within the international legal system through expansion of the legal obligations imposed on states through the international trade regime, and increased levels of direct legal protection through bilateral and regional investment treaties. Therefore, a foreign company can win millions of dollars worth of damages through international investment arbitration, or strongly influence countries to bring cases under the international trading system so as to promote their access to markets. Global corporations have proven to be outstandingly competent economic entities, "formidably effective and swift machine[s]," capable through their coordinated operations of far outperforming smaller scale, national business models.

The multinationals exploit to great effect their ability to coordinate operations and to trade and invest internally, seeking the greatest return for the group as a whole. In short, "multinational groups pursue a policy of group profit maximisation in which the interests of the individual constituent members of the group are subordinated to the interests of the parent, that is, the group as a whole" (Beth, 2002).

Capping Off the Regulatory Arbitrage

It is in this globalised regulatory environment that questions are raised about the ability of governments individually, particularly in developing countries, to effectively regulate the actions of TNCs. Developing countries, in particular, are often competing with other countries for investment by TNCs and are therefore not in a strong position to impose effective regulatory measures unilaterally. This situation is exacerbated by other factors, e.g., by weak governance structures in many developing countries; by the fact that TNCs have hugely complicated networks of subsidiaries and suppliers; and by the fact that corporations may become complicit in the human rights violations of governments (Ratner, 2001; Ruggie, 2008). Assessment of the policies and practices by which governments in developing countries actually regulate with regard to the human rights conduct of multinational companies supports these concerns; studies indicate that legislation is virtually non-existent and states largely rely on voluntary initiatives. Such regulatory frameworks are widely perceived as inadequate for holding TNCs accountable for their conduct (Muchlinski, 2007; Ruggie, 2007).

Ruggie defines these issues as the "predicament" of business and human rights stems from "governance gaps created by globalisation"—where the impact of corporations on human rights (and indeed on other issues) exceeds the ability of states and societies to manage the adverse consequences. These critics want to create a global 'floor of responsibilities' that MNCs must observe in relation to workers rights, human rights and the environment. This in turn assumes that social and cultural relativism is unimportant, or conversely, that there is sufficient common ground among the world's major ethical systems that we can agree on a common floor of ethical responsibilities for business. The strongest site in this area is that which places the adherence of fundamental human rights at the heart of ethical business practice. Responsibility for any infringement of human rights was historically with the state. However, in the context of business ethics, the exercise of human rights standards seeks to extend their relevance and applicability to private non-state actors as well.

As Clapham (2006) has forcefully argued, changes in the nature and location of power in the contemporary international system, including an increase in the power of private non-state actors such as MNCs (which may allow them to bypass traditional state-centred systems of governance), have forced a reconsideration of the boundaries between the private and the public spheres. This, in turn, has brought into question the traditional notion of the corporation as a private entity with no social or public obligations, with the consequence that such actors, including MNEs, may in principle be subjected to human rights obligations. This argument corresponds with the apprehension that these dominant entities may discount human rights and, by this means, infringe human dignity. Notwithstanding the compelling academic and ethical argument for extending liability for human rights violations to MNEs, the legal accountability of MNEs for such contraventions remain tentative and imprecise. As a consequence, much of the writing on this subject put forward an approach to restructuring and enlarging the law towards full legal responsibility, rather than documenting actual juridical findings of human rights violations by MNCs or, indeed, other non-state actors.

Ruggie observes that progress has been made in the past decade in attempting to fill these 'governance gaps.' However, while the steps taken, for example, initiatives such as the Kimberley Process and the UN Global Compact, are to be welcomed, the fundamental problem "is that there are too few of them...and they do not cohere as parts of a more systemic response," Ruggie says. The aim of his report is therefore to propose a systematic framework for the management of business responsibility and accountability for maintaining human rights. These concerns about the inherent inability of countries to effectively regulate the human rights impacts of TNCs have led to alternative strategies to address such conduct. A host of international campaigning groups have appeared wanting to take action with regard to the negative social impact of multinationals—organising consumer boycotts, protests, and naming and shaming of misbehaving TNCs and pressing for effective regulation of their activities (Shamir, 2004).

> The fact that they have multiple production facilities means that TNCs can evade state power and the constraints of national regulatory schemes by moving their operations between their different facilities around the world.

Regulatory schemes are largely domestic, based upon national laws, administrative bodies and judicial systems, while transnationals operate across borders. Over 30 years ago, Prof Detlev F. Vagts (1970) pointed out that "the present legal framework has no comfortable, tidy receptacle for such an institution," producing a tension between the legal theory of independent corporate units, each "operating as a native within the country of its incorporation," and the reality of the "economic interdependence" of the MNC. Soros (1998) has decried the lack of a global system capable of regulating global capitalism (Beth, 2002).

The Edifice for Business Accountability for Human Rights

Despite calls for more, there is already a surprising amount of documentation, both legally binding and non-binding, that can offer an insight into the content of global social responsibility standards in business. The sources vary from voluntary codes of conduct developed by individual companies or industry sectors, NGO codes, codes drawn up by governments or IGOs and binding conventions on specific issues. The implication of human rights and the compass of the subject-matter of international human rights instruments have extended gradually over the decades after the adoption of the Universal Declaration of Human Rights (UDHR) in 1948 by the UN. The UDHR, followed by two binding Covenants adopted in 1966, and their two Optional Protocols shaped the prominent part of human rights law included in the UN system of international regulation. Distant from these human rights mechanisms there are various others, committed to prevention of discrimination, rights of the child, rights of women, etc., as well as a range of human rights standards, proposals and statements. In spite of the human rights instruments, they fall short to mitigate human right infringement and governance gaps particularly in case of TNCs. The evident cause is that TNCs are not covered in international law, and they are subjected to jurisdictions of States where they operate. TNCs have lot of economic and political power especially in the current milieu of globalisation and liberalisation. They can directly impinge on the lives of millions of people but placing a direct liability on a TNC for human rights violation. Nevertheless, the abundance and wide scope of international human rights instruments does not oblige corporations. Therefore, they cannot bear responsibility arising from the breach of these instruments. The table illustrates the sectors in the relevant human rights instruments.

Table 2.1

Human Rights Regulations in Relevant Sectors

Sector/industry Referred in Concluding Observations of Treaties	
Treaty	*Sector/industries*
Civil and Political Rights (ICCPR)	Labour market, commercial and agricultural sectors (including the cotton industry), logging and mining concessions and media.
International Convention on Economic, Social and Cultural Rights (ICESCR)	Labour market, private prisons, natural resource extracting companies (including transnational companies), "mineral, timber and other commercial interests", development projects, private social security schemes and funds, private health care system
International Convention on the Elimination of All Forms of Racial Discrimination (ICERD)	Extractive and forestry industries, transnational corporations, large business centures (particularly in indigenous areas), media and communication networks, private employers, private banks, housing agencies, hotels, restaurants and cafes.
The Convention on the Elimination of All Forms of Discrimination against Women (CEDAW)	Private companies, public companies, private enterprises, business, labour market, private sector, media and advertising agencies, credit facilities, media, service sector, agricultural sector and informal sector, maquila (textile) industries.
Convention on the Rights of the Child (CRC)	Radio and television broad casters, educational institutions, childcare professionals, institutions for mental illness, legal persons, Internet service providers, private adoption houses, private institutions, labour market, informal sector.
International Convention on the Protection of the Rights of All Migrant Workers and Members of their Families (ICRMW)	Agricultural sector

Source: Human Rights Council, Implementation of General Assembly Resolution (2007).

The preamble of the 2003 UN Norms on the Responsibilities of Transnational Corporations and Other Business Enterprises recognises states as primary actors to protect, respect and remedy human rights; it also recognises the obligation of TNCs to respect human rights following the UDHR. Nevertheless, this broad interpretation lacks wider international recognition. The complex relation between human rights, TNCs and international law is 'horizontality.' As noted earlier, rights traditionally concern the state–citizen relation, emerging to protect citizens against their state on the vertical level and companies, on the horizontal (where private law subjects interact), are not included. Traditionally, only states can violate human rights directly. Yet, companies may have liability or responsibility for human rights. Ruggie's (2008) framework defines 'differentiated but complementary responsibilities of states and businesses' *vis-à-vis* human rights. An approach to holding TNCs directly responsible for human rights violations has been taken by various international organisations by creating initiatives in this respect. From the mid-1970s, four initiatives have been drawn up. Those were the UN Draft Code of Transnational Corporations (1977), the Sullivan Principles (1970), the OECD Guidelines for Multinational Enterprises (1976) and the International Labour Organisation Tripartite declaration of principles concerning MNEs (1977). Starting with the new millennium, more initiatives were drafted, such as the Global Compact (2000), the UN Norms on the Responsibilities for Transnational Corporations and Other Business Enterprises with Regard to Human Rights (2003), the Report of the Special Representative of the Secretary General on the issue of human rights and transnational corporations and other business enterprises, John Ruggie—*Protect, Respect and Remedy: A Framework for Business and Human Rights* (2008).

Regardless of the fact that these initiatives had an ambitious goal for TNCs to respect human rights, to gain publicity through reporting system, and voluntary nature, they had serious shortcomings that made these initiatives only a little more than mere declarations. These drawbacks were lack of monitoring and enforcement mechanisms and voluntary nature. Voluntary nature can be both advantage and disadvantage here because TNCs are more willing to be part of these initiatives when they are not forced into them, but then again due to voluntary nature they implement these initiatives the way they see fit only so as to continue their profitable operation (Katuoka and Dailidaitè, 2012).

Decoding the Ruggie's "Protect, Respect and Remedy" Matrix

The Special Representative presented this framework to the Human Rights Council in June 2008. The "Protect, Respect and Remedy" framework rests on three pillars: the state duty to protect against human rights abuses by third parties, including business, through appropriate policies, regulation and adjudication; the corporate responsibility to respect human rights, which means to act with due diligence to avoid infringing on the rights of others and to address adverse impacts that occur; and greater access by victims to effective remedy, both judicial and non-judicial. The Human Rights Council unanimously welcomed what is now referred to as the UN Framework, marking the first time that a UN intergovernmental body had taken a substantive policy position on this issue. The council also extended the Special Representative's mandate with the task of 'operationalising' and 'promoting' the framework.

In May 2011, at the end of his second mandate, Ruggie submitted his Guiding Principles on Business and Human Rights. These principles are intended to implement his Protect, Respect and Remedy policy framework, elaborated in his 2008 report and further developed in his 2009 and 2010 reports. They were the final product of six-year mandate as the Secretary General's Special Representative on Business and Human Rights. The policy framework and Guiding Principles focused on addressing the regulatory gaps in relation to the human rights impacts of business activity, and in particular, business activity in developing countries. One cannot have a difference of opinion regarding the implication of Ruggie's contribution to the global dialogue on corporate accountability. Moreover, his articulation of the policy framework and Guiding Principles intended at the framework's operationalisation has been imperative for the concern of corporate human rights accountability, and for the inclusive mapping of existing international standards and so-called 'governance gaps,' and crucially for the link that Ruggie has constructed to bring states and business on the issue of responsibilities towards humans .

Finally in June 2011, the United Nations Human Rights Council collectively endorsed the UN Guiding Principles on Business and Human Rights, which Ruggie developed with support from all stakeholder groups. The Guiding Principles of 2011 puts down the steps requisite for states and businesses to implement the "Protect, Respect and Remedy" framework on business and human rights. It reaffirms that states have a duty to protect human rights and prevent and sanction abuses by third parties, including business; it establishes that companies have a responsibility to respect human rights; and it stresses the need for greater access to effective remedy, both judicial and non-judicial, for victims of business-related human rights abuses.

The UN Framework was received well by key stakeholder groups: a number of individual governments have utilised it in conducting their own policy assessments; several major global corporations are realigning their due diligence processes based on it; civil society actors have employed it in their analytical and advocacy work; and several major international organisations have drawn on it in adapting their own business and human rights policies and standards.

The State Duty to Protect

The first pillar of the UN Framework is the state duty to protect against human rights abuses committed by third parties, including business, through appropriate policies, regulation and adjudication. It highlights that states have the primary role in preventing and addressing corporate-related human rights abuses. The Special Representative documented the duty's legal foundations, policy rationales and scope in his 2008 and 2009 reports to the Council.

Although states interact with business in numerous ways, many currently lack adequate policies and regulatory arrangements for effectively managing the complex business and human rights agenda. While some states are moving in the right direction, overall state practice exhibits substantial legal and policy incoherence and gaps, which often entail significant consequences for victims, companies and states. The most common gap is the failure to enforce existing laws. Legal and policy incoherence arises because the departments and agencies which directly shape business practices—including corporate law and securities regulation, investment, export credit and insurance, and trade—typically work in isolation from, and uninformed by, their government's own human rights obligations and agencies (UN, 2011).[3]

In Ruggie's reports to the Council, the Special Representative has proposed five priority areas through which states can work to promote corporate respect for human rights and prevent corporate-related abuse. They include: (a) striving to achieve greater policy coherence and effectiveness across departments working with business, including safeguarding the state's own ability to protect rights when entering into economic agreements; (b) promoting respect for human rights when states do business with business, whether as owners, investors, insurers, procurers or simply promoters; (c) fostering corporate cultures respectful of human rights at home and abroad; (d) devising innovative policies to guide companies operating in conflict-affected areas; and (e) examining the cross-cutting issue of extraterritoriality.

The Corporate Responsibility to Respect

The corporate responsibility to respect human rights means acting with due diligence to avoid infringing on the rights of others, and addressing harms that do occur. The term 'responsibility' rather than 'duty' is meant to indicate that respecting rights is not currently an obligation that international human rights law generally imposes directly on companies, although elements of it may be reflected in domestic laws. It is a global standard of expected conduct acknowledged in virtually every voluntary and soft-law instrument related to corporate responsibility, and now affirmed by the Human Rights Council itself.

A company's responsibility to respect applies across its business activities and through its relationships with third parties connected

---

3. *http://www.business-humanrights.org/SpecialRepPortal/Home*

with those activities—such as business partners, entities in its value chain, and other non-state actors and state agents. In addition, companies need to consider the country and local contexts for any particular challenges they may pose and how those might shape the human rights impacts of company activities and relationships.

Companies can affect virtually the entire spectrum of internationally recognised rights. Therefore, the corporate responsibility to respect applies to all such rights (although some rights typically will be more at risk than others in particular contexts). For an authoritative list of internationally recognised rights, companies should look to the Universal Declaration of Human Rights, the International Covenants on Civil and Political Rights and on Economic, Social and Cultural Rights, and the core conventions of the ILO. The principles those instruments embody are the most universally agreed upon by the international community, and they comprise the human rights benchmarks by which other social actors judge companies.

Many companies say that they respect human rights. In order to 'know and show' that they are meeting this responsibility, companies need a human rights due diligence process, whereby they become aware of, prevent and address their adverse human rights impacts. Drawing on well-established due diligence practices and combining them with what is unique to human rights, the UN Framework describes the core elements of human rights due diligence: based on a statement of commitment to respecting rights and supporting policies, human rights due diligence should include assessing human rights impacts, integrating respect for human rights across relevant internal functions and processes, and tracking as well as communicating performance. (The Special Representative is currently running a public online forum to seek views on various aspects of the corporate responsibility to respect.)

Access to Effective Remedy

Even where institutions operate optimally, adverse human rights impacts may still result from a company's activities and victims must be able to seek redress. Effective grievance mechanisms play an important role in both the state duty to protect and the corporate responsibility to respect.

As part of their duty to protect against business-related human rights abuse, states must take appropriate steps within their territory and/or jurisdiction to ensure that when such abuses occur, those affected have access to effective remedy through judicial, administrative, legislative or other appropriate means. Currently, access to judicial mechanisms for business-related human rights claims is often most difficult where the need is greatest as a result of both legal and practical obstacles. And there is currently an uneven patchwork of non-judicial mechanisms, including mechanisms at the company level, national level (such as national human rights institutions or National Contact Points in states that have signed the OECD Guidelines on Multinational Enterprises) and at the international level [such as the Compliance Advisor Ombudsman for the International Finance Corporation (IFC)].

Non-judicial mechanisms, whether state-based or independent, should conform to principles of legitimacy, accessibility, predictability, rights-compatibility, equitability and transparency. Company-level mechanisms should also operate through dialogue and engagement rather than the company itself acting as adjudicator of its own actions. To support improved access to information, learning and expertise in pursuit of more effective non-judicial grievance mechanisms, the Special Representative established an online resource to assist parties in navigating their available options—Business and Society Exploring Solutions.

Convergence and Alignment

The Guiding Principles have rapidly become an authoritative focal point and have been incorporated into a range of other standards. The OECD Guidelines for Multinational Enterprises were revised in 2011 and now specifically address human rights. Building on the guiding principles, they also include business relationships. The OECD's NCPs hear complaints about 'specific instances' of corporate implementation of the OECD Guidelines: since business relationships were at the heart of many past complaints, they are likely to become even more prominent as a result. The convergence of standards around the Guiding Principles can be seen in other areas too: in the International Standards Organisation's International Standards Organisation (ISO) 26000: 16 in references to the UN "Protect, Respect and Remedy" (PRR) Framework in the updated Performance Standards of the IFC (World Bank Group); in the OECD's Common Approaches for Officially Supported Export Credits and Environmental and Social Due Diligence, which was recently updated, and in national legislation and other national and regional initiatives.

The increasing number of references to the Guiding Principles in these and other standards, as well as in business contracts, industry association policies, corporate guidance, and multi-stakeholder initiatives suggest that a culture of expectation is forming. By extension, given the alignment of standards, businesses are far more likely to face consistent expectations about their responsibility regarding human rights from business partners as well as from governments, investors and wider society.

At differing levels, efforts are underway within the EU, ASEAN and the African Union to assess the state of implementation of the Guiding Principles within their member countries and to promote compliance. Similar developments are visible at the national level. The US government has already incorporated elements of the Guiding Principles in Section 1502 of the Dodd-Frank Wall Street Reform Act addressing conflict minerals from the Democratic Republic of Congo, and points to the principles as a benchmark in its reporting requirements for investments exceeding the USD 500,000 threshold in Myanmar. In Europe, the European Commission invited all EU member states to develop national plans for the implementation of the UN Guiding Principles by the end of 2012. The European Commission is currently in the process of developing guidance on the corporate responsibility to protect in three sectors: information and communications technology (ICT), oil and gas, and employment and recruitment agencies.

In May 2011, investors representing $2.7 trillion of assets under management, and who have signed the UN supported Principles on Responsible Investment (PRI), publicly declared their support for the UN Guiding Principles and the UN Framework. They noted that these documents would help them to analyse how companies address human rights risks, and would "enable credible benchmarking of company efforts in a way that has not been possible to date." They also pointed to "significant gaps" in the UN Guiding Principles. Specifically, they suggested that the UN Guiding Principles do not take enough account of investors' "special position of influence" with regard to companies' human rights due diligence processes, and had missed an opportunity to examine fiduciary duty "with a human rights lens." In a report published in August 2011, Sustainalytics, a research firm specialising in ESG matters, outlined the implications for investors of the UN Guiding Principles (Schoemaker, 2011).

The UN Guiding Principles have already acted as a catalyst, aligning different standards and guidelines that address specific aspects of business responsibility with regard to human rights. Over time, moreover, some of the core precepts of the UN Guiding Principles "may slowly become binding" as states adopt legislation 'consistent with Ruggie's recommendations.' For these reasons, the UN Guiding Principles provide a robust analytical framework for investors and are likely to remain the most widely accepted global standard on business and human rights.

An Assessment on UN Guiding Principles

Let us begin with some review questions. How do these observations impact upon the role business plays in the human rights agenda? What happens in practice? How can respect for such rights be part of corporate responsibility in the globalised economy? Can TNCs, from a legal perspective, be held accountable at all for human rights' breaches? The answers are unquestionably complicated. An expansive view of human rights at the very least challenges existing conduct. Questioning the very idea of progressing human rights risks a displacing of the potential of reason in a critique of and in an intervention to improve governance practices. These questions also recount to scepticism regarding rights enforceability. Meyer and Rowan define the notion of 'ceremonial conformity' to express how companies adapt their structures and norms to signal conformity with societal norms and expectations. Dimaggio and Powell refer to this phenomenon as 'isomorphism' (iso = same; morp = form or shape). Organisations and corporations take on similar forms because they want to be recognised as legitimate institutions in society.

One of the paramount concerns has been the lack *modus operandi* for making obligatory the human rights in international law. Till date only national law officially regulates companies. If there are various concrete international contracts and fundamentals of international law exclusively for companies, the norms thereby defined have to be put into operation at state level. An illustration is the UN anti-corruption treaty. It lays down international standards that are only enforceable by national laws. The equivalent pertains for international human rights conventions and treaties. Their application and enforcement depends on national laws and procedures. So we now envisage a condition where most nations have incorporated human rights into their legislation, hitherto the paper law does not prevent regular rights' breaches.

The another flaw in the Ruggie's framework is that instead of squarely dealing with the difficult question of precise human rights responsibilities of corporations that operate in diverse business environments, the report debunks any requirement for cataloguing human rights responsibilities of corporations. The justification runs like this: because "business can affect virtually all internationally recognised rights ... any limited list [as attempted in the UN Norms] will almost certainly miss one or more rights that may turn out to be significant in a particular instance, thereby providing misleading guidance." It is, nevertheless, critical that responsibilities of corporations *vis-à-vis* rights (defined originally with reference to states) are identified (Deva, 2011).

According to Deva (2011), it is also doubtful if the responsibility of corporations to merely respect human rights will prove satisfactory, for human rights cannot be fully realised unless 'multiple kinds of duties' are obligated on all those actors which could abridge rights. If human rights law could obligate states to ensure that their agents as well as private actors within their respective jurisdictions do not violate human rights, why cannot we impose an obligation on a parent company to ensure that its *de facto* agents (subsidiaries, affiliates, contractors and suppliers) respect human rights obligations? In fact, if the responsibility of corporations is limited to respecting human rights, this might encourage them to contract out human rights abuses to their business partners and supply chain participants, over which they often exercise effective control but at the same time keep distance by design. Amnesty International criticised the Guiding Principles' failure to adequately address key corporate accountability issues and suggested mandating rather than only recommending a due diligence approach, effectively preventing and punishing extraterritorial human rights abuses, and explicitly recognising the right to a judicial remedy as a human right. According to Amnesty International (2011),[4] without a stronger mandate, the Working Group would be unable "to take proactive steps to tackle the need for greater clarity and increased legal protections. If not corrected, this will be a missed opportunity."

Many scholars also scrutinise the permitted scope of home state jurisdiction by framing the problem as one relating to 'extraterritorial' jurisdiction. Yet, 'extraterritorial' is not only notoriously difficult to define, but is often associated with notions of illegality. Indeed, continued reference to extraterritoriality undermines the recognition of existing territorial links between home state institutional structures and the global economic activities of TNCs, unintentionally reinforcing home state reluctance to regulate in the first place. Generally speaking it is difficult to establish an agency relationship between a TNC and a home state. This is in part because an agency relationship presumes that the state is in the position of principal while the TNC is a subordinate. Yet, home states are not 'puppeteers' who direct the actions of TNC 'marionettes.' Instead, home state involvement is more about 'acquiescence than direction and control, more about facilitation by quiet encouragement than specific instructions, more about omission than commission.' While the TNC is clearly the driving force behind its own conduct, the home state 'may be a key facilitator' of the activity through 'complex acts and omissions.' Thus, the use of agency as a standard for direct home state

4. *http://killercoke.org/buying_respectability.php*

responsibility for private actor conduct by TNCs may be 'not just impractical but also self-defeating'. Notably, the agency paradigm "not only neglects the subtle relationships between the private and public sphere ... it encourages them," as states can pursue indirect support of activities without creating an agency relationship (Wettstein, 2010).

In recognition that extraterritorial jurisdiction 'constitutes a range of measures,' the Special Representative of the UN Secretary-General for Business & Human Rights (SRSG) ultimately proposes a matrix. It has two rows: direct extraterritorial jurisdiction over parties or activities abroad, and domestic measures with extraterritorial implications. And it has three columns: public policies, prescriptive regulations and enforcement action. The combination yields six cells—six broad types of measures with differing extraterritorial reach—not all of which are equally controversial or as likely to trigger objections and resistance. Yet, the SRSG concludes, 'all cells' are 'under-populated', 'not only the most difficult and controversial'. While the SRSG clearly acknowledges the legitimacy of concerns expressed by home states, host states and corporations about extraterritorial jurisdiction, he is clear: "the debate [about extraterritorial jurisdiction] must be had because the business and human rights agenda ultimately is about closing governance gaps." However, these laws may in principle help fill a governance gap by encouraging corporate attitudes and practices conducive to human rights support and by re-enforcing the same through inter-linkages with potentially influential stakeholder movements.

Despite the ubiquitous nature of the discourse on human rights, there is currently little research on the emergence of disclosure by MNCs on their human rights obligations or the regulatory dynamic that may lie behind this trend. The UN Working Group conducted a survey in December 2012 "Report of Pilot Business Survey on Implementation of the Corporate Responsibility to Respect Human Rights on the Responses to Guiding Principles". The UN Working Group on Business and Human Rights created a pilot survey to assess the views of business representatives regarding their company's implementation of the corporate responsibility to respect human rights. Their aim was to gather a solid baseline of credible and complete data that can support the UN and other actors as they progress their work to disseminate, implement and embed the UN Guiding Principles globally (Institute for Human Rights and Business, 2012).

The survey reflects the diversity of business, notwithstanding industry, size, ownership and geographic background by taking into consideration corporate responsibility to respect human rights. The survey suggests that companies are considering and actively working to address human rights with reference to international human rights standards and the UN Guiding Principles. After nearly 18 months their endorsement (as the survey was conducted in December 2012), there appears to be a strong trend in awareness and engagement by business with the UN Guiding Principles and dialogue at the international level including at the UN. According to survey results, efforts are being put into human rights policy commitments; identifying, assessing and addressing adverse human rights impacts; communicating with a range of stakeholders; and supporting or providing for access to remedy. The survey also indicates that a deepening and more nuancing of business action may still be necessary. One of the most striking patterns of the survey results was that when asked general questions about the components of the responsibility to respect (policy commitment, addressing impacts, communication and reporting) a high number of companies (around 80% and above) were confident that their company does have some form of practice in place. However, when respondents were asked questions pertaining to how mature or embedded practices were, the response rate dropped considerably—often (and interestingly) with a spike in 'unsure' responses.

By way of illustration, 82 per cent of respondents agreed that "when an actual or potential human rights impact is identified, responsibility is allocated to the relevant business unit and/or department to resolve the issue and report on progress when necessary." But when the respondents were asked if their company tracks progress through developing "qualitative and quantitative indicators, informed by experts and relevant stakeholders," 53 per cent agreed, 47 per cent disagreed or were unsure. So the results were fairly divided. When asked to respond to the statement "My Company is using grievance data for management systems review and continuous learning," only 55 per cent agreed and 45 per cent disagreed or were unsure. This may indicate that elements of Human Rights Due Diligence and engaging in Access to Remedy requires innovation or that existing innovation needs to be more effectively scaled and spread. This survey may be conclusive as it is more indicative of trend. However, it may indicate the beginnings of a more global and diverse dialogue (Institute for Human Rights and Business, 2012).

Conclusion

To re-examine the value and strength of the UN norms in light of the newly endorsed Guiding Principles and the 'Protect, Respect and Remedy' framework, we can say that these norms were key example of Business and Human Rights thrust on the necessity of it being accepted by all stakeholders and it does not propose a rigid binding framework. However a more thorough investigation of the Guiding Principles may suggest that the difference between the earlier two documents is more nuanced and this 'soft law' document may show the way to a prospect development of 'hard law' regulation (Miretski and Bachmann, 2011). The decanting of novel legal concepts defining a new paradigm of corporate legal responsibility becomes particularly relevant in the context created by the SRSG's Report and by its promise of operationalisation. Human rights issues like health and safety or environmental re-enforces the signal that certain corporate harms are serious enough to bring them under the remit of criminal law (Aurora, 2009). The SRSG deserves credit for recognising that developing countries lack capacity or will to regulate TNCs' activities, that extraterritorial regulation of TNCs' activities could be a legitimate option, that governments should work to change the corporate culture of doing irresponsible business, and that the notion of 'sphere of influence' conflates two different meanings of influence (impact and leverage). Professor Ruggie also deserves praise for pointing out that "defining a limited set of rights linked to imprecise and expansive responsibilities, rather than defining the specific responsibilities of companies with regard to all rights" is probably the better approach.

Normatively these norms are an accomplishment. Notwithstanding the letdown of not having become binding law, the norms are generating a tangible impact on stakeholders at the non-state level as discussed and revealed in 2012 survey mentioned above. Investment institutions are applying the norms to persuade companies to improve their social responsibility, NGOs began using the norms as a basis for their advocacy of corporate social responsibility, companies have expressed general support for the Norms, while others even began 'road-testing' the norms.

Perhaps after all, the norms are fulfilling the role designed for them, even if they were not adopted officially. Being the less preferred alternative for the corporations, they have certainly turned out to be one of the fundamental building blocks of the new UN 'Protect, Respect and Remedy' framework. Rule suggests that the norms were designed to stimulate societal change, rather than to become a binding legal document and that it should therefore be read as relating to an ideal structure of *de lege ferenda* as regards the connection between business and human rights (Miretski and Bachmann, 2011). Kinley *et al.* (2007) point out in their analysis of the politics behind the draft standards, one of the most contested and polarising characteristics of the norms was "their apparent attempt to impose obligations directly on companies, in addition to parallel obligations on states." In fact, the earliest critiques by the business community focused primarily on the fact that the norms contemplated legally binding international obligations for corporate actors. Thus, the norms were criticised for their "binding and legalistic approach," and it was argued that "any shift toward mandatory compliance would violate accepted international practices." Subsequent critiques of the norms have focused on more technical issues. Throughout his tenure as SRSG, Ruggie skilfully avoided the controversy created by the norms. He made the decision early in his first mandate to leave them behind, dismissing them as a 'distraction.' Adopting an approach he termed 'principled pragmatism', Ruggie trod a careful and strategic path, consulting with a wide range of stakeholders and keeping business and government 'on side' (Simons, 2011). Backer argues that the norms were constructed as to have a certain constitutional dimension on a supra-national level. One can conclude with the words of Baxi, whereas the more successful attempts to legislate were often the ones were the original ambitions constituted legal utopias *de lege ferenda*, which managed to transform existing legal and factual frameworks altogether (Miretski and Bachmann, 2011).

References

Alejandro, T. and M. Özden, (2011). *Transnational corporations Major Players in Human Rights Violations*. Critical Report No 10. Issue: Business and Human Rights. Part of a series of the Human Rights Programme. December. CETIM. Available at: *http://cetim.ch/en/publications_cahiers.php*

Aurora, Voiculescu (2009). "Human Rights and the New Corporate Accountability: Learning from Recent Developments in Corporate Criminal Liability", *Journal of Business Ethics* 87: 419-32.

Bachmann, Sascha-Dominik Oliver Vladimir and Pini Pavel Miretski (2011). "Global Business and Human Rights: The UN 'Norms on the Responsibility of Transnational Corporations and Other Business Enterprises with Regard to Human Rights'—A Requiem", *Deakin Law Review* 17(1).

Backer, Larry Catá (2010). "On the Evolution of the United Nations' 'Protect-Respect-Remedy' Project: The State, the Corporation and Human Rights in a Global Governance Context", *Santa Clara Journal of International Law* 9(1).

Bakan, J. (2004). *The Corporation: The Pathological Pursuit of Profit and Power*. London: Constable and Robinson.

Barnett, Richard J. and Ronald E. Muller (1974). *Global Reach: The Power of the Multinational Corporations*. New York: Simon and Schuster. p.508.

Baxi, U. (2006). *The Future of Human Rights* (2nd ed). New Delhi: OUP, p.252.

Berle, Adolf A. and Gardiner C. Means (1967). *The Modern Corporation and Private Property*. New York: Harcourt, Brace & World.

Beth, Stephens, (2002). "The Amorality of Profit: Transnational Corporations and Human Rights", 20 *Berkeley J. Int'l Law*. 45.

Blanpain, R. (ed.) (2000). "Multinational Enterprises and the Social Challenges of the XXIst Century", *Bulletin of Comparative Labour Relations* 37-2000. Kluwer Law International.

Campbell, John L. (2007). "Why would Corporations Behave in Socially Responsible Ways? An Institutional Theory of Corporate Social Responsibility", *Academy of Management Review* 32(3): 946–67.

CETIM (2011). "Transnational Corporations Major Players in Human Rights Violations", Critical Report no. 10 available at: *http://cetim.ch/en/publications_cahiers.php*

Chandler, G. (1999). "Keynote Address: Crafting a Human Rights Agenda for Business", in M.K. Addo (ed.) (1999), *Human Rights Standards and the Responsibility of Transnational Corporations*. The Hague: Kluwer Law International. pp.39-45.

Clapham, A. (1993). *Human Rights in the Private Sphere*. Oxford: Clarendon Press, pp.137-38.

Campbell, T. and S. Miller (eds.) (2004). *Human Rights and the Moral Responsibilities of Corporate and Public Sector Organisations*. Netherlands: Kluwer Academic Publishers.

Cutler, A.C. (2001). "Critical Reflections on the Westphalian Assumptions of International Law and Organization: A Crisis of Legitimacy", *Review of International Studies* 27: 133–50.

Deva, Surya (2011). "Protect, Respect and Remedy: A Critique of the SRSG's Framework for Business and Human Rights", in Karin Buhmann, Lynn Roseberry and Mette Morsing (ed.) (2011), *Corporate Social and Human Rights Responsibilities Global Legal and Management Perspectives*. New York: Palgrave Macmillan.

———. (2012). "Guiding Principles on Business and Human Rights: Implications for Companies", *European Company Law* 9(2).

Ellen, Israel Rosen (2002). *Making Sweatshops: The Globalisation of the US Apparel Industry*. Berkeley: University of California Press.

Edna, Bonacich and Richard P. Appelbaum (1999). *Behind the Label: Inequality in the Los Angeles Apparel Industry*. Berkeley: University of California Press.

Freeman, R.E. and S.R. Velamani (2006). "A New Approach to CSR: Company Stakeholder Responsibility", in Kakabadse M. Moring (ed.), *Corporate Social Responsibility: Reconciling the Aspiration with Application*. Hound Mill: Palgrave MacMillan. pp.9-23.

Harrison, J. (2010). "Human Rights and Trans-national Corporations: Establishing Meaningful Obligations", in J. Faundez and C. Tan (eds.), *International Law, Economic Globalisation and Developing Countries*. Cheltenham: Edward Elgar. pp.205-33.

Hepple, B. (2000). "The Importance of Law, Guidelines and Codes of Conduct in Monitoring Corporate Behaviour", in R. Blanpain (ed.) (2000), *Multinational Enterprises and the Social Challenges of the XXIst Century Bulletin of Comparative Labour Relations* 37-2000. Kluwer Law International.

Held, D., A. McGrew, D. Goldblatt, and J. Perraton. (1999). *Global Transformations: Politics, Economics and Culture*. Polity and Stanford University Press.

Institute for Human Rights and Business (2012). "Global Business Initiative on Human Rights", *State of Play: The Corporate Responsibility to Respect in Business Relationships*, December 2012. *http://www.ihrb.org/ publications/reports/state-ofplay. html.*

International Labour Office (2005). *Forced Labour and Human Trafficking: Estimating the Profits* by Patrick Belser. Geneva: International Labour Office. March.

ISO (n.d.), "ISO 26000–Social Responsibility". *http://www.iso.org/iso/iso26000.*

Jägers, Nicola and Willem van Genugten (2011). "Corporations and Human Rights: Moving Beyond 'Principled Pragmatism' to 'Ruggie-Plus," Available at *http://ssrn.com/abstract=1844203*

John, Ruggie (2008). *Protect, Respect and Remedy: A Framework for Business and Human Rights*, Report of the Special Representative of the Secretary-General on the issue of human rights and Transnational corporations and other business enterprises,: *http://www.reports-and-materials. org/Ruggie-report-7*

———. (2011). *UN Guiding Principles on Business and Human Rights: Implementing the United Nations 'Protect, Respect and Remedy' Framework*, Report business enterprises, A/ HRC/17/31, March.

Katuoka, Saulius and Monika Dailidaitė (2012). "Responsibility of Transnational Corporations for Human Rights Violations: Deficiencies of International Legal Background and Solutions Offered by National and Regional Legal Tools", *Jurisprudence* 19(4): 1301-16.

Kinley, D., J. Nolan and N. Zerial (2007). "The Politics of Corporate Social Responsibility: Reflections on the United Nations Human Rights Norms for Corporations".

Klein, Naomi (2000). *No Logo*. London: Flamingo Harper-Collins.

Kobrin, S.J. (2008). "Globalisation, Transnational Corporations, and the Future of Global Governance", in A.G. Scherer and G. Palazzo (eds.), *Handbook of Research on Global Corporate Citizenship*. Edward Elgar, Cheltenham, pp.249-72.

Matthews, J.B., K.E. Goodpaster and L.L. Nash (1985). *Policies and Persons: A Casebook in Business Ethics*. New York: McGraw-Hill.

Mayer, A.M. (2009). "Human Rights as a Dimension of CSR: The Blurred Lines between Legal and Non-Legal Categories", *Journal of Business Ethics* 88: 563.

McCorquodale, R. and P. Simons (2007). "Responsibility Beyond Borders: State Responsibility for Extraterritorial Violations by Corporations of International Human Rights Law", *Modern Law Review* 70(4).

Morrison, J. and D. Vermijs (2011). *The "State of Play" of Human Rights Due Diligence Anticipating the Next Five Years.* London: Institute for Human Rights and Business.

Muchlinski, P. (2007). *Multinational Enterprises and the Law*. London: Oxford University Press.

OECD (2011). *OECD Guidelines for Multinational Enterprises, http://www.oecd.org/daf/internationalinvestment/guidelinesformultinationalenterprises/*

OHCHR (2011). *The Corporate Responsibility to Respect Human Rights–An Interpretive Guide.* pp.35-36.

Pogge, Thomas (2002). *World Poverty and Human Rights*. Cambridge Polity Press, p.142.

Ratner, Steven R. (2001). "Corporations and Human Rights: A Theory of Legal Responsibility", *Yale I.J.* 443, 446.

Rondinelli, Dennis A. (2003). "Sovereignty on Line: The Challenges of Transnational Corporations and Information Technology in Asia", in J.D. Montgomery and N. Glazer (eds.), *Sovereignty Under Challenge.* New Brunswick: Transaction Publishers.

Ruggie, J.G. (2005). "Reconstructing the Global Public Domain: Issues, Actors, and Practices", *European. Journal of International Relations* 10: 499-531.

———. (2007). "Business and Human Rights: The Evolving International Agenda. Corporate Social Responsibility Initiative", *Working Paper* No. 31. Cambridge, MA: John F. Kennedy School of Government, Harvard University.

———. (2008). *Protect, Respect and Remedy: A Framework for Business and Human Rights.* Report of the Special Representative of the Secretary-General on the issue of human rights and transnational corporations and other business enterprises. 7 April A/HRC/8/5,

Scheffler (2001). "Individual Responsibility in a Global Age, Boundaries and Allegiances: Problems of Responsibility and Justice", in *Liberal Thought.* Oxford: Oxford University Press, p.39.

Scheffler, Samuel (1994). *Families, Nations, and Strangers. The Lindley Lecture.* Lawrence: Dept. of Philosophy, University of Kansas. p.11.

Scherer, A.G. and G. Palazzo (2007). "Toward a Political Conception of Corporate Responsibility: Business and Society Seen from a Habermasian Perspective", *Academy of Management Review* 32: 1096-120.

Schoemaker, Daan (2011). "*Raising the Bar on Human Rights: What the Ruggie Principles Mean for Responsible Investors", http://www.sustainalytics.com/sites/default/files/ruggie_principles_and_human_rights.pdf.*

Shamir, R. (2004). "Between Self-Regulation and the Alien Tort Claims Act: On the Contested Concept of Corporate Social Responsibility", *Law & Society Review* 38(4).

Simons, Penelope C. (2011). "International Law's Invisible Hand and the Future of Corporate Accountability for Violations of Human Rights", *Journal of Human Rights and the Environment* 3(1).

Sonja, Gallhofera, Jim Haslamb and Sibylle van der Waltc (2011). "Accountability and Transparency in Relation to Human Rights: A Critical Perspective Reflecting upon Accounting, Corporate Responsibility and Ways Forward in the Context of Globalisation", *Critical Perspectives on Accounting* 220: 765-80.

Soros, George (1998). "Towards a Global Open Society", *The Atlantic Monthly* 281(1): 20-32.

Strange, Susan (1996). *The Retreat of the State: The Diffusion of Power in the World Economy.* Cambridge: Cambridge University Press.

Su-Ping Lu (2000). "Corporate Codes of Conduct and the FTC: Advancing Human Rights through Deceptive Advertising Law", *Columbia Journal of Transnational Law* 603: 603-04.

Ulrich, P. (2008). *Integrative Economic Ethics: Foundations of a Civilized Market Economy.* Cambridge/New York: Cambridge University Press.

United Nations Conference on Trade and Development (UNCTAD) (2012). *World Investment Report—Towards a New Generation of Investment Policies*, p. xLvi. At: *http://www.unctad-docs.org/files/UNCTAD-WIR2012-Full-en.pdf*

UNO (2012). The Corporate Responsibility to Respect Human Rights: An Interpretive Guide. New York and Geneva: UNO.

Vagts, Detlev F. (1970). "The Multinational Enterprise: A New Challenge for Transnational Law", *Harvard Legal Review* 83: 739, 756.

Young, I.M. (2004). "Responsibility and Global Labour Justice", *Journal of Political Philosophy* 12(4): 365–88.

Weissbrodt, David and Muria Kruger (2003). "Norms on the Responsibilities of Transnational Corporations and Other Business Enterprises with Regard to Human Rights", 97 *American Journal of International Law*.

Wettstein, Florian (2010). "The Duty to Protect: Corporate Complicity, Political Responsibility, and Human Rights Advocacy", *Journal of Business Ethics* 96: 33-47.

Wright, Michael (2008). "Corporations and Human Rights: A Survey of the Scope and Patterns of Alleged Corporate-related Human Rights Abuse", *Corporate Social Responsibility Initiative Working Paper* No. 44. Cambridge, MA.

Documents:

Business and Human Rights: Mapping International Standards of Responsibility and Accountability for Corporate Acts: Report of the Special Representative of the Secretary-General (SRSG) on the issue of Human Rights and Transnational Corporations and Other Business Enterprises, *http://www.business-humanrights.org/Documents/SRSG-report-Human-Rights-Council-19-Feb-2007.pdf*

Human Rights Council, 35 (19 Feb. 2007). *Report of the SRSG—Business and Human Rights: Mapping International Standards of Responsibility and Accountability for Corporate Acts,* A/HRC/4.

3

DILLIP KUMAR KAR

Social Auditing

An Essentiality to Effective Corporate Social Responsibility

Introduction

Financial audit deals with reviewing of credit, debit, matching the process of transaction, pointing out the issues related to accounts and recommends how to improve. It is carried out either by an internal auditor or external auditor. Social audit is a process of reviewing the programmes planned and executed in the ground, and how far the stakeholders are aware of the programme components, process and outcome. It is not only helpful for the stakeholders but also for the company to strategise for future. It is carried out by the stakeholders at the end of each programme or at the end of each year.

Social audit is a management tool and accountability mechanism which enhances the capacity of the organisation to understand the effectiveness of the strategy, determines how the organisation meets the expectation of the stakeholders and impact of their activities on the stakeholders. Social audit is organised with the stakeholders for whom the programme is organised.

The concept of corporate social responsibility (CSR) is governed by clause 135 of the Companies Act, 2013, which was passed by both the Houses of the Parliament, and received the assent of the President of India on 29 August 2013. Companies undertake various programmes to support the project-affected community, peripheral development and support to other stakeholders directly and indirectly. For any company, it is important to recognise that its business activities have wide impact on the societies in which it operates and therefore an effective practice is required giving due consideration to the interests of its stakeholders including shareholders, customers, employees, suppliers, business partners, local communities and other organisations.

Objectives of Social Audit

- Accurate identification of requirements of the community in either project-affected area or peripheral area.
- Prioritisation of developmental activities as per requirements.
- Proper utilisation of funds.
- Conformity of the developmental activity with the stated goals.
- Improving quality of service.

Components of Social Audit

Social audit contains the following components:

- Sharing of information on programmes planned and executed in a specific period by company.
- Receiving stakeholder feedback (quantitative and qualitative) on the programme executed.
- Obtaining suggestions from the stakeholder for better planning and execution of programmes in future.

Why Social Audit?

- To permit the company to effectively monitor performance (know what is happening).
- To permit the 'stakeholders' in the company affect its behaviour (understand what people think and want).
- To allow company to report on its achievements based on verified evidence rather than on unsubstantiated claims (tell people what you are achieving).

- Permits those who invest in the company and its stakeholders to judge if it is achieving the values set out to achieve (strengthen loyalty/commitment).
- Enhance decision-making.
- Improve overall performance.

Social audit has excellent promise as a management tool but some potential problems which exist are as follows:

- Reporting organisation can deliberately limit audit scope in order to avoid controversies.
- Process can be managed internally to the disadvantage of some external stakeholders.
- Some significant stakeholders may be omitted.
- Organisation may use arbitrary or inappropriate indicators to evaluate outcomes.
- The standards, independence and honesty of the auditor may be open to question.
- Mindset of people: Even after 50 years of independence, people do not understand the concept of government for the people of the people, and by the people. Most of the people still think themselves as being ruled by the politicians, while politicians think that they are the rulers. Due to this reason, common people do not get involved in the developmental activities.
- Lack of any legal proceedings for not following social audit principles. Unless there is a stringent penalty on authorities for not implementing social audit, they will not give up control because it reduces their kickbacks and authority.
- Lack of education among the common masses. Since common people are not that educated, they do not know their rights, let alone get them enforced.

Social audit is compulsory in major rural development programmes like Mahatma Gandhi National Rural Employment Guarantee Act (MNREGA), Indira Awas Yojana (IAY), etc., in which government facilitate organising the social audit at the end of the programme/financial year at the village level. Community gets together and listens to the information described by *gram panchayat*, opine on the process, benefits of the programme and give suggestions for improvement in future.

The information is displayed publically in the villages at a central point. The social audit is also to be compulsory in the CSR activities of corporates so that it would establish better understanding among the stakeholders and help to have sustainable benefits of the CSR activities. This would lead to proper stakeholder engagement and management in implementing the programmes. Involvement of stakeholders in preparation and dissemination of performance reports, production details, income and loss details, etc., allows stakeholders to be a part in decision-making. In corporates who follow disclosure, report and compliances on regular basis, the stakeholders are mostly aware of the status of the company in regular interval in market and internal management practices.

The business organisations need to take proactive and sensible steps to provide privileges for the stakeholders and facilitate smooth business operations that ensure good transactions with indirect stakeholders. To run the business smoothly companies must be very careful and strategic in operations too. Public disclosure of facilities and changes or processes dedicated for the stakeholders must also be managed in systematic and strategic manner.

The corporates where social audit is not done face the following issues:

- Community dissatisfaction.
- Unsustainable output of the programmes.
- Enhanced community expectations from the corporate.
- No evidence to show the outcome of the CSR activities.

Benefits of Social Audit

- Involvement of people in developmental activities ensures that money is spent where is it actually needed.

- Reduction of wastages.
- Reduction in corruption.
- Awareness among people.
- Promotes integrity and a sense of community among people.
- Improves the standard of governance.

In short, by doing social audit regularly, there is development of brand equity, better governance, improved investor trust and reduction of risk for the corporate.

How to Organise Social Audit

Towards the end of the financial year, a specific date needs to be fixed in consultation with the community for doing the social audit. The information including date, venue, agenda must be displayed in the concerned villages. At the social audit meeting, majority of the community members including leaders need to be present.

A document on the programme components, cost, beneficiaries and benefits obtained or expected to get should be provided to all the participants. The success story of a beneficiary needs to be explained by him/her. The issues can be discussed amongst the community and resolution can be made for replication of good practices. The report of the social audit needs to be considered for future programme planning and implementation.

Implementation of Social Audit

Empowerment of People

Social audit is most effective when the actual beneficiaries of an activity are involved in it. However, people can only get involved in the process when they are given appropriate authority and rights. To this end, the 73rd Amendment of the Constitution has empowered the *gram sabha* to conduct social audit. This is relevant only in the villages. In the cities, the Right to Information (RTI) Act empowers the people to inspect public records.

Proper Documentation

Every activity right from the requirement gathering to planning and implementation must be properly documented. Some of the documents that should be made mandatory are:

- applications, tenders and proposals;
- financial statements, income-expense statements;
- registers of workers; and
- inspection reports.

Accessibility of Documents

Merely generating documents is useless if they are not easily accessible. In this information age, all the documents must be put online.

Disciplinary Action

The final and most important provision, about which nothing is being done yet, is to have punitive actions for non-conformance of the process of social audit. Unless legal punishment is prescribed, there will be no incentive for the people in authority to implement the processes in a fair manner.

Generic Steps for Social Audit

- Clarity of purpose and goal of the local elected body.
- Identify stakeholders with a focus on their specific roles and duties. Social auditing aims to ensure a say for all stakeholders. It is particularly important that marginalised social groups, which are normally excluded, have a say in local development issues and activities and have their views on the actual performance of local elected bodies.
- Definition of performance indicators which must be understood and accepted by all. Indicator data must be collected by stakeholders on a regular basis.
- Regular meetings to review and discuss data/information on performance indicators.

- Follow-up of social audit meeting with the *panchayat* body reviewing stakeholders' actions, activities and viewpoints, making commitments on changes and agreeing on future action as recommended by the stakeholders.
- Establishment of a group of trusted local people including elderly people, teachers and others who are committed and independent. Such a group to be involved in the verification and to judge if the decisions based upon social audit have been implemented.
- The findings of the social audit should be shared with all local stakeholders. This encourages transparency and accountability. A report of the social audit meeting should be distributed for *gram panchayat* auditing. In addition, key decisions should be written on walls and boards and communicated orally.
- Assemble organisation and secure agreement and commitment.
- Define and prioritise the organisation's objectives and establish the action it intends to perform to meet them.
- *Gram sabha* is the best forum to do social audit and RTI is the best powerful weapon to get information for the public to know all information.

After introduction of RTI and power to *Gram Sabha* many changes have come to the society as transparency of information improved.

Relevance of Social Audit in CSR Activities of the Corporates

Introduction of new CSR rules for corporates to spend 2 per cent of their net profit provides scope for community to streamline their role, understanding and expected outcome of the supports provided by corporates to them.

The concept of charity, donation and demand for getting something from corporate will be changed. Community will try to use the benefits of the CSR supports of the corporate in a sustainable development process.

Let us now discuss some of the cases where social audit can be applicable for CSR programmes.

Case 1: One corporate has reported that they have supported 20 farmers in one village to grow ground nut with full package of capacity building, input provisioning and market linkage, and 50 fishermen with similar approach of giving inputs, training and market linkage. By this, farmers got about ₹8,000 per acre and fishermen got about ₹6,000 in one acre of pond.

The corporate wanted to expand these supports in the next year also and therefore conducted social audit in the villages. Proper documentation was prepared including the name of the beneficiaries, supported given, yield results and sell value obtained by the farmers/fishermen, etc., and fixed social audit dates in separate days in the two villages. Community, panchayati raj institution (PRI) members and community from other villages were also invited to the social audit. The report of the corporate was explained to the participants and the beneficiaries themselves explained what they got and how they were benefited. Others who participated were so impressed that they were convinced to go for ground nut and fishing in the similar manner. The corporate was inspired and planned to continue supporting ground nut and fishing value chain in a bigger way.

Case 2: One corporate reported that they have dug 10 tube wells in four villages to provide drinking water to the community. But a group of villagers complained to district collector that the tube wells are not giving water. So collector organised social audit in these villages. Specific dates were informed to the villagers and *panchayat*. On the day of social audit, community openly expressed that the tube wells were executed through a contractor who had not done it properly and within 3 months none of the tube wells were working. The report by community was submitted to the Collector, and the corporate was charged penalty for such bad work and instructed to repair the tube wells immediately.

Case 3: One corporate had established a hospital with an aim to provide health services to the community. After 6 months, it was found that very few patients were coming to the hospital. The corporate wanted to find out the real cause and ways of improving the situation. Therefore, the corporate organised social audit in the villages. The findings of the social audit were that the non-functioning of the hospital is due to:

- Doctor not available most of the time.
- Common medicines were also not available.
- The registration charge was higher than other hospitals.

These findings helped the corporate to change the doctor and pharmacist, etc. Within a period of 3 months of action, more and more community members started coming to hospital for treatment.

Conclusion

Social auditing is "a process of measuring and reporting, in order to understand and ultimately improve, an organisation's social performance." Including social audit in the CSR policy of all corporate would bring sustainability development, reduce tension and community understanding and benefits would be enhanced.

References

Berthin, G. (2008). *A Practical Guideline to Social Audit as a Participatory Tool to Strengthen Democratic Governance, Transparency and Accountability*. UNDP.

Timane, R. and M. Chavan (2012). "A Study of Stakeholder Engagement in Social Audit", *International Journal of Research in IT & Management* 2(12).

Documents:

"Overview of Social Auditing", Presentation by Interpraxis, *www.interpraxis.com*

"Social Audit", *http://en.wikipedia.org/wiki/Social audit* (accessed on 2 October 2014).

"Social Audit and Meeting Management", *http://socialaudit.gov.in/* (accessed on 2 October 2014.

"The National Rural Employment Guarantee Act 2005 (NREGA)—Operational Guidelines." Transparency and Accountability: Public Vigilance and Social Audits: Chapter 11, p.55. NREGA.

"What is Social Audit? Definition and Meaning", *http://www.businessdictionary.com/definition/social-audit.html* (accessed on 2 October, 2014).

4

BIBHU PRASAD MOHANTY

R&R *versus* Corporate Social Responsibility

A Curtain Raiser

Introduction

After the transition of Land Acquisition Act 1894 to enactment of the Right to Fair Compensation and Transparency in Land Acquisition, Rehabilitation and Resettlement Act, 2013 ('LARR13'), resettlement and rehabilitation (R&R) activity got a new thrust and force in the process of implementation. Resettlement and Rehabilitation Policy 2007 could make a road setting for many corporate houses in India on this aspect. Eventually R&R got a place in land acquisition as per several directions and displeasure of Supreme Court of India in different verdicts across last so many years. Honourable Supreme court is aware and sensible on one thing that is the existing R&R activities are not adequate and adhering to expected outcomes. It is a fact that displacement in India has several development issues. There are huge number of unsolved questions related to this. However due to several struggles and pressure from national and international forum and intellectual interventions today this country has the privilege of having a human centre approach to land acquisition to public good. It is definitely a new vista of new thinking, a transition from colonial thinking to a practice of true humanitarian services to people of independent India. At the same time Company Act 2013 had also come up with making company law more conducive for business in India. It has several advantages and facilities for corporate houses. Corporate social responsibility (CSR) came up in a bigger way in Section 135, Schedule VII. CSR is now mandatory for all the corporate bodies with ₹500 crore investments/with ₹1,000 crore annual transactions/making an annual net profit of ₹5 crore. Except a few points of Millennium Development Goal (MDG) (such as reducing child mortality and improving maternal health, combating human immunodeficiency virus (HIV), acquired immune deficiency syndrome (AIDS), malaria and other diseases and social business, etc.) many major points are now included in this for development activities under CSR by corporate houses. It is a fact that while obliging land of law, corporate houses knowingly and unknowingly confuse with R&R and CSR. Although both have same kind of activities, the focus groups and objectives are different.

R&R Practices

Corporate houses have been valuing R&R activities as a humanitarian support practice under designed R&R activities for displaced people those who have been forced to give land to large-scale development projects as the development projects like dams, roads, industries, etc., are meant for large-scale benefit to people of this country at large number. In return, they are given compensation for the land, constructed houses or community resettlement infrastructures, different income generation trainings as the projects disturb their existing livelihood and livelihood skill, also employment facility to some of the members of the family, etc., under R&R package activity. Effort is made to take care of smooth living of the people after displacement. People get benefit of better facilities to the education of their children, health facilities, sports and so on. In some of the cases, scholarship and health insurance were administered for these stakeholders of the projects.

The underlying socio-economic and political impact becomes far reaching for the people. And the objective is also to encompass such impacts in purposeful and healthy manner. The beautiful fact of this R&R activity is the increasing awareness of displaced people about their entitlement. They come across a situation where they compensated for land and they learn about the processes followed in land alienation process, their entitlements for that. They loose livelihood and they go through a process where they shift from one to many livelihood activities, related skills and scope of adopting multiple income sources enriching their economic and social status.

However, the scope of livelihood in the areas of large-scale projects is enormous which is known to many. Therefore, people in this century invite such changes.

In many of the cases, all the great intentions and processes found bringing adversity in life of those displaced people. Those intended facilities for displaced people become formalities of government and project authorities and bring more displeasure and annoyance towards the dreamed projects which would bring prosperity for many. The delays or pending cases or resentments of displaced people across the country are the evidence of faulty approaches and mechanical implementation of R&R supports to displaced people by government and private large-scale projects. Since 1962 to recent days, it was found that millions of cases are pending in different courts of India on this subject. Many complainants and responders both have left their body of heavens abode but the cases remain unsolved in those courts. The judgements still locked in the name of inadequacy in supportive documents, sometime magistrate is not available, R&R officer is out of office, analysis if documents need more time and so many pleas and excuses. Lack of time limitation and urgency of addressing such cases is never ever though of. Magistrates are considered as the God in this country. They can come and go to office as they wish. They can ask or speak any irrelevant and humiliating questions in court and there is no restriction or limitation for them in this regard. It must be mentioned here that these are the public opinion and observation so far. It does not mean all the magistrates are of such character and behaviour in regard to R&R or sensitive problems are concerned. However because of these bottlenecks both the project and displaced people suffer years in terms of money, time and mental sufferings. At times, stay orders of court make the life of displaced mass miserable. Due to such situation all the R&R benefits are stopped for indefinite time that brings substantial loss to all the people in community too. Judiciary system need more sensibility to such situations and provide justice in time to expedite the progress or change in condition in right direction for the benefit of the country and individual or group of people displaced or suffered injustice or delay in justice.

R&R is a project activity and its expenditure is inbuilt in the project. Its time and benefit to people are well organised and designed under government rules and regulations. Now after new law, the process is further strengthened, that become more people oriented than previous law. Therefore it is a mandatory activity for a project. It is a statutory obligation of the project and stakeholders involved in the implementation including government and project authorities with relevant power and responsibilities bestowed on them.

CSR: A Beginning

It is a fact that corporate houses are paying taxes and availing benefits of government facilities. Their tax money and contribution for Compensatory Afforestation fund Management and Planning Authority (CAMPA) are supposed to be spent for the benefit of people. In an ideal situation, there is no need of spending on social and economic development of target mass or community around the development projects. But the reality is different. Government is unable to implement the desired and planned changes in the communities from where projects are mostly operated and gain huge profit. Corporate houses face stringent law and order situation as government fails to address basic problems and aspiration of communities around the industries, dams and large-scale development projects of urban infrastructure development. As the corporates usually paid off charges and taxes to government and remain abide with the law of the soil, they do not heed to the demands of those communities. But delaying supports to community demands creates several law and order situations. Several studies say thus companies bear huge losses and progress of both communities and companies or projects get delayed.

CSR Practices

Therefore it is decided at apex level of democracy of India to involve corporates or big projects of huge investments to participate actively in basic development of communities around them out of their profit money. There are several best reasons credited to this change those are attuned with national development purpose.

Thus CSR is now a vital operation that adds value to the product and services of large companies along with other International Organization for Standardization (ISO) standards they oblige. Therefore, it is definitely a great step of the Government of India (GoI) and Federations of Industries and Mines owners in India those who are actively supporting this decision of including CSR in new Companies Act 2013. Again it is humanitarian and adds value to the product and services of the corporates those who adopt it. Now most of the companies are aware of the new law and procedures to be followed in reporting and consequences of neglecting those law. Of course by doing that, there is an increase in accountability of the companies towards development of nation and its social and economic status. Under CSR the best thing would be to facilitate national and state government schemes to reach people in remote parts of India. India being a country of villages has several villages which require supports in education, health, girl child development, economic empowerment of women and handicapped people, sports, peace process, youth with good livelihood options, strengthening value chains of food and livelihood security, conservation of biodiversity, popularising science and technology in rural area, water and sanitation, drinking water, communicable diseases, strengthening governance of the *panchayat* and so on.

MDG is consulted and incorporated in Company Act 2013 in precise manner under Schedule 123 of Section VII where CSR is described. Government programmes as commitment to MDG are already linked to CSR of any company so that the facilities reach poor. Corporate houses must arrange the missing gaps of MDG implementation and bring down the benefit to poor in their operational or focus area. For example if the region is having infrastructure problem like road connectivity, corporate engaged in CSR should not construct the road rather make arrangements, use several lobby tools to motivate government machinery to work there to facilitate different schemes which will enable people to get the benefit of Pradhan Mantri Sadak Yojana or any other state level facilities. It is found in many cases and many places government is not able to distribute iron tablets for adolescent girls through their system. Without crticising system, we should organise necessary arrangements and facilities and make sure that our girl children take those tablets and remain healthy. It is not spending which is important rather making the facilities reach the people is very important. In reality government can do things far better than any company. Because its competency is long continuation of the programme. Similar are other areas of development.

Table 4.1

Fundamental Differences between R&R and CSR

Resettlement & Rehabilitation	*Corporate Social Responsibility*
It is very much required and mandatory to resettle the displaced family from project area at other location than the project area. Its cost is inbuilt in the project of the company.	Initially it was voluntary but under MoEF direction through environmental clearance certificate it is very much mandatory to do good in surrounding villages of project or company which is affecting the environment of the location. Therefore good for public starts through socio-economic development of the public around the company set-up.
Displaced person or family must be rehabilitated as he lost his/her livelihood in the process of project implementation	This is connected to the profit of company. Only after the implementation of project and when it makes profit, CSR should be planned and executed.
In the process of resettlement of pAF or land sellers, project/company has to look into the issues pertaining to complete payment of compensation of land either sold to the company or the land is acquired through Land Acquisition Act under government intervention. Necessary counselling to affected people and land sellers is to be cared for by the company and the appropriate authority from government which ever is easier and appropriate.	Strategically CSR activities are conducted in villages or surrounding human settlements which are influenced socially, economically and environmentally. People in these locations are taken as first neighbour of the company and a peaceful relationship is built up by helping them in fulfilling their aspirations of development. Surrounding population is taken care in terms of health, education, infrastructure, livelihood, livestock, women empowerment, youth development, addressing issues pertaining to malnutrition, sports development, girl child development and so on.
R&R is connected to land acquisition or land purchase by the company for public purpose.	CSR is connected to the profit of company and it can go beyond the project area and its location.
Under R&R, the land seller or project-affected family must abide with law of the land. This is restricted to support only those targeted mass.	CSR deals with people beyond project-affected families and land sellers. In the process of implementation of CSR, those critical masses of PAF or Land seller may be benefited.

contd...

.contd...

R&R terms and conditions should be made public so that there would be no binding on company and no resentment among the land sellers and project-affected people. Necessary information dissemination should be made as per possible legal measures existing and innovated mostly sensible and practical in terms of business and human rights.	CSR is technically a great approach that talks about holistic development of entire location without discriminating any family and natural inhabitants. It only aims good for all. It is sensible to human drudgery and future prospect of location and beyond that. Therefore, CSR is mostly long term and allows broad innovations for public good.
Under rehabilitation mostly companies provide job opportunities in own projects or set-ups with different conditions. The other approach is self-employment options are created by increasing employability of those targeted mass through skill development and trainings or hand holding approaches. Also they are employed in better companies and government through designed recruitment process. It is an enabling process where the targeted mass get employment opportunities. It is binding and the extent of good for the targeted people is calculated along with the project.	CSR also looks into livelihood projects with designed and desired activities to increase employability of its target location or focused location. It has to be very logical in its designs and operation where the maximum benefit can reach people it focused. It sets own targets as per the size of the project and degree of good it aims for the people. Its cost is dependent on the profit of the organisation. Loss making organisations usually cannot make CSR. But recent Company Act 2013 has taken a different stand on this.

Source: Prepared by Author.

Conclusion

Therefore, companies must take the opportunity to be closer to community and should not get afraid of the criticisms by opinion leaders, media or other people of conflicts. They should also remain alert of differences between CSR and R&R so that after R&R activities they should implement CSR work in those R&R areas. R&R cannot continue for indefinite time, but CSR can continue till the company continues to make profit. So it should be the willful wish of the company to develop the community in such a manner that the community will be able fulfil the company requirements like human resource (HR), infrastructure, support and restrict different types of exploitation by unscrupulous people in the region. It is advisable to keep R&R and CSR separate from each other till R&R is over.

References

Ghosh, S. (2014). "A Study of the Participation of the Private Sector Companies of India in Corporate Social Responsibility Activities through Conjoint Analysis", *Vision: The Journal of Business Perspective* 18: 91-108.

Government of India and UNDP (2008). *Land Rights Ownership.*

Mathur, Hari Mohan (2011). *Resettling Displaced People: Policy and Practice in India.*

PricewaterhouseCoopers (2008). PPP Techno-Economic Feasibility Study and Transaction Advisor for Selected State Roads in the State of Orissa—Draft Sia And R&R Action Plan.

Raghu Raman, S. (n.d.). *Corporate Social Reporting in India—A View from the Top*. Chennai: Institute for Financial Management and Research.

Wankhade, Vivek (2014). *Corporate Social Responsibility: Towards New Agenda,* 3(4). Abhinab Publication.

Documents:

Notification of Provisions Relating to Corporate Social Responsibility under the Companies Act, 2013- KPMG, February 2024.

Training-Workshop reports Gandhian Trusteeship and Corporate Responsibility Foundation.

5

KIRTI CHAWLA

Corporate Governance and Corporate Social Responsibility in Perspective

Introduction

There is increasing attention towards global impact of large corporations. The global impact includes both social and economic elements. Wealthy economies are not willing to passively accept the decisions made by firms, especially when these amount to inflicting costs to society. A few decades ago, companies could pollute environment with no punishment, and still be considered as beneficial to the community in their role of job providers. Today, there are rules which are sometimes implemented strictly as to threaten the survivorship of misbehaving companies. Social communities try to influence firms in their normal operations from a variety of opinions, including their goals, transparency and code of behaviour. This influence is exerted by means as legislation, regulation, pressure groups and political contacts. In such a complex environment, it is natural that firms react by upgrading their working mechanism.

National governance has been defined by the World Bank as the exercise of political authority and the use of institutional resources to manage society's problems and affairs. This is a view of governance which prevails in the present, with its assumption that governance is a top-down process decided by those in power and passed to society at large. In actual fact, the concept is originally democratic and consensual, being the process by which any group of people decides to manage their affairs and relate to each other. Such a consensual approach is, however, problematic for any but the smallest of groups, and no nation has actually managed to institute governance as a consensual process. With the current trend for supranational organisation (e.g., the European Community), this seems even more of a remote possibility; nor is it necessarily desirable. Thus, a coercive top-down form of governance enables a society to accept leadership and to make some difficult decisions which would not otherwise be made. Equally, of course, it enables power to be usurped and used dictatorially—possibly beneficially—but most probably in a way in which most members of that society do not wish.

Governance is however an issue which has come to the fore recently as a direct cause of problems associated with the financial and economic crisis. This applies to governance in general but to 'corporate governance' in particular. Corporate governance can be considered as an environment of trust, ethics, moral values and confidence—as a synergic effort of all the constituents of society, that is the stakeholders, including government; the general public and so on; professional/service providers—and the corporate sector. One of the consequences of a consideration of the actions of an organisation, and the consequences of those actions, has been an increasing awareness of corporate governance (Hermalin, 2005). Corporate governance is therefore a current buzzword the world over. It has gained tremendous importance in recent years. Two of the main reasons for this upsurge in interest are the economic liberalisation and deregulation of industry and business, and the demand for new corporate ethos and stricter compliance with the law of the land. One more factor that has been responsible for the sudden exposure of the corporate sector to a new paradigm for corporate governance that is in tune with the changing times in the demand for greater accountability of companies to their shareholders and customers (Bushman and Smith, 2001).

Thus, the term corporate governance has become ubiquitous in considering the governance of every type of organisation—corporate or not—in order to distinguish this from societal or civic governance.

Good governance is essential for good corporate performance and one view of good corporate performance is that of stewardship and thus, just as the management of an organisation is concerned with the stewardship of the financial resources of the organisation so too would management of the organisation be concerned with the stewardship of environmental resources. The difference, however, is that environmental resources are mostly located externally to the organisation. Stewardship in this context, therefore, is concerned with the resources of society as well as the resources of the organisation. As far as stewardship of external environmental resources is concerned, the central tenet of such stewardship is that of ensuring sustainability. Sustainability is focused on the future and is concerned with ensuring that the choices of resource utilisation in the future are not constrained by decisions taken in the present (Aras and Crowther 2007a). This necessarily implies such concepts as generating and utilising renewable resources, minimising pollution and using new and advanced techniques of manufacturing and distribution. It also implies the acceptance of any costs involved in the present as an investment for the future.

Of equal concern is the question of corporate social responsibility (CSR), what this means and how it can be operationalised (Aras and Crowther 2007b). Although there is an accepted link between corporate governance and CSR, the actual association and dependence on each other has not been defined clearly. Thus, for many firms their governance is adequate as the compliance with the applicable codes and regulatory obligations is met. The more enlightened ones recognise that there is a clear and required relationship between both and they implement in the same manner. Often this is no more than making a claim that good governance is a part of their CSR policy as well as part of their good relationship with the shareholders.

Corporate Governance

One of the main issues which have been exercising the minds of business managers, accountants and auditors, investment managers and government officials—all over the world—is that of corporate governance. Often a company's main target is to become global, while at the same time remaining sustainable as a means to gain competitive power. But the most important question is concerned with what will be a firms' route to becoming global and what will be necessary in order to get global competitive power. There is more than one answer to this question and there is a variety of routes for a company to achieve this.

Probably since mid-1980s, corporate governance has attracted a great deal of attention. The early impetus was provided by Anglo-American codes of good corporate governance. Stimulated by institutional investors, other countries in the developed as well as in emerging markets established or adapted versions of these codes for their own companies. Authorities like Organization for Economic Co-operation and Development (OECD) and the World Bank did not remain passive and developed their own set of standard principles and recommendations. It is understandable that investors' protection has become a much more important issue for all financial markets. Investors are demanding that companies implement rigorous corporate governance principles in order to achieve better returns on their investment and to reduce agency costs. Most of the time investors are ready to pay more for the companies to have good governance standards. Similarly, a company's corporate governance report is one of the main tools for investors' decision. Because of these reasons, companies cannot ignore the requirement and importance of good governance from shareholders, potential investors and other market actors.

Corporate Governance Principles

Since corporate governance can be highly influential for firm performance, firms must know what the corporate governance principles are and how it will improve strategy to apply these principles. In practice, there are five principles of good corporate governance:

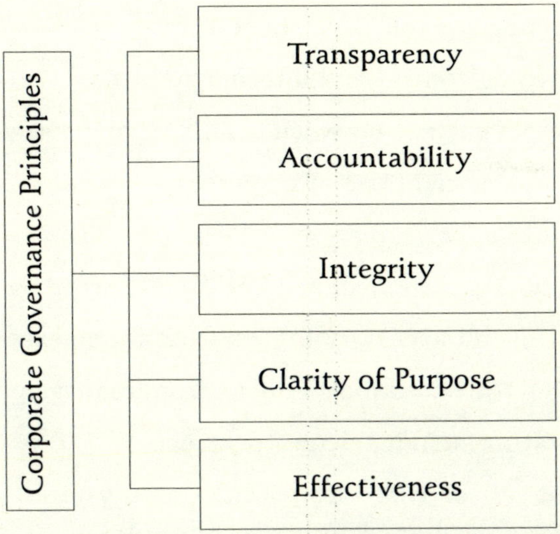

Corporate governance procedures determine every aspect of the role for firm's management to try and maintain balance and to develop control mechanism in order to increase both shareholder value and stakeholder satisfaction. In other words, corporate governance is concerned with creating a balance between the economic and social goals of a company including aspects like efficient use of resources, accountability in the use of its power and the behaviour of the corporation in its social environment.

The definition and measurement of good corporate governance is still subject to debate. However, good corporate governance will address all these main points:

- Creating sustainable value.
- Ways of achieving firm's goals.
- Increasing shareholder's satisfaction.
- Efficient and effective management.
- Increasing credibility.
- Ensuring efficient risk management.
- Providing an early warning system against all risk.
- Ensuring a responsive and accountable corporation.

- Describing the role of a firm's units.
- Developing control and internal auditing.
- Keeping a balance between economic and social benefits.
- Ensuring efficient use of resources.
- Controlling performance.
- Distributing responsibility fairly.
- Producing all necessary information for stakeholders.
- Keeping the board independent from management.
- Facilitating sustainable performance.

As evident, all of these issues have many ramifications and ensuring their compliance must be thought of as a long-term procedure. However, firms naturally expect some tangible benefit from good governance, so good governance offers some long-term benefits for firms, such as:

- Increasing the firm's market value.
- Increasing competitive power.
- Attracting new investors, shareholders and adding equity.
- More or higher credibility.
- Enhancing flexible means for a smooth functioning with financial institutions.
- New investment opportunities.
- Attracting good manpower.
- Capturing new markets.

It is also an acceptable fact that all these long-term benefits are directly related to the sustainability of a firm's success.

Development of CSR

There has been considerable debate about the relationship between CSR and corporate governance, but in recent years, the term CSR has gained prominence, both in business and in the press to such an extent that it seems to have become ubiquitous.

There are probably many reasons for the attention given to this phenomenon, not least of which is the corporate excesses witnessed in recent years.

CSR therefore involves a concern with the various stakeholders to a business but there are several problems in identifying socially responsible behaviour:

- Research shows that the concern is primarily with those stakeholders who have power to influence the organisation. Thus organisations are most concerned with shareholders, less with customers and employees and very little with society and the environment. CSR would imply that they are all of equal importance.
- The definitions imply that CSR is a voluntary activity rather than enforced through regulation, whereas in actual fact, it is an approach and the voluntary-regulated debate is irrelevant.
- Claiming a concern is very different to actually exhibiting that concern through actions taken (Crowther, 2004).

Definitions of CSR abound but all can be seen as an attempt to explain and define the relationship between a corporation and its stakeholders, including its relationship with society as a whole. Many too are phrased in terms of the triple bottom line, in a way which, we argue, trivialises the concept. Because of the uncertainty surrounding the nature of CSR activity it is difficult to evaluate any such activity. It is therefore imperative to be able to identify such activity and Aras and Crowther (2007b) argue that there are three basic principles which together comprise all CSR activities. These are:

- Sustainability.
- Accountability.
- Transparency.

No matter whether the discourse is of CSR or of sustainability, there exists a high degree of skepticism about the reality of corporate activity. There have been arguments on a perception that CSR is a developmental process and changes as organisations mature in their behaviour and attitude towards both their stakeholders and their ideas concerning social responsibility. Of course, there is growing body of evidence to show that social responsibility behaviour becomes reflected positively in financial performance of a company, thereby providing a financial imperative for changing behaviour. It would be relatively easy to develop a typology of CSR activity based on the treatment of various stakeholders to an organisation but as Cooper *et al.* (2001) show, all corporations are concerned with their important stakeholders and make efforts to satisfy their expectations.

Thus, a concern with employees and customers is apparent in all corporations, being merely a reflection of the power of those stakeholder groupings rather than an expression of social responsibility. Similarly, in some organisations, a concern for the environment is less a representation of social responsibility and more a concern for avoiding legislation or possibly a reflection of customer concern. Such factors also apply to some expressions of concern for local communities and society at large. It is therefore inappropriate to base any typology of CSR activity upon the treatment of stakeholders as this is often based upon power relationships rather than a concern for social responsibility, and it is not realistic to distinguish the motivations.

A different typology was therefore proposed—one which is based upon the three principles of social responsibility outlined earlier. Moreover, it shows the way in which CSR develops in organisations as they become more experienced and more convinced of the benefits of a commitment to this form of corporate activity. The development of this typology is based upon research conducted with concerned managers in a considerable number of large corporations, many of which are committed to increasing social responsibility. It demonstrates stages of increasing maturity.

Table 5.1

Stages of Maturity of CSR Activity

Stages of Development	*Dominant Feature*	*Typical Activity*	*Examples*
1	Window dressing	Redesigning corporate reporting	Changed wording and sections to reflect CSR language (see Crowther, 2004)
2	Cost containment	Re-engineering business processes	Energy efficiency programmes
3	Stakeholder engagement	Balanced scorecard development	Customer/employee satisfaction surveys (see Cooper *et al.*, 2001)
4	Measurement and Reporting	Sophisticated tailored measures	CSR reports
5	Sustainability	Defining sustainability: re-engineering processes	Sustainability reporting
6	Transparency	Concern for the supply chain: requiring CSR from suppliers	Human rights enforcement: e.g., child labour
7	Accountability	Reconfiguration of the value chain	Relocating high value added activity in developing countries

Source: Crowther (2006).

Relating Corporate Governance and CSR

It is of course no longer questioned that the activities of a corporation impact upon the external environment and therefore such an organisation should be accountable to a wider audience than simply its shareholders. This is a central tenet of both the concept of corporate governance and the concept of CSR. Implicit in this is a concern with the effects of the actions of an organisation on its external environment and there is recognition that it is not just the owners of the organisation who have a concern with the activities of that organisation. Additionally there are a wide variety of other stakeholders who justifiably have a concern with those activities, and are affected by those activities. Those other stakeholders have not just an interest in the activities of the firm but also a degree of influence over the shaping of those activities. This influence is so significant that it can be argued that the power and influence of these stakeholders is such that it amount to quasi-ownership of the organisation.

Corporate governance and CSR are therefore complementary in their shaping of the objective function and the constraints faced by corporations. They can reinforce each other in the modern vision of the firm as an institution which does not disregard various relevant constituencies in its search for increase in value. The modern and socially responsible firm can go beyond the simple definition of accounting profits if it realises that such a definition ignores pieces of value which are practically relevant. It does not matter whether accounting profits neglect negative consequences on the environment, violation of human rights and other elements. These elements are crucial to the evaluation of the corporation which is given by the society. Fortunately, the modern environment has an increasing number of tools which may be used to induce corporations to move beyond the traditional bottom line and towards an extended bottom line.

Socially responsible firms with good corporate governance are often also the most respected and profitable firms. Therefore, socially responsible actions are not selected by firms from the pool of profit-decreasing choices. Therefore, good corporate governance protects the stakeholders which contributes to the life of the firm. Corporate governance and CSR are strong compliments. The positive relation existing between both on one hand and the market value of the firm on the other hand suggests the market competition is somehow able to detect the companies which are best also from the point of view which are not included in the accounting definition of profit. This is reassuring hypothesis, which merits more theoretical and empirical analysis.

Role of Board Members

The corporate governance framework should ensure the strategic guidance of the company, effective monitoring of management by the board, and the board's accountability towards the company and the shareholders.

Board structures and procedures both vary:

- Some countries have two-tier boards that separate the supervisory function and the management functions into different bodies. Such systems typically have a 'supervisory board' composed of non-executive board members and a 'management board' composed entirely of executives.
- Other countries have 'unitary' boards, which bring together executive and non-executive board members.
- In some countries, there is also an additional statutory body for audit purposes.

The principles are intended to be sufficiently general to apply to whatever board structure is charged with the functions of governing the enterprise and monitoring management.

Together with guiding corporate strategy, the board is also responsible for monitoring managerial performance and achieving an adequate return for shareholders, while preventing conflicts of interest and balancing competing demands. In order for the board's to effectively fulfil their responsibilities, they must be able to exercise objective and independent judgement. Another important responsibility is to oversee system's designed to ensure that the corporation obeys applicable laws, including tax, competition, labour, equal opportunity, health, safety and environmental laws.

In some countries, companies have found useful to explicitly articulate the responsibility that the board assumes and those for which management is accountable. In addition to monitoring and disclosure of corporate governance practices on a regular basis, a number of countries have moved to recommend or indeed mandate self-assessment by boards of their performance as well as performance reviews of individual board members and the chief executive officer (CEO)/chairman.

The board is not only accountable to the company and its shareholders but also has a duty to act in their best interest. In addition, boards are expected to take due regard of and deal fairly with other stakeholders interests including those of employees, creditors, customers, suppliers and local communities. Observance of environmental and social standards is relevant in this context.

Concept of Global Governance

All systems of governance are concerned primarily with managing the governing of associations and therefore with political authority, institutions and ultimately control. Governance in this particular sense denotes formal political institutions that aim to coordinate and control interdependent social relations that have the ability to enforce decisions. Increasingly, however, in a globalised world, the concept of governance is being used to describe the regulation of interdependent relations in the absence of overarching political authority, such as in the international system. Thus, global governance can be considered as the management of global processes in the absence of a form of global government. There are some international bodies which seek to address these issues and prominent among these are the United Nations (UN) and the World Trade Organization (WTO). Each of these have met with mixed success in instituting some form of governance in international relations but are part of a recognition of the problem and an attempt to address worldwide problems that go beyond the capacity of individual states to solve.

To use the term global governance is not of course to imply that such a system actually exists, let alone to consider the effectiveness of its operations. It is merely to recognise that in this increasingly globalised world, there is a need for some form of governance to deal with multinational and global issues. The term global governance, therefore, is a descriptive term, recognising the issue and referring to concrete problem-solving arrangements. These may be formal, taking the shape of laws or formally constituted institutions to manage collective affairs by a variety of bodies—including states, intergovernmental organisations, non-governmental organisations (NGOs), other civil society actors, private sector organisations, pressure groups and individuals. The system also includes of course informal or temporary units. Thus, global governance can be considered to be the complex of formal and informal institutions, mechanisms, relationships and processes between and among states, markets, citizens and organisations, both inter- and non-governmental, through which collective interests on the global plane are articulated, rights and obligations are established, and differences are mediated.

Global governance is not of course the same as world government; indeed it can be argued that such a system would not actually be necessary if there was such a thing as a world government. Currently however various state governments have a legitimate monopoly on the use of force—on the power of enforcement. Global governance therefore refers to the political interaction that is required to solve problems that affect more than one state or region when there is no power of enforcing compliance. Improved global problem-solving need not of course require the establishing of more powerful formal global institutions, but it would involve the creation of a consensus on norms and practices to be applied. Steps are of course underway to establish these norms and one example that is currently being established is the creation and improvement of global accountability mechanism. In this respect, for example, the United Nations Global Compact10—described as the worlds' largest voluntary corporate responsibility initiative—brings together companies, national and international agencies, trade unions and other labour organisations, and various organs of civil society in order to support universal environmental protection, human rights and social principles. Participation is entirely voluntary, and there is no enforcement of the principles by an outside regulatory body. Companies adhere to these practices both because they make economic sense and because their stakeholders, including their shareholders, are concerned with these issues, and this provides a mechanism whereby they can monitor the compliance of companies easily. Mechanisms such as Global Compact can improve the ability of individual and local communities to hold companies accountable.

CSR as a Mode of Global Governance

Calls for multinational corporations (MNCs) to demonstrate greater responsibility, transparency and accountability are leading to establishment of a variety of new governance structures: rules, norms, code of conduct and standards. The day-to-day production, employment, research and marketing practices of large companies play a critical role in shaping environmental impacts, labour practices, income distribution and even consumer identities. MNC's global reach highlights spatial differences in living and labour standards, health care and individual rights. MNCs have *de facto*, become part of the fabric of global governance, the emerging multi-layered and multi-actor system of global authority. Their strategies and operations are thus inherently political.

MNCs have been put in the spotlight by the confluence of the rise of CSR discourse and the growth of social movements with the capacity to monitor and publicise MNC operations.

CSR, as a system of rules, standards, norms and expectations, serves as a form of global governance that shapes MNC practices and constructs them as moral agents. CSR can be viewed as a more socially embedded and democratic form of governance that emanates from civil society or alternatively, as a privatised system of corporate governance that lacks public accountability. We argue that CSR represents contested political terrain as well as a strategic tool deployed in struggles over corporate governance. The meaning of CSR itself is a key point of political struggle: business could assume a degree of responsibility for social outcomes, while retaining full authority and autonomy, or it could be held responsible and accountable to society in ways that cede substantive authority to multiple stakeholders. Where CSR differs most sharply from historical efforts to restrain markets is in its reliance on the private realm rather than the state. CSR can shape assumptions regarding consumer behaviour, competitors' reactions and regulatory responses, thus molding the market environment within which corporate strategy is developed. Although CSR has clearly achieved considerable success in shifting corporate practices and attitudes, it does not compromise the core economic structures and managerial prerogatives of contemporary market societies. Indeed, it proclaims the harmony of financial and social interests. Yet the harmony of business and social interests posited by CSR advocates is thus not something to take for granted, but rather represents a discursive and material compromise that emerges from the strategies of various parties. Advocates for CSR can generate legitimacy for stakeholders, shift societal expectations of business, create media attention, directly pressure business, bring attention to win-win opportunities, and even shape market environments. For business, CSR compromises an element of corporate political strategy that offers social legitimacy, some attractive market opportunities, and protection against more severe activist demands and regulatory pressure. CSR therefore rests on a rather precarious balance of conflict and cooperation.

CSR is thus an emergent form of governance that can redress, to some degree, the governance deficit that exists in the international arena. This political-strategic approach stands in sharp contrast to more conventional perspectives that develop an ethical and business case for CSR. CSR is not just a struggle over practices, but over the locus of governance authority, offering a potential path towards the transformation of stakeholders from external observers and petitioners into legitimate and organised participants in decision making.

Conclusion

It is clear that the definition of corporate governance has extended considerably beyond investor relations and encompasses relations with all the stakeholders including the environment. This is essential for the longer-term survival of a firm and is therefore a key component of sustainability. There is evidence that some firms understand this but they are in minority. Therefore, it is possible to say that good corporate governance will address this but that not all firms recognise this. It is equally possible to state that a firm which has a more complete understanding of the relationship between social responsibility, sustainability and corporate governance will address these issues more completely. By implication, a more complete understanding of the inter-relationships will lead to better corporate governance, and therefore to better economic performance.

The other tentative conclusion is concerned with the extent of disclosure manifested through the reporting of such things as corporate governance and CSR, and is more in the nature of a prognosis. Crowther (2000) traces an archaeology of corporate reporting which shows that, over time, the amount of information provided—first to shareholders, then to potential investors (Gilmore and Willmott, 1992), then to other stakeholders—has gradually increased throughout the last century, as firms recognised the benefit in providing increased disclosure. Similarly, the amount of disclosure regarding CSR activity has been increasing rapidly over the last decade, as firms have recognised the commercial benefits of increased transparency. Therefore, it is reasonable to argue that the amount of information regarding the relationship between governance and social responsibility will also increase, not just as firms gain a clearer understanding of that relationship, but also as they understand the benefits of greater disclosure in this respect. Thus, we consider that this will become more apparent over time.

References

Aras, G. and D. Crowther (2007a). "Is the Global Economy Sustainable?", in S. Barber (ed.) (2007a), *The Geopolitics of the City*. London: Forum Press. pp.165-94.

———. (2007b). "The Development of Corporate Social Responsibility", *Effective Executive* X(9): 18-21. September.

———. (2007b). "Sustainable Corporate Social Responsibility and the Value Chain", in M. Zain and D. Crowther (eds.), *New Perspectives on Corporate Social Responsibility*. Kuala Lumpur: Mara University Press; pp.119-40.

———. (2010). *A Handbook of Corporate Governance and Social Responsibility*.

Beltratti, A. (2005). "The Complementarity between Corporate Governance and Corporate Social Responsibility", *The Geneva Papers* 30: 373-86.

Bushman, R.M. and A.J. Smith (2001). "Financial Accounting Information and Corporate Governance", *Journal of Accounting and Economics* 32: 237-333.

Cavico, F.J. and B.G. Mujtaba (2012). "National and Global Perspectives of Corporate Social Responsibility", *International Journal of Management Sciences and Business Research* 1(3).

Cooper, S., D. Crowther, M. Davies and E.W. Davis (2001). *Shareholder or Stakeholder Value? The Development of Indicators for the Control and Measurement of Performance*. London: CIMA.

Crowther, D. (2000). "Corporate Reporting, Stakeholders and the Internet: Mapping the New Corporate Landscape", *Urban Studies* 37 (10): 1837-48.

———. (2004). "Limited Liability or Limited Responsibility", in D. Crowther and L. Rayman-Bacchus (eds.) (2004), *Perspectives on Corporate Social Responsibility*. Aldershot: Ashgate. pp.42-58.

———. (2006). "Standards of Corporate Social Responsibility: Convergence with the European Union", in D. Njavro and K. Kirkuk (eds.) (2006), *Business Ethics and Corporate Social Responsibility*. Zagreb: MATE. pp.17-34.

Gilmore, C.G. and H. Willmott (1992). "Company Law and Financial Reporting: A Sociological History of the UK Experience", in M. Bromwick and A. Hopwood (eds.) (1992). *Accounting and the Law*. Hemel Hempstead: Prentice Hall. pp.159-91.

Hermalin, B.E. (2005). "Trends in Corporate Governance", *Journal of Finance* LX (5): 2351-84.

OECD Principles of Corporate Governance (2004). OECD Publications.

Rahim, M.M. (2013). *Legal Regulation of Corporate Social Responsibility, CSR, Sustainability, Ethics & Governance*. Heidelberg: Springer-Verlag Berlin.

Reilly, E. (2009). *Guide to Principles of Good Governance*. British and Irish Ombudsman Association.

6

DHARMESH PUSHPA DHAWANKAR

Social Auditing and Public Policy

A Mass Media Critique

Introduction

Policy makers have traditionally viewed the media as a shortcut to public opinion because they rightly or wrongly assume that the general public is heavily influenced by what they read in the papers or watch on television. Adapting to the priorities of the media is therefore a strategy to respond to what are believed to be the demands and preferences of the electorate. In some cases, the response will be confined to symbolic politics; in others, it will be more substantial as proposals might be altered, postponed to a time when public opinion is strategically less crucial, or even aborted altogether. At the same time, policy makers are expected to demonstrate leadership and vision, which is why public announcements of policy changes are usually interpreted as giving in to the pressure of the media or the whims of public opinion—as the example at the beginning of this chapter illustrates—rather than as the responsiveness to citizens' concerns. Therefore, political actors routinely evaluate policy proposals in view of the reaction they might trigger in the media before pursuing them through the legislative process. The media have become such an indispensable part of modern democratic life that they often seem to dominate the political process. Many observers would answer the question positively whether media govern, pointing to numerous instances where media campaigns have put pressure on policy makers to revise their decisions. Given the widespread concerns of political insiders, it comes as a surprise that the academic disciplines that are mainly concerned with issues of the relationship between politics and the media—political science and communication studies—have paid relatively little attention to the role of the media in the policy process. So far, most research on the political impact of the media has focused on two main areas of enquiry: the media's influence on citizens' political attitudes and political behaviour, and the professionalisation of election campaigns and the emergence of political marketing. This study aims to fill this gap by exploring whether, to what extent and under what circumstances the media affect public policy, i.e., the processes and outcomes of political decision making.

New Media: A Fair Tool of Audit for Social Issues

The emergence of new media tool has given a fillip to the overall understanding of how the social issues be tackled. These issues can be sublimely to the overlapping phases of the social order in a given circumspective society. The social audit of media is not a control process to be used during a crisis, although it can pinpoint potential problem areas and generate solutions. A social audit of media may be comprehensive and encompass all of the social impact areas of a business, or it can be specific and focus on one or two areas. There are obvious reasons to assume that the media have little chance to influence policy decisions. One argument is the volatility of media coverage. The news rarely focuses on an issue over a sustained period of time, and thus generates only spotlights of attention that hardly leave any traces in the memory of the audience. In contrast, the policy agenda develops over long time spans, often involving several legislative terms. Further, the media's representation of politics is mainly concerned with personalities, whereas the policy process revolves around highly specialised fields of regulation. Finally, the substance of the media agenda differs from the policy agenda in that it is driven by newsworthy events rather than structural problems, such as the health system, economic growth or the budget. Thus, there seems to be a fundamental mismatch between the way in which the media operate and the processes of policy making. What then are the mechanisms that could be considered to provide possible entry points for media influences?

While policy makers pay attention to the media as a manifestation of public opinion, they also follow the news as a way of monitoring the political environment in which they operate. Given the growing specialisation and segmentation of the policy process, it has become virtually impossible even for long-serving politicians to keep abreast of what is going on elsewhere in government, in the opposition or even within their own party. The media have a unique capacity to bridge these different spheres and to serve as the 'nerves of government' that link the divergent parts. Not only do the media cover a broad range of issues, from developments in society at large to actual government actions, but they are also consumed by everybody which in turn creates a sphere of shared knowledge where each actor in the system knows what the others know. Unlike ordinary citizens, policy makers use the media mainly for strategic purposes. Information obtained from the media provides them with clues that help them to monitor the movements of their opponents and to gauge their own standing within an ever-shifting constellation of policy coalitions. They can then adjust their own strategies, which may include re-framing an issue or policy proposal, distracting attention from unfavourable issues to safer ones, or using the media to attack the position of opponents. These implications of the media's monopolistic characteristics have to be rooted out if they have to be absorbed in total congregation of corporate issues.

Role of Media in Social Issues

The increased visibility of corporate social responsibility (CSR) has encouraged companies to better account for their actions in a wide range of areas, including human resources, environmental policies, ethics programmes, and community involvement. At one extreme, a company may want to achieve the best social performance possible, whereas at the other extreme, a firm may desire to project a good image to hide misconduct. Still other companies may see the auditing process as a key component of organisational improvement. Here comes the role of media to rake in issues that concern the social milieu. In order to explain the often contradicting evidence of the media's influence on policy, some scholars have suggested policy uncertainty and elite consensus as intervening variables that reduce, or enhance, the media's ability to change the course of policy making (Robinson, 2001). Policy uncertainty is assumed to make political decision makers more susceptible to the pressure of media coverage, in particular when the issue involved can be portrayed with sensational images that have the potential to mobilise public opinion up to a point of moral panic. Conversely, consensus among policy makers works like a protective shield because it reduces the interest of the media in the topic. Typically, the media's attention is drawn to a policy debate when internal splits or sharp divisions between political parties become obvious. Once the media have become involved, the dynamic and direction of a policy can change dramatically. Increased media coverage usually intensifies the conflict and invites new actors to enter the debate and to join one of the opposing camps. Policy alternatives must then be formulated in a manner that suits the media's thirst for sound bites and catchy headlines, and since the conflict is now enacted in front of the public eye, compromises and backstage deals become less likely. Besides the complexity of the conditionality of media influences in the policy process, the attempt to systematise the media–policy nexus is further aggravated by the dubious relationship between cause and effect. Research approaches that follow this logic of enquiry have frequently shed important light on the forces that shape public policy. In particular, longitudinal agenda research that compares the changes of issue salience on the media and policy agenda, often complemented by measures of public opinion, has proven extremely effective in establishing empirical evidence for the power of the media and its limitations in public policy (Baumgartner and Jones, 1993; Page and Shapiro, 1992). However, this approach might miss out some of the processes that are going on. As mentioned above, policy makers and journalists are continuously engaged in an exchange of information where it becomes impossible to work out who is influencing whom. Mutual dependency has led to each side developing new strategies to respond to the attempts of influence of their counterparts a constant 'arms race' to control the public agenda. As a consequence, the dynamics of media coverage of political activities and the response of external actors and public opinion does not follow a linear pattern that can be captured by common stochastic modeling. Therefore the role of the new media is very schematic, as its reach and access have specific boundaries to achieve. The social issues that concern the policy and the implementation occur here. This may give a scholastic approach to the CSR activity to rake in a new philosophy of policy matter that can be loaded with the introduction and sanction of the popular choices of media use by the corporate and the people alike.

Is Policy Making Correlated to Media?

The literature at hand suggests that the media and public policy is patchy and provides a rather incoherent picture. This meta-analysis thus indicates that the media can be a relevant force in the policy process that needs to be taken more systematically into account if we are to better understand the dynamics of public policy in modern democracies. Predicting and adapting to media response has become ever more vital because journalists seem to have given up their traditional 'sacerdotal' orientation toward politicians and political institutions to adopt a more adversarial, even aggressive style of political reporting. Thus, supportive media coverage of new policy initiatives has become less likely than in the past, which further increases the pressure on policy makers to engage in active news management. Another factor that has contributed to uncertainty in the policy process is the dramatic development of communication technologies over the past decade. In particular, the Internet has opened up new opportunities to communicate directly with citizens without the interference of journalistic gatekeepers and to establish policy networks with allies that have formerly been isolated from national politics. But the Internet has also provided new actors with a forum to disseminate alternative views to large audiences, which has significantly diminished the ability of policy makers to control the communication environment in which they operate.

New communication technologies, such as satellite transmission and digital cameras, have also changed policy making in the international realm. Here 24-hour news coverage with instant global reach and live reporting have altered the mode and pace of decision making, especially in the context of international crises, military operations and humanitarian interventions (Gilboa, 2005; Livingston and Bennett, 2003). Utilising the media may enable policy makers to gain control over the public agenda, but they can only achieve this by accepting the media's rule of the game. These in turn affects the process and, to some extent, even the outcome of policy making. 'Mediatisation' can therefore be regarded as another mechanism through which the media affect public policy. The term refers to a situation 'where political institutions are increasingly dependent on and shaped by mass media'. The central role of the media in the policy process has made the political arena into an extremely unpredictable, even dangerous, terrain where a slip of the tongue, a leaked email or a premature public statement can damage not only a policy proposal but also political careers (Kepplinger, 2007). However, the media rarely generate policies; they have, according to Meyer (2002), 'colonised' the political process by imposing their operational logic on the institutional procedures of public policy. With regard to policy making, mediatisation involves tailoring policy decisions with a view to their communication through the media.

A further mechanism of media influence on policy making is the closeness of interaction between politicians and journalists in the day-to-day routines of politics. Although journalists like to see themselves as watchdogs and adversaries *vis-à-vis* political power holders, most of the time the two sets of actors—journalists and politicians—cooperate rather than work against each other. Research on media–source relationships has shown that news is a joint product emerging from frequent interactions and shared norms between journalists and political actors. Conversely—and more significant in the context of the present analysis—politicians regularly seek the exchange of ideas with journalists and form issue coalitions with those who hold similar views either to promote a particular proposal or to attack oppositional ones (Davis, 2007). Hence, policy makers and journalists, especially at the top level of each elite group, can be seen as interpretative communities with each part having an impact in the formation of policy.

One crucial condition that sets the frame for the media–policy link is the policy field and its specific dynamic. Policy fields constitute complex settings of constellations of actors, legal and procedural frameworks and specific policy instruments. Policy fields that can be assumed to limit, or even exclude, media involvement are those that are characterised by a high degree of path dependency and the dominance of civil servants. It is unlikely that the media will take notice of the highly specialised, often esoteric, debates going on in these arenas—unless a gross policy failure occurs that has the potential for a full-blown media scandal. In contrast, less established policy fields provide plenty of opportunities for new actors to enter the arena, and they usually do this by mobilising the media for their cause. Equally, policy fields that are closely linked to electoral politics can be assumed to be more vulnerable to media interference because politicians are highly dependent on the media to win the support of voters. A special case is policy fields that directly affect the professional or economic interests of the media because here the media enter the field as interested parties. Media policy is the obvious case where the media are both reporters of events and a lobby group, but other areas, such as economic policy and taxes, could be affected too.

Function of Media in CSR Policy Matter

Does the mass media have the capacity and power to influence the CSR policy making agenda? Media models of agenda-setting have focused mostly on the relationship between public opinion and media coverage rather than on the CSR policy making process itself (McCombs, 1997), but clearly there is an underlying assumption in these studies that public opinion influences public policy. But, of the many stages of the social policy process in which the media surely plays a role, media agenda-setting studies tend to focus on how the media influences electoral vote choice or other forms of civic participation. While these are clearly important components of the policy process, scholarly attention should shift to how the media affects other stages, especially macro political agenda-setting, decision-making and bureaucratic behaviour. Tests of the indexing hypothesis are unable to identify causal mechanisms to explain who is leading whom. The problem with existing studies is that they never compare systematically the agenda-setting power of the media with that of government officials. We have devised a scheme that allows for this explicit comparison. This is a natural, and at the same time crucial, extension of the existing literature comparing media agenda-setting and indexing. What cannot be overemphasised is that an overwhelming amount of scholarship to date examining press–state does so in settings that are event-driven (focusing on events or policy failures) rather than issue-driven and more on international crises or local events rather than on and in domestic (national) policy arenas. The role of the media in the public policy process can be broadly characterised by four distinct theories. These theories fundamentally focus on the interactions between the media, collectively characterised, and politicians, again collectively characterised. The theories are:

- Influence theory: the media tell the politicians what to think.
- Agenda-setting theory: the media tell the politicians what to think about.
- Indexing theory: the politicians tell the media what to write about.
- Detection theory: Politicians and the media struggle to identify, characterise and prioritise multiple complex streams of information.

We advocate moving away from understanding the media–policy maker relationships outlined in the influence, agenda-setting and indexing theories, which imply direct, mostly linear, causal relationships, to a complex systems framework focusing on information flows, which implies nonlinear, interactive relationships. Influence theory depicts the media as private businesses producing profit, increasingly conglomerate and non-competitive. These corporate interests pursue government policies that benefit the bottom line. While this may indirectly affect the flow of information, it is of less interest here than other theories of media influence because it falls more in the domain of interest group politics and can be understood through those models of policy making.

A major problem with existing models of mass media effects on public policy is that they are rooted in an influence framework. The question of who has power is certainly not irrelevant, but it has led to overly simplistic models of the interaction between government officials and the media. The media is intimately involved in this process, but it is a mistake to think of its role in direct, causal terms. Causation implies influence; influence implies intentionality. Clearly, corporate leaders intend to influence the media, but it is less clear that the media intends to influence the corporate world, once we get beyond the issue of corporate self-interest. It is even less clear that any one set of actors be they from the media or the political elites, or from business or from 'the public' in any sense 'controls' policy making. However, what anecdotal evidence is presented on the effects of media consolidation does not seem to cut in one direction. On the one hand, surely consolidation has led to the concentration of power in the hands of fewer individuals, and the drive for profits has led to less news content, more hype and episodic frames. On the other hand, new media outlets, including the internet and the propensity of news organisations, even in oligopolies, to compete may offset this tendency, but evidence for this cuts both ways as well.

As far as the 'pandering to mass tastes' complaint, we suspect that has been a part of the media mix as long as there has been media. Our notion of the role of the media in the policy making process changes when we incorporate elements of an information-processing approach to press–state dynamics. It is likely that for many issues, both the press and policy makers are responding to changes in indexes of objective conditions. Responses of either or both may be disproportionate—a long period of under-reaction with bursts of over-reaction (Jones and Baumgartner, 2005). This means that the relationship between the press and policy makers is characterised by non-linearities and positive feedback effects, such as tonal, context-setting effects and policy outbursts. In some respects, it does not matter whether the media acts as agenda-setters, as indexers, or as information detectors. Once a positive feedback reaction sets in, the rule of policy outcomes becomes different, large changes are more probable, and public opinion becomes more important. In the information processing framework, we suggest that information about the importance and salience of issues are transmitted as signals, which can be amplified or attenuated by the interaction of media coverage and public opinion in a complex environment with multiple streams of information. The media can reweight the strength of these signals. The stronger the signal, the clearer and more urgent the message, the more likely government will respond, and the larger the response. While this implies that our notions of causation, and hence influence, must become more sensitive to context, it by no means implies we need to give up on the development of theory. It does mean that these theories will be increasingly related to the 'complex systems' perspective common in the natural sciences today.

Conclusion/Discussion

Of course the idea of social audit and the social issues that coincide with the holistic policy of CSR activity has to be addressed here to get the maximum advantage in terms of the corporate objectives. There are basically two broad views propping up in holistic media environment. First, media can have a direct impact on what people think about certain policy decisions. Media campaigns for a 'hard line on crime' may shift the policy preferences of the electorate towards more repressive policies. Politicians trying to secure public support for their policies will feel compelled to follow suit, at least to certain degree, if they want to avoid being exposed by their political rivals for not 'listening to the people.' Second, media make politicians believe that certain issues need to be addressed by determining the agenda of the public debate and by claiming to voice the opinions of the proverbial ordinary man. Again, politicians may react to such agenda setting even though there may be no evidence that public opinion actually shares the concerns expressed by the media. To be sure, this dichotomy simplifies the intricate relationship between media and policy makers. In many cases, it is found that, by occupying a position at the end of a 'chain of influence,' politicians may themselves be in a position to influence the media contents and hence the conditions under which they act. However, this simple dichotomy reminds us that some of the alleged media influence may actually happen in the minds of the politicians who may simply lack the confidence to keep faith to their principles if they come under media fire. Furthermore, our perception of media influence is largely influenced by the media discourse itself, and it can come as no surprise that journalists will lean towards exaggerating their own role in any significant policy shift. As such, many accounts of media influence contain an element of a self-fulfilling prophecy. This brief sketch clearly shows that there is sufficient scope for carefully disentangling the complex web of mutual influence. However, there is no simple answer. While some high profile policy decisions are exposed to the limelight of the public debate, many policy decisions are simply too uninteresting or too complex and will therefore not attract much media attention. Furthermore, the complex policy cycle frequently exhausts media attention. In other words, media attention tends to be rather short-term and focused on specific events, while policy making is slow and often driven by intricate detail. It follows from this that the general question for the policy impact of the media is too simple. Specific types of policies are more susceptible to media influence than others. Furthermore, to conclude, media influence is rarely 'the result of intentional intervention on the part of the journalists.' Rather, it works indirectly through the discursive power of the media. Yet, this discursive power is not always directed at the most important political problems of society. While individual high profile crimes regularly lead to a considerable overestimation of the relevant crime rates by mass publics, structural problems like poverty or unemployment are often underrepresented in the media. To be sure, some of these biases are simply due to the inherent media logic driven by the news value of certain policies or events.

This is very imperative to understand that the role of media is not subjected to one view of understanding. The basic apprehension has to be glued properly if the media has to undergo the pluralistic changes. However, it would be naïve to neglect the fact that those who own or control the media owners can and will influence editorial policies and hence the discursive power of the media.

We expect the media to have under certain circumstances the capacity to bring new issues and new frames into the policy debate. This in turn may lead to a reconfiguration of policy institutions by providing opportunities for new actors to enter the arena. A redefinition of a problem that is already part of the policy agenda can also result in the reorganisation of existing responsibilities and structures. We do not suggest, though, that the media's influence in the policy process is paramount or that policy making is dominated by the dynamic of public communication, as theories of 'media democracy' suggest. There are large areas of policy making that are entirely unaffected by the media. However, we argue that if the media enter the policy arena, they are able to change the course of decision making and the policy outcome in significant ways. Whether and to what extent political decision makers adopt the media's constructions of reality in their own perceptions and evaluations remains an open question, however. First, political professionals might be excessive media users, but they have elaborated information-processing strategies that largely immunise them against media influence on their attitudes. Second, because the political elites are also embedded in various channels of direct communication and have access to insider documents, they are able to access numerous alternative sources of information. The specific function of the media is to process and consolidate different streams of information, thus providing an overall picture of the situation, beyond the highly specialised communication networks of experts. The dysfunctions of the scattered and uneven corporate policies relating to the social audit have an unbecoming impact on the social milieu. In fact, the new media has come up with the unending abilities to give you a social platform of your character which will serve a long way to fulfil all the objectives of the social obligations related to the CSR initiatives. Thus, the media has its slice of functional intervention which the corporate world has to understand and negotiate properly for maximum benefit.

References

Baumgartner, Frank R. and Bryan D. Jones (1993). *Agendas and Instabilities in American Politics*. Chicago: University of Chicago Press.

Blumler, J.G. and M. Gurevitch (1995). *The Crisis of Public Communication*. London: Routledge.

Coleman, S., J. Taylor and W. van de Donk (eds.) (1999). *Parliament in the Age of the Internet*. Oxford: Oxford University Press.

Chaffee, S.H. and S.F. Kanihan (1997). "Learning about Politics from the Mass Media", *Political Communication* 14(4): 421-30.

Davis, A. (2007). "Investigating Journalist Influences on Political Issue Agendas at Westminster", *Political Communication* 24(2): 181-99.

Entman, R.M. (1989). "How the Media Affect what People Think: An Information Processing Approach", *Journal of Politics* 51(2): 347-70.

Gandy, O. (1982). *Beyond Agenda-setting*. Norwood, NJ: Ablex.

Gans, H.J. (1979). *Deciding What's News*. New York: Pantheon Books.

Gilboa, E. (2005). "The CNN Effect: The Search for a Communication Theory of International Relations", *Political Communication* 22: 27-44.

John, P. (2006). "Explaining Policy Change: The Impact of the Media, Public Opinion and Political Violence on Urban Budgets in England", *Journal of European Public Policy* 13(7): 1053-68.

Jones, B.D. and F.R. Baumgartner (2005). *The Politics of Attention: How Government Prioritises Problems*. Chicago, IL: University of Chicago Press.

Kennamer, D.J. (ed.) (1992). *Public Opinion, the Press, and Public Policy*. Westport, CT: Praeger.

Kernell, S. (1997). "The Theory and Practice of Going Public", in S. Iyengar and R. Reeves (eds.) (1997), *Do the Media Govern*? Thousand Oaks: SAGE Publications: pp.323-33.

Kepplinger, H.M. (2007). "Reciprocal Effects: Towards a Theory of Mass Media Effects on Decision Makers", *Harvard International Journal of Press/Politics* 12(2): 3-23.

Livingston, S. and W.L. Bennett (2003). "Gatekeeping, Indexing, and Life-event News: Is Technology Altering the Construction of News?", *Political Communication* 20: 363-80.

Mazzoleni, G. and W. Schulz (1999). "Mediatization of Politics: A Challenge for Democracy?", *Political Communication* 16(3): 247-61.

McCombs, M.E. (1977). "Newspapers versus Television: Mass Communication Effects Across Time", in D.L. Shaw and M.E. McCombs (eds.) (1977), "The Agenda-setting Function of the Press", *Public Opinion Quarterly* 36(2): 176-87.

Meyer, T. (wlth Lew Hinchman) (2002). *Media Democracy: How the Media Colonize Politics*. Cambridge, UK: Polity.

Moy, P., E. Manosevitch, K. Stamm and K. Dunsmore (2005). "Linking Dimensions of Internet Use and Civic Engagement", *Journalism and Mass Communication Quarterly* 82(3): 571-86.

Molotch, H.L., D.L. Protess and M.T. Gordon (1987). "The Media–Policy Connection. Ecologies of News", in D.L. Paletz (ed.) (1987), *Political Communication Research: Approaches, Studies, Assessments*. Norwood, NJ: Ablex: pp.26-48.

Page, B.I. and R. Shapiro (1992). *The Rational Public: Fifty Years of Trends in Americans' Policy Preferences*. Chicago: University of Chicago Press.

Robinson, P. (2001). "Theorising the Influence of Media on World Politics", *European Journal of Communication* 16: 523-44.

Waddock, Sandra and Neil Smith (2000). "Corporate Responsibility Audits: Doing Well by Doing Good", *Sloan Management Review* 41 (Winter): 7-83.

Street, J. (2005). "Politics Lost, Politics Transformed, Politics Colonised: Theories of the Impact of Mass Media", *Political Studies Review* 3: 17-33.

Weaver, D.H. (1977). "Political Issues and Voter Need for Orientation", in D.L. Shaw and M.E. McCombs (eds.), *Did the Media Matter? Journalism and Mass Communication Quarterly* 78(4): 787-98.

SECTION II

Corporate Social Responsibility and Emerging Issues

7

ARUN KUMAR RATH

Corporate Social Responsibility and Sustainability

New Mantras of Corporate Strategy

Introduction

Issues concerning ethics, good governance and social responsibility of business corporations have gained prominence in the last two decades all over the world. Scandals and frauds in high profile corporations have adversely affected the shareholders and other stakeholders. These events have proved beyond doubt that mismanagement and unethical practices in corporations can play havoc with the economic and social order. It has been realised that proper governance of business corporations has become as crucial to the world economy as proper governance of countries (Wolfensohn, 1998). There is an increasing demand on the corporations to be fair and ethical and fulfil their responsibility towards society and environment.

Corporate social responsibility (CSR) and sustainable development are emerging as major issues of corporate strategy. Earning profit is crucial for any business organisation. A company is formed to carry on business with the object of profit or gain. But earning profit is no longer acceptable as the sole purpose of business. The non-profit objectives of ethics, social responsibility and sustainable development have wider implications for society and environment. These factors are becoming increasingly significant for future prospects of business organisations.

There is growing acceptance that, in addition to complying with the provisions of law and economics, it is imperative for corporations to invest more into human capital, environment and society. The emerging non-profit corporate goals are taken under different terminology like corporate citizenship, social issues management, stakeholder management, corporate sustainability, business ethics, social trust and corporate social responsibility. All these terms have similar philosophical foundations. There is a clear overlap between business ethics and social responsibility of business. Both concepts concern values, and decisions based on goals other than the mere pursuit of profits. A socially responsible corporation must act ethically (Crane and Matten, 2010).

The modern corporation has emerged as the powerful engine of economic development. As the state is withdrawing from industry, trade and business corporations are assuming bigger role in the economy. They have become dominant and omnipresent producing goods and services, creating jobs and generating income for the people. Corporations have become the principal factors in economic organisation (Organization for Economic Co-operation and Development [OECD], 1999).

Profit *versus* Social Good

Attitude of experts and corporate leaders towards CSR has undergone remarkable change in last four decades. The view prevalent in the early 1970s was that "there is one and only one social responsibility of business—to use its resources and engage in activities designed to increase its profits" (Werther and Chandler, 2010). The ground has now shifted. Business ethics and CSR have risen up the corporate governance agenda. It is now accepted that the purpose of business is not just to make profit as an end by itself, but to make profit so that the business can do something more or better; "profit would be the means to that larger end" (Handy, 2002). "Profit for a company is like oxygen for a person. If you don't have enough of it, you're out of the game. But if you think your life is about breathing, you're really missing something" (Drucker, 2008). CSR needs to be integrated into the long-term corporate plan. The vision should be to earn profit by doing good business. Sustainable business strategy must harmonise the twin objectives of profit and social good.

The Stakeholder Theory

A stakeholder in an organisation is any group or individual who can affect or is affected by the achievement of the organisation's objectives. Stakeholders are those groups who are vital for the survival and success of the corporation. Modern large corporations are affecting society in contemporary world. Groups/individuals/institutions who can substantially affect/be affected by the company are stakeholders (Solomon and Solomon, 2004). A stakeholder holds a stake, rather than just a share. Managers should take decisions in the interest of all stakeholders. This theory raises the fundamental ques-tion of purpose of the corporation. Shareholders, the employees, customers, creditors, suppliers, community, government, society and environment are stakeholders, since they all contribute to long-term value addition in the company.

CSR: A Rationale

CSR is a multilayered concept having four main aspects namely: (a) economic responsibility required by society, (b) legal responsibilities also required by society, (c) ethical responsibilities as expected by society and (d) philanthropic responsibilities being desired by society. True CSR requires satisfaction of all four levels consecutively. It leads to definitions of CSR like: "CSR includes the economic, legal, ethical and philanthropic expectations placed on organisations by society at a given point of time."[1]

Following are other definitions of CSR:

> A view of the corporation and its role in society that assumes a responsibility among firms to pursue goals in addition to profit maximisation and a responsibility among a firm's stakeholders to hold the firm accountable for its actions (Werther and Chandler, 2010).

> A concept whereby companies integrate social and environmental concerns in their business operations and in their interaction with their stakeholders on a voluntary basis (European Commission Green Paper, 2001).

1. *Carroll's Pyramid of CSR*, Crane and Matten (p.53).

Unethical Business: Adverse Consequences

Unethical business practices may lead to expensive court cases, bad publicity, damage to reputation, loss of brand value, fall in share price. There are examples galore to show that corporate irresponsibility has been costly. Multinational Shell earned bad publicity in 1995 due to: (a) attempted disposal of Brent Spar oil rig in North Sea and (b) failure to oppose human rights violations by Nigerian government in spite of Shell's corporate influence. Cases of Nike facing adverse criticism for its supplies using child labour, Dow Chemicals getting involved in 2012 Olympics Sponsorship controversy are few more examples. Monsanto was criticised for aggressively marketing and political lobbying for its GM products. Nestlé's aggressive advertisement and marketing of milk products in developing countries resulted in decrease in breast feeding and use of dirty water in feeding infants. This resulted in boycott of Nestlé's milk products.[2]

Business organisations are increasingly realising the potential risk of their unethical business practices. They are aware that there should be ethics in marketing of dangerous products, transparency about environmental risks, declaration about product ingredients, possible health risks to consumers, honesty in advertising and fairness in pricing.[3] The damage that unethical behaviour can do to a company's reputation and brand value can be up to 25 per cent of world's financial health (Ruston, 2001).

CSR: Acquiring Competitive Edge

"Companies with an eye on their triple bottom line-economic, environmental, and social sustainability—outperform their less fastidious peers on the stock market."[4] CSR ensures advantages to the company, boosts its brand value, and avoids activists taking on directors in AGM on unethical practices. Employees feel happy to work in an ethical firm. It builds trust among shareholders, employees, customers and society. Socially responsible investment

2. *The Economist* , *Business Ethics*, Edited (2010).

3. Ibid

4. Ibid.

(SRI) is now a criteria used by many fund managers for investment decisions. It also helps attract talented people in the company and retains customers and suppliers.[5]

It is also necessary to be ethical in human resource management. Companies need to avoid discrimination by gender, race, religion and disability even in the absence of a national policy on affirmative action for the private sector. There should be ethical practice in financial management. Companies must avoid creative accounting, misleading financial analysis, insider trading, bribery or kickbacks and accounting scandals as happened in Enron, World.com and Satyam. Some critics claim business ethics to be an oxymoron, which means bringing two apparently contradictory concepts together. To say that business ethics is an oxymoron suggests that business is in some way unethical. In reality, despite scandals and scams in business corporations, ethics in business situations is not entirely redundant. In fact, everyday business activities require the maintenance of basic ethical standards like honesty, trustworthiness and cooperation between directors, managers, buyers, sellers, creditors and people. Business activity would be impossible if people do not trust each other or do not depend upon certain mutual expectations of ethical conduct. Ethical issues include the rights and duties between a company and its employees, suppliers, customers and neighbours, its fiduciary responsibility to its shareholder. "Ultimately, companies may have to accept that virtue is sometimes its own reward."[6]

Business: A Social Trust

Profit alone cannot ensure sustainability. Vision, social and ethical values are emerging as crucial factors. Visionary companies with social relevance and contribution to social cause sustain and survive in the long run. Mahatma Gandhi in his concept of Trusteeship of Property visualised that the rich and wealthy should be trustees of property. They hold economic power on behalf of society only as custodians. They may enjoy only a portion of their

5. Ibid.
6. Ibid.

wealth up to a reasonable limit but major portion of their wealth must be available for benefit of society (Sethi, 1986). The concept of trusteeship of property gives a strong philosophical foundation to business ethics and social responsibility.

UN Global Compact

The United Nations Global Compact, also known as Compact or UNGC, is a United Nations (UN) initiative to encourage businesses worldwide to adopt sustainable and socially responsible policies, and to report on their implementation. The Global Compact is a principle-based framework for businesses, stating 10 principles in the areas of human rights, labour, the environment and anti-corruption. The Global Compact is the world's largest corporate citizenship initiative.

The Global Compact was first announced by the then UN Secretary-General Kofi Annan in an address to The World Economic Forum on 31 January 1999 and was officially launched at UN Headquarters in New York on 26 July 2000. The UN acknowledged the power and social responsibility of business entities when it was announced, "Let us choose to unite the power of markets with the authority of universal ideals. Let us choose to reconcile the creative forces of private entrepreneurship with the needs of the disadvantaged and the requirements of future generations." The world body promoted the concept of corporate citizenship among global companies.[7]

CSR: Issues and Challenges

CSR is an obligation beyond requirement of law and economics. A firm is expected to pursue long-term goals that are good for society and environment. It is the continuing commitment by business to behave ethically and contribute to economic development leaving an overall positive impact on society. CSR means conducting business in an ethical way and in the interests of the wider community balancing shareholder interests against the

7. UN Global Compact Website.

interests of the wider community. It ultimately amounts to being a good citizen in the community (Werther and Chandler, 2010).

There are a number of drivers of CSR in the current context. The shrinking role of government, demand for greater disclosure, increased customer interest, growing investor pressure, competi-tive labour markets and conducive supplier relations force companies to be socially responsible.

Does business have responsibilities to society broader than making profits for business owners and investors? In the 1950s, even the legality of corporate philanthropy was questioned. There are debates whether the strategy of CSR and moral obligations to society contradicts the principle of corporate profit maximisation.

The advocates of CSR argue that shareholders and investors prefer investing in companies with high social responsibility. CSR attracts ethically conscious customers. It differentiates the firm from its competitor and can be a source of competitive advantage. Benefits of CSR include improved financial performance, increased customer loyalty, attraction and retention of employees, greater motivation of workforce, better public image and long-term sustainability of the corporation (Dianne and Suzanne, 2010).

There are also arguments against CSR. The critics argue that the corporation's principal purpose is to maximise return to shareholders. If unchecked, managers may squander away scarce resources on CSR activities. Corporations may just create appearance of social responsibility only for public relation and end up doing just "green washing" (Dianne and Suzanne, 2010). The critics feel that ethical corporation is an oxymoron, since CSR is against the principle of maximisation of profit. Under corporate law, directors are prohibited from any activity that would reduce returns and profits to the company. A corporation may espouse CSR and sustainable development, while its activities may be damaging to society and environment. Corporate management cannot decide on what is in the social interest. Costs on CSR will be passed on to consumers and can reduce economic efficiency and profit (Crane and Matten, 2010).

Nevertheless business organisations are decidedly taking a view in favour of CSR. Businesses feel that they do not have an unquestioned right to operate in society. Those managing business realise that they depend on society. Business relies on resources from society and on socially created institutions. There is a social contract between business and society involving mutual obligations. Society and business recognise that they have to depend upon each other. Business can see advantages in adopting a CSR approach in doing business (Balton and Benn, 2010).

Sustainable Development

CSR is also closely linked to the concept of sustainable development. Sustainable development seeks to "meet the needs of the present without compromising the ability of the future generation to meet their own needs."[8] The concept of sustainable development gave rise to the triple bottom line approach for business corporations. The objectives of business should be threefold namely profit, people and planet. Business must subserve the economic, social and the environmental concerns in their growth strategy. The twin principles of working for long term while causing least harm must guide the actions of corporations.

The Ethical Corporation

The modern corporations are assuming significant role in economic development. They are expected to earn profit and add value to the shareholders' investment, but profit alone is not enough to ensure sustainability of their business. In addition to shareholders and investors, there are other stakeholders who contribute to long-term value maximisation of the corporation. Society has emerged as a major stakeholder of the corporation. Business is seen as a social trust aimed at satisfying social expectations. The non-financial parameters like ethics, social responsibility and sustainable development are increasingly being regarded as factors responsible for lending competitive edge to the corporations. Social good in addition to profit is basis for judging the performance of business.

---

8. UN Brandtland Commission Report, Sustainable Development (1987).

The investors, employees, customers, suppliers, community and society expect the corporation to conduct its affairs in an ethical and transparent manner, protecting environment and discharging its social obligations.

CSR initiatives should rise above the limited perspective of resource allocation and expenditure activity. The CSR plan should be integrated into business strategy of the corporation. The organisational culture in the corporation should be conducive to acceptance of social responsibility of business. The entire organisation needs to be sensitised. The employees and executives must feel a sense of commitment to society and environment. CSR vision supported by action plan, CSR audit and public reporting would enhance the image and credibility of the company.

Ethical, well-governed and socially relevant companies are preferred as the investment destinations. Social responsibility of business and ethical conduct are the hallmarks of good corporate governance. In a nutshell, the ethical and socially responsible corporation is emerging as a model for business all over the world.

CSR Law: Mandate for Indian Companies

India took a bold initiative while amending the company law. In addition to substantial changes in the law, a new provision in the act was introduced to give a legal status to corporate social action. Directors were also given legal responsibility to ensure implementation of such provisions in the following manner.

(i) Duties of Directors

Under Sec 166 (2) "A director of a company shall act in good faith in order to promote the objects of the company for the benefit of its members as a whole, and in the best interests of the company, its employees, the shareholders, the community and for the protection of environment."

(ii) Corporate Social Responsibility

Under Sec 135 (1), it is provided that:

- Board of every company shall make every endeavour to ensure that the company spends, in every financial year, at least two per cent of the average net profits of the company made during the three immediately preceding financial years, in pursuance of its CSR policy.
- If the company fails to spend such amount, the board needs to specify the reasons in its report.

The CSR rules drafted under the law, provided for eligibility criteria as:

Companies (includes foreign companies with branches or project in India) having:

- Minimum net worth of ₹500 crore.
- Turnover up to ₹1000 crore.
- Having a net profit of at least 5 crore during any financial year, are covered by this provision.

Further activities not included under the CSR:

- Business run in the normal course.
- Outside the territory of the India or abroad.
- For the welfare of the employees and their families.
- Political party contribution of any amount directly and indirectly as defined u/s 182 of the Act.

(iii) Schedule VII

This schedule lists out the activities related to CSR like education, women and child welfare, social security, employment generation, etc. The CSR rules elaborated activities which may be included by companies in their CSR policies as:

- eradicating extreme hunger and poverty;
- promotion of education;
- promoting gender equality and empowering women;
- reducing child mortality and improving maternal health;

- Combating human immunodeficiency virus (HIV), acquired immune deficiency syndrome (AIDS), malaria and other diseases;
- ensuring environmental sustainability;
- employment enhancing vocational skills;
- social business projects;
- contribution to the Prime Minister's National Relief Fund or any other fund set up by the central government or the state governments for socio-economic development and relief and funds for the welfare of the scheduled castes (SCs), the scheduled tribes (STs), other backward classes (OBCs), minorities and women; and
- such other matters as may be prescribed.

CSR as Law: A Critique

There are a number of uncovered areas in the Company Act 2013 with respect to the provisions of CSR. A number of questions remain unanswered.

- Mandatory CSR spending is nothing but disguised taxation. This comparison may not be entirely sound. It is trite managerial and corporate philosophy today that companies which fail to take into account the social and environmental aspects of their activities will eventually become unsustainable and only companies that create 'stakeholder value' will reap long-term benefits and remain profitable. In other words, CSR is a sound business policy and is good for companies. Tax, on the contrary, has no such *quid pro quo* benefits.
- The act does not specify proper enforcement mechanism. Only minimum requirements are prescribed, and the actual implementation of the policy is left to the company itself. It does not seek to implement, enforce or correct the CSR policies of individual companies or monitor and regulate the activities under it. CSR policies and reports are usually designed to inform investors, shareholders and

other stakeholders about the social and environmental performance and philosophy of a company rather than to satisfy government scrutiny.

- Creating additional financial burdens will hurt investments. The total expected CSR spending under this new law is estimated at somewhere between ₹10,000 and ₹15,000 crore. Collectively, it is a significant contribution. There are some inherent problems with such corporate spending, especially when it is philanthropic or even as partnerships with civil society organisations. As Buffett (2013) asserts in his article in *The New York Times*, corporate philanthropy "just keeps the existing structure of inequality in place." Some studies have even shown that it may even aggravate absolute inequality (Dasgupta and Kanbur, 2011). Therefore, the bill only has businesses and governments "searching for answers with their right hand to problems that others in the room have created with their left."
- CSR, as imagined, is ineffective without corporate accountability.
- The CSR spending on activities in the schedule has to align with and complement the overall public policies and not create tangential corporate enclaves of CSR activities (Venkatesan, 2013).
- Voluntary, if not mandatory, reporting of social and environmental compact is the right idea for 21st century corporate governance. "Unfortunately, the National Voluntary Guidelines, which would have put India's institutions of corporate governance in the forefront with world leaders, have been given short shrift in the new Company Law. They have been drowned by the buzz around the retrograde 2 per cent CSR provision in the law" (Maira, 2013).
- Social action is generally voluntary in nature. By making it a legal liability, the voluntary spirit is lost. Companies should be allowed to see their own advantage in spending on CSR. The Schedule VII of the act prescribes corporate

social projects just like governmental programmes with little innovation left for the corporations

Department of Public Enterprises Guidelines on CSR and Sustainability

In order to fill the gap in the Company Act of not including corporate responsibility on sustainability, the Department of Public Enterprises (DPE) issued fresh guidelines in line with its earlier guidelines. The new guidelines issued effective from 1st April 2014 reiterated its earlier guidelines issued on 1st April 2013 (before rules under Company Act 2013). These guidelines emphasise on the need of responsible business practices in the context of sustainability in its entirety. DPE stated:

- "Corporate Social Responsibility and Sustainability is a company's commitment to its stakeholders to conduct business in an economically, socially and environmentally sustainable manner that is transparent and ethical."
- All Central Public Sector Enterprises (CPSEs) shall have to comply with the provisions of the Act and the CSR rules. Any amendment notified by the Ministry of Corporate Affairs in the CSR rules, or in Schedule VII of the Act, will also be binding on the CPSEs.
- CPSE's commitment to CSR and their willingness to voluntarily take a few extra steps to address social, economic and environmental concerns, which may be beyond the realm of CSR as envisaged in the act and the CSR rules, but are nevertheless worthy of attention for promotion of sustainable development in its diverse dimensions. All CPSEs must adopt a CSR and sustainability policy specific to their company with the approval of the board of directors.
- CPSEs are advised to align their CSR and sustainability policy with their business policies and strategies to the extent possible, and select such CSR activities/projects which can be better monitored through in-house expertise. All CPSEs are expected to act in a socially, economically

and environmentally sustainable manner at all times. Even in their normal business activities, public sector companies should try to promote sustainable development through sustainability initiatives by conducting business in a manner that is beneficial to both business and society.

- As a part of their sustainability initiatives, CPSEs are expected to give importance to environmental sustainability even in their normal mainstream activities by ensuring that their internal operations and processes promote renewable sources of energy, reduce/re-use/recycle waste material, replenish groundwater supply, protect/conserve/restore the ecosystem, reduce carbon emissions and help in greening the supply chain. CPSEs are expected to behave in a responsible manner by producing goods and services which are safe and healthy for the consumers and the environment, resource efficient, consumer friendly, and environmentally sustainable throughout their life cycles, i.e., from the stage of raw material extraction to production, use/consumption, and final disposal.
- The philosophy and spirit of CSR and sustainability should be understood and imbibed by the employees at all levels and get embedded in the core values of the company.
- CPSEs should extend their reach and oversight to the entire supply chain network to ensure that as far as possible, suppliers, vendors, service providers, clients and partners are also committed to the same principles and standards of CSR and sustainability as the company itself. CPSEs are encouraged to initiate and implement measures aimed at 'greening' the supply chain.
- CPSEs should devise a communication strategy for regular dialogue and consultation with key stakeholders to ascertain their views and suggestions regarding the CSR activities and sustainability initiatives undertaken by the company. However, the ultimate decision in the selection

and implementation of CSR activities would be that of the Board of the CPSE.

- In case a company fails to spend such amount, it shall have to specify the reasons for not spending it. However, in case of CPSEs, mere reporting and explaining the reasons for not spending this amount in a particular year would not suffice and the unspent CSR amount in a particular year would not lapse. It would instead be carried forward to the next year for utilisation for the purpose for which it was allocated.

In other words, CSR needs to be integrated with business strategy. CSR initiatives should rise above the limited perspective of resource allocation and expenditure activity. The organisational culture in the corporation should be conducive to acceptance of social responsibility of business. The entire organisation needs to be sensitised. The employees and executives must feel a sense of commitment to society and environment. CSR vision supported by action plan, CSR audit and public reporting would enhance the image and credibility of the company.

CSR in PSUs : An Evaluation Study

An evaluation study by *Economic Times* (2012-13) reveals the following deficiencies in the implementation of CSR by public sector undertakings (PSUs) in India:

- Ten large PSUs managed to disburse less than half of target amount. 10 large PSUs, which were together mandated to spend ₹1,313 crore in FY12, managed to disburse less than half that amount.
- Some PSUs struggle for want of dedicated CSR professionals, others for mindset.
- Lack of partnerships with expert agencies, inability to identify good social projects, lack of top management vision for CSR, lack of teams dedicated to CSR work are reasons for low CSR spend by PSUs.

- In some cases, working process is cumbersome and bureaucratic structures cause delays in money reaching projects in time.
- Problem of finding good social projects is another problem. "Companies (often) don't know how to address these issues which are so different from their particular industry and core competencies." (John Elkington, a global authority on CSR and sustainability who conceived the concept of 'triple bottom line.')
- However it also reported that PSUs are showing interest in taking CSR seriously. There has been an enormous shift in the mindset of top management of companies. There is clear indication that they are taking CSR seriously. PSUs need to revise their CSR strategies.

Road Ahead

CSR strategy should include the following 10-point action plan:

- Ownership and commitment is necessary at all levels beginning from top to bottom.
- Business Strategy should integrate CSR and sustainability into business plan.
- The entire corporate culture must be sensitised. The company should encourage employee voluntarism, so that willing and committed employees can join and strengthen corporate efforts.
- CSR need to be internalised in order to build a mindset in the functioning of the CSR activities.
- Board should allocate CSR fund from profit in advance to facilitate prompt action in the field formations.
- There must be a dedicated wing for CSR in the company.
- CSR must be implemented in project mode with definite timelines and budget commitments.
- Outcome and impact must be monitored.

- Audit and evaluation must be carried out at the end of the CSR projects to assess the impact.
- Lastly the company needs to report and communicate to all shareholders and other stakeholders about the progress and achievements in the area of CSR and sustainability.

All the above components are necessary for effective social action. It is for the board of directors of the company to take the lead and design an imaginative policy and effective implementation strategy for CSR and sustainability.

Conclusion

Business corporations have been created for the objective of earning profit and ensuring return on investment to the shareholders and investors. Nevertheless profit motive alone cannot assure long-term survival of the enterprises. In addition to the shareholders, other stakeholders also contribute to the sustainability of business. Society has emerged as the most important stakeholder providing social capital and resources for the growth of the corporate entities. India has provided legal status to responsibility of corporations to society. However the mandate of two per cent spend on CSR should be regarded as the minimum level of commitment of the corporations to society. Corporations need to go beyond this minimum commitment as prescribed in the CSR law. They need to address the issues of sustainable development and demonstrate their responsibility as corporate citizens. The activities of the business operations are adversely affecting nature, ecological balance and the general environment. As such, the corporations owe moral responsibility to people and the planet to restore ecological balance and conserve nature. The very purpose of business is undergoing change. Whereas earning profit remains the compulsion for business, social responsibility and sustainable development should engage the attention of the board and top management as the emerging objectives of the modern corporations.

References

Balton, Dianne and Suzanne Benn (2010). *Key Concepts in Corporate Social Responsibility*.

Crane, Andrew and Dirk Matten (2010). *Business Ethics*. Oxford University Press.

Dasgupta, I. and R. Kanbur (2011). "Does Philanthropy Reduce Inequality?", *Journal of Economic Inequality* 9(1): 1-21, March. Springer.

Drucker, Peter (2008). "Peter Senge's Necessary Revolution", *Business Week*, June 11.

European Commission Green Paper (2001). *Promoting Corporate Social Responsibility*.

Handy, Charles (2002). "What's a Business For?" *Harvard Business Review*, December, p.54.

Maira, Arun (2013). "India's 2% CSR Law: The First Country to Go Backwards", *Economic and Political Weekly,* September 21.

OECD (1999). *Principles of Corporate Governance* (May).

Ruston, K. (2001). "Cracking the Code", IoD Director's Guide: Sustainable Development, May.

Sethi, J.D. (1986). *Trusteeship: The Gandhian Alternative*. Gandhi Peace Foundation.

Solomon, Jill and Aries Solomon (March 2004). *Corporate Governance and Accountability*, p.2.

UN Brandtland Commission Report, Sustainable Development, (1987).

Venkatesan, Rashmi (2013). "Ordering Corporate Responsibility—A Misplaced Faith?", *Economic and Political Weekly*, 21 September,.

Werther, William B. Jr. and Chandler, David (2010). *Strategic Corporate Social Responsibility*. Sage Publication.

Wolfensohn, James D. (1998). "Battle for Corporate Honesty", *The Economist*, World in 1999.

8

TULSI JAYAKUMAR

Turning the Wheel of Social Responsibility

Towards Integrating Corporate Social Innovation with the Corporate Social Responsibility Agenda

Introduction

Corporate social responsibility (CSR) is the new buzzword in the Indian lexicon. The passage of the Companies Act 2013 in August 2013 and the implementation of the accompanying Companies (Corporate Social Responsibility) Rules 2014, mandating large Indian companies—i.e., those public or private limited companies having a net worth of INR 500 crore or a turnover of INR 1,000 crore or net profit of INR 5 crore—to spend at least 2 per cent of their average net profit for the preceding three financial years on corporate social responsibility activities with effect from 1 April 2014, has turned the spotlight on CSR. In an increasingly globalised world, Indian companies were nowhere close to adoption of global best practices regarding CSR spends, measurement as also reporting. This is clear from the fact that even as late as in March 2013, most of the top 100 Indian companies by revenue were neither spending enough on CSR, nor reporting their CSR spends (Jayashankar and Bhat, 2013). How should Indian companies respond to the new legal requirements, as also the growing societal concerns for corporate responsibility? In particular, can Indian corporate use this growing emphasis on CSR as an opportunity to drive corporate social innovations (CSIs)? What business models should such CSR-driven social innovations follow?

The CSR discussion increasingly is directed towards a call for sustainable development. Sustainable development has been defined

(Brundtland Commission, WCED, 1987: 43) as "meeting the needs of the present generation, without compromising the ability of future generations to meet theirs." Firms, in the conduct of their activities thus, are required to not just behave responsibly in the present, but also be mindful of inter-generational claims. Such activities falling within the ambit of a firm's CSR or sustainable development goals traditionally were viewed as distinct in scope from a firm's innovation activities. In a sense, CSR and innovations were seen as mutually exclusive.

Turning to innovations, drivers of firm innovations ranged from economic profits to regulation to technological progress. Moreover, most innovations arose within the firm. Increasingly, however, it is being recognised that sources of innovations may lie more within the firms' external environment (Chesbrough, 2003). Firms by opening up their business models to such external resources may do better in the process of value-creation and capture.

Problem Definition

Research on CSR-driven CSIs, especially in the context of emerging countries like India, is scant.

This paper attempts to fill the void in existing CSR literature by exploring the relationship between CSR and social innovations, particularly in the Indian context. The main research question considered is: Can an innovating firm be driven by its desire to be socially responsible or are innovation and CSR mutually exclusive? Specifically, what is the particular path that an innovating firm, desirous of marrying the economic and social (and/or environmental) goals of profits and sustainability (people/planet), pursue? How can open innovations help in this pursuit?

The paper proposes a theoretical model for incorporating open innovations as a means of driving CSI and hence national competitive advantage. The source for such innovations, comes primarily not from within but from outside the firm. By co-opting NPOs, customers, competitors and suppliers in the value co-creation and capture process, Indian firms can integrate CSIs with the CSR agenda. Such a shared CSR agenda can drive national competitive advantage, especially in a factor-driven economy like India.

The paper is organised thus: the first section studies the extant literature on CSR in India, as well as innovations, with particular emphasis on open innovations. It also reviews extant studies on CSI. The second section proposes a theoretical model for transforming the firm into a CSI-driven firm. The third section discusses cases of successful Indian as also global firms that have adopted CSIs. The final section gives concluding remarks and provides directions for further research.

Literature Review

CSR in India

The CSR concept relates closely to corporate citizenship, corporate social responsiveness, corporate social performance, and stakeholder management (Carroll, 1979; McWilliams and Siegel, 2001; Kotler and Lee, 2005; World Business Council for Sustainable Development, 2005). Common to these concepts is the idea that organisations should not only be concerned about making a profit but also engaged in actions that appear to further some social good, beyond the interests of the firm and that which is required by the law. In this sense, CSR generally refers to business decision making related to ethical values, compliance with legal requirements, and respect for people, communities and the environment.

Conceptually, CSR implies some sort of commitment through corporate policies and action, reflected in a firm's social performance. Such activities should go beyond the law and exceed a firm's 'minimum obligations.' CSR activities are discretionary and cannot be enforced in any court of law. Corporations that embrace CSR do so by means of voluntary codes of conduct at local, regional, national and international levels, but these are not legally binding in any way. Further, the emphasis in recent years has shifted to stakeholders (Freeman, 1984) rather than on 'society' as was the case with conceptualisations of CSR in the 1970s.

Several surveys have been conducted since 2000 to study various aspects of CSR in India. These include:

- The survey conducted by the Tata Energy Research Institute (TERI-Europe), The New Academy of Business and ORG-MARG Research (Kumar *et al.*, 2001);
- The Centre for Social Marketing survey in early 2001 (Brown, 2001);
- The Indian *NGOs.com* data and interview-based survey 2002 (*IndianNGOs.com*, 2002);
- The survey by the United Nations Development Programme (UNDP), the British Council, the Confederation of Indian Industry and PricewaterhouseCoopers in 2002 (UNDP, 2002);
- The PiC-IMRB survey of 2003 [Partners in Change (PiC), 2003];
- The NSE administered questionnaire-based survey of 50 companies in the NSE NIFTY Index in 2003 to determine how CSR is being considered or implemented in these organisations (NSE/NIFTY, 2003); and
- The Karmayog CSR ratings.

Kumar *et al.* (2001) identified four models of corporate responsibility as operating in India: voluntary commitment to public welfare based on ethical awareness of broad social needs: the Gandhian Ethical model; state-driven policies including state ownership and extensive corporate regulation and administration: the Nehruvian Statist model; corporate responsibility primarily focused on owner objectives: Milton Friedman's Liberal model; and stakeholder responsiveness which recognises direct and indirect stakeholder interest: R. Edward Freeman's Stakeholder model.

While there is a growing recognition among Indian companies that passive philanthropy is no longer sufficient in the realm of CSR (UNDP, 2002), the studies point to an inadequate appreciation of CSR as a means of gaining strategic competitiveness (Bhattacharya, 2007; PiC, 2003).The Karmayog CSR ratings of companies operating in India in 2009 (Karmayog CSR Ratings, 2009) indicated that 26 per cent of the top 500 Indian companies were not performing CSR at all, while a majority of Indian companies [including multinational corporations (MNCs)] were performing very little CSR. Very few companies had a clearly defined CSR philosophy and most implemented their CSR in an *ad hoc* manner, unconnected with their business process. Similar results were borne out by a survey conducted by *CSRidentity.com* in collaboration with Forbes India even as late as 2013 (Forbes, 2013). Other studies have indicated that financial support was taken as the prime CSR orientation, alongside foundation creation, public relations activity and philanthropic work. Further, such surveys and studies pointed to the lacunae in implementation of CSR, as also impact assessment (NSE/NIFTY, 2003).

We found no evidence of studies which try to capture the link between CSR and social innovations in the Indian context. This is not surprising considering the low awareness regarding CSR translated into *ad hoc* and limited CSR spends and activities by Indian companies up until now.

Innovations

There are several definitions of innovation. We can understand innovations as "the process through which productive resources are developed and utilised to generate higher quality and/or lower cost products than had been previously available " (O'Sullivan, 2000: 393).

Innovations can be characterised on the basis of several criteria as well. Important distinctions are those between radical and incremental innovation (based on their extent and scale); sustaining and disruptive innovations (based on their ability to strengthen a firm's existing capabilities and market position or to disrupt them by rendering competencies obsolete or reaching out to new customers and so-far unserved markets (Christensen, 1997; Kim and Mauborgne, 1997); and open *versus* closed innovations (Chesbrough, 2003; Chesbrough *et al.*, 2006).

In fact that Indian companies lack an innovative environment is captured in the Global Innovation Index (GII) 2014, which reported that India had fallen 10 notches in the innovation rankings (from 66 to 76) among 143 economies. This was as compared to its remaining four BRICS (Brazil, Russia, India, China and South Africa) compatriots, all of which had improved their rankings (Global Innovation Index, 2014).

Open innovation refers to "the use of purposive inflows and outflows of knowledge to accelerate internal innovation and expand the markets for external use of innovation, respectively" (Chesbrough *et al.*, 2006). It suggests that valuable ideas can come from both within and outside the firm, and can similarly follow a path to the market from both within and outside the firm. In contrast to traditional models of value creation focused on firms or firms' value chains (Porter, 1980), open innovation models admit of ideas germinating in a variety of settings.

Research on open models for carrying out corporate social innovations is scant. Holmes and Smart (2009), for instance, explored eight voluntary dyadic relationships between corporate and not-for-profit organisations in the United Kingdom (UK), resulting in innovation outcomes. Such open innovation models however have been hardly used to explore the case of corporate social innovations, especially within emerging economy contexts like India.

Corporate Social Innovations

CSI—a term introduced by Rosabeth Moss Kanter (1999: 125)—referred to "social issues that could serve as learning laboratories for firms to identify unmet societal needs and for developing solutions that could create new markets." Three variants of such innovations are products designed for the bottom-of-pyramid (BoP), social entrepreneurship and eco-innovations (Hockerts and Morsing, 2008).

However, as pointed out by Hockerts (2007) through his study of 12 multinationals, firms hardly thought of CSR as a means of driving product innovations; CSR was nothing more than a tool to reduce risks and operational costs. As such, it was only corporate learning processes and development of knowledge structures that resulted from investments in corporate social performance that could lead to CSI.

Global Cases in CSIs: Heterogeneous Approach

With the 'Triple Bottom Line' gaining importance, large global corporations are working towards CSI in different ways. We outline two innovative ways in which global corporates have introduced innovative practices across their value chains to impact the society and the environment.

Nike's Zero Discharge of Hazardous Chemicals Project: A Case of Collaborative CSI

Nike's 'Zero Discharge of Hazardous Chemicals Project' represents a case of competitors joining together to implement collaborative CSI. Under this project, 13 apparel companies including Nike, Puma, Adidas, etc., with linked value chains joined hands to develop a shared roadmap on how they could make an environmental difference through eliminating discharge of hazardous chemicals (*http://nikeinc.com/news/nike-roadmap-toward-zero-discharge-of-hazardous-chemicals*).

The Joint Roadmap prepared in 2011 commits Nike to achieving this goal of Zero Discharge of Hazardous Chemicals by 2020. It read:

> By issuing the following joint roadmap (a living document), Adidas Group, C&A, H&M, Li Ning, NIKE, Inc., and PUMA further demonstrate our commitment to collaborate and lead the apparel and footwear industry towards zero discharge of hazardous chemicals for all products across all pathways in our supply chains by 2020.
>
> This roadmap is based on statements that were issued on an individual basis by each of the founding brands. In the future, the intention is that all public individual statements conform to one model statement, which is currently in development.

Any company or entity wishing to join the collaborative process is invited to publish an individual statement and sign up to the roadmap. In doing so, the entity commits itself to support the group and to dedicate resources towards implementation of the roadmap. *(http://nikeinc.com/system/assets/5408/111118_JointRoadmap_original.pdf?1321567189)*

Puma's Environmental Profit & Loss Account: A Case of CSI in Financial Disclosure

Puma published its Environmental Profit & Loss Account (EPL) in 2011, which attempted to put a cost on business' impact on environment throughout their supply chains. An attempt to calculate its environmental impact "from cradle-to-gate", PUMA sought to put a monetary value on nature's services that Puma used in its business—such as fresh water, clean air, healthy biodiversity and productive land—and also on the negative impacts the company had on the environment. This would help the company to identify where in the value chain such costs were being incurred, and how these costs could be mitigated.

While such costs wouldn't impact the company's financials, they had an impact on environment and society. The planet was taken as the service provider and the costs were accounted for as accruing to the planet (for instance, the first costs that were reported in 2011 were greenhouse gas emissions and water usage, followed later by land use, air pollution and packaging throughout its operations and supply chain). They found, further, that €8 million (£6.4 million) or 6 per cent of the costs occurred through the company's own direct operations, such as offices, warehouses and stores. A further 9 per cent (€13 million) arose with its tier 1 suppliers, the companies responsible for manufacturing Puma shoes and clothing, while the remaining €124 million—or 85 per cent of the impacts—were distributed through its Tier 2, 3 and 4 suppliers going right back the actual sourcing of raw materials, such as leather, cotton and rubber.

Thus, Puma could understand better those impacts which lay within its control, as also those for which it would need to work with other companies which were part of its supply chain in order to make a difference.

The company has used this analysis to develop its sustainability strategy and targets. In 2010, it used a Sustainability Scorecard to draw up a list of goals to be achieved by 2015. It used its EPL to refine the scorecard and direct investment into relevant areas. For instance, one project of Puma involved developing Puma Re-Suede made of 100 per cent recycled polyester fibres, recovered from manufacturing scrap waste, which cut energy use and emissions by 80 per cent (Puma: Business and the Environment, 2011). "A new business paradigm is necessary and a transformation of corporate reporting will be central to this—one that works WITH nature and not AGAINST it" (Executive chairman, Jochen Zeitz, Puma, 2011).

Theoretical Framework for Incorporating CSI into the CSR Agenda

Traditionally, business models were 'closed,' in that business development processes, as also the marketing of new products took place within the firm boundaries (Figure 8.1).

Figure 8.1

A Closed Innovation Model

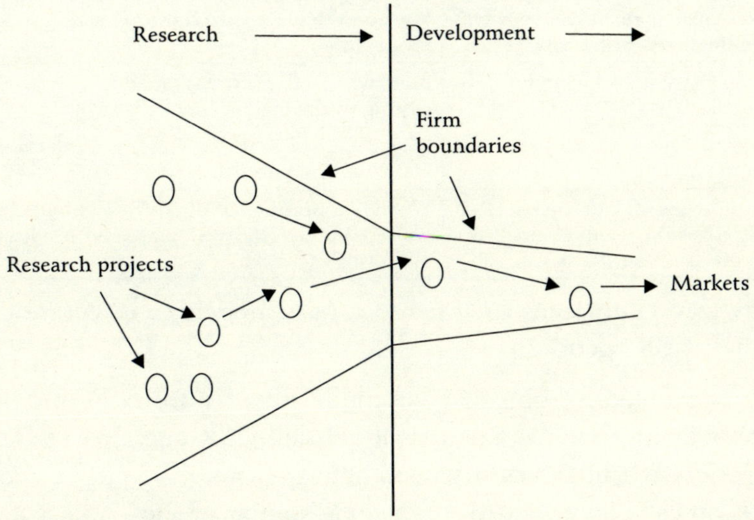

Source: Chesbrough, 2003.

The innovating firm would carry out all research projects within itself and supply to existing markets. Value creation thus was confined to within the boundaries of the firm. Value capture in the case of such innovations was again restricted to the firm. Table 8.1 illustrates the difference between open and closed innovation principles.

Recent literature on open innovations and open business models emphasises the irrelevance of the rigid firm boundaries inherent in past models. Firm boundaries, in such open business models, are seen as porous-combining internal and external ideas, as well as internal and external paths to market to advance the development of new technologies (Chesbrough, 2003). Such innovations, however, have been used to explain the for-profit agenda of firms in modern setting

Table 8.1

Closed versus Open Innovation Principles

Closed Innovation Principles	*Open Innovation Principles*
The smart people in the field work for us.	Not all the smart people work for us, so we must find and tap into the knowledge and expertise of bright individuals outside the company.
To profit from R&D, we must discover it, develop it, and ship it ourselves.	External R&D can create significant value: internal R&D is needed to claim some portion of that value.
If we discover it ourselves, we will get it to the market first.	We don't have to originate the research to profit from it.
The company that gets an innovation to the market first will win.	Building a better business model is better than getting to the market first.
If we create the most and the best ideas in the industry, we will win.	If we make the best use of internal and external ideas, we will win.
We should control our Intellectual Property (IP) so that our competitors don't profit from our ideas.	We should profit from others' use of our IP, and we should buy others' IP whenever it advances our business model.

How can companies use open business models to integrate CSIs with their CSR agenda?

We can visualise the firm as made up of porous boundaries. The innovating firm 'A' has a well-defined CSR agenda—typically synergistic with business interests. Thus, firms may either choose to focus on the planet and/or the people's pillar of the Triple Bottom Line approach, along with the profits pillar. This does not mean that the firm would ignore the environmental or social concerns. It simply acknowledges a more realistic approach, wherein firms may choose a CSR agenda closer to their line of business. For instance, an FMCG company may choose a CSR agenda focusing on sustainable livelihoods, whereas a chemicals company may choose one focusing on environmental protection.

The company's own research laboratory may come up with ideas and innovations serving its needs for economic profits. At the same time, it may license out or put out for further development, ideas and technologies, which it may not find useful for its own strategies. Simultaneously, as seen in Figure 8.2, it may also receive ideas in line with its CSR agenda (whether social or environmental) from various external sources—competitors, suppliers, not-for-profit organisations, BoP customers, as also its regular customers. Such ideas, however, may prove to be useless, unless they are all coordinated through some underlying architecture/system that puts all such open knowledge together.

Such an umbrella system may be present at the firm level. However, in countries like India with scarce economic resources, the government may draw the architecture of such an umbrella system. Using appropriate incentive systems, it may nudge firms in the same CSR space to pool such common knowledge to come up with corporate social innovations in the given sphere. Several companies, united by a common social cause, may pool resources to come up with product, process or service innovations in the social sphere.

Figure 8.2

Open Model for CSIs

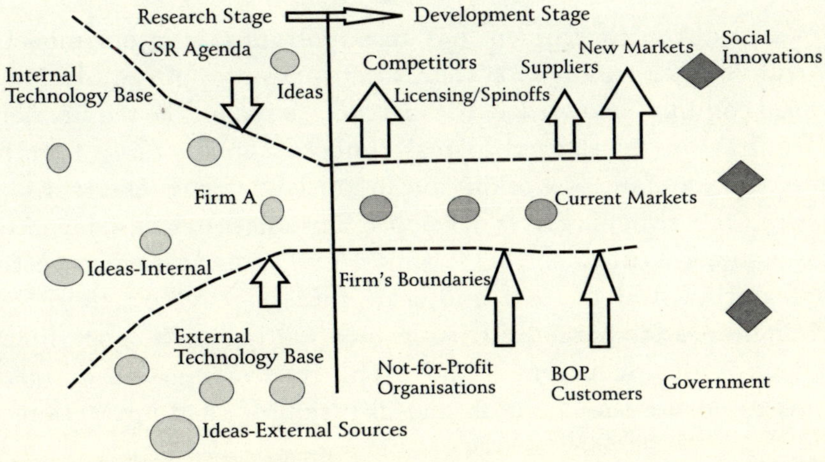

Source: Adapted from Chesbrough, 2003.

Thus, as seen in Figure 8.2, ideas at the research stage may come from both within and outside the firm's core research facility. Important external resources for such ideas include NPOs, BOP customers, suppliers and competitors working in similar CSR space. At the same time, ideas may also permeate through the firm's boundaries to the external environment.

Not all such ideas at the research stage may be developed within the organisation. The firm may share intellectual property with other firms operating in the same CSR space. Such ideas may be developed outside the firm and may cater to new markets. At the same time, the firm may access ideas from outside at the development stage, and use such ideas to develop products and services to cater to new/existing markets.

Our model differs from traditional open innovation models in the following ways.

An important distinction in our model compared to traditional open innovation models is a more proactive role for NPOs, not only as implementers of firms' CSR agenda, but as active collaborators and contributors to product, service and process innovations which will better achieve the firm's CSR agenda. NPOs, with their ear to the ground, may be in a better position to highlight key social concerns, as also provide practicable solutions to social and developmental problems. The firms or a cluster of firms operating in that social space may use such insights to provide appropriate social innovations.

Second, the government has an important role in our model as providers of an umbrella system to ensure optimum utilisation of pooled common knowledge. For instance, based on the requirements of sanitation, as also ecological concerns and pooling together ideas from architects working on urban landscapes (external ideas resources), a firm may have developed bio-toilets to be used in cities/ urban slums. With such toilets almost one and a half times costlier than normal toilets, cost and scale factors may constrain their production and thereby diffusion into markets. The government may provide incentives to both the innovating and adopting firms to ensure the adoption and diffusion of such innovations in the form of pecuniary (tax reliefs), as also non-pecuniary means (national recognition for firms contributing to social good). The returns from health and productivity improvements through such measures would outweigh the fiscal considerations, if any.

The resultant benefits from such a shared CSR agenda and integrating CSI with such agenda would not be restricted to a single level. Such an integration of stakeholder efforts would generate multiplier effects on national competitive advantage, thereby creating a virtual cycle.

Case Studies on CSIs: The Indian Context

As discussed in the first section, we look at three variants of CSI: the BOP model, social entrepreneurship and eco-innovation.

Bottom-of-Pyramid (BoP) Models of CSI

Hindustan Unilever Ltd.'s (HUL's) Project Shakti: A User-led Model: HUL's project Shakti was a rural distribution initiative in small villages. The project blended the business objective for HUL of enhancing its direct rural reach, with the social objective of creating livelihood opportunities for underprivileged rural women. The unique micro-entrepreneurship model with the aim of integrating business interests with societal need represented a social innovation of HUL in the 1990s.

The choice of such a micro-entrepreneurship model—which co-opted users—had clear benefits for the rural community:

- Sustainable investment opportunity for village community/ rural women.
- Increase in the household income of poor families of Shakti Entrepreneurs (SEs).
- Empowerment to rural women.
- Better standards of living through access to health and hygiene products.
- Basic business management training for sustained livelihood to rural underprivileged women. In this unique model, the

company sold the products at additional discounts to the SEs thus enabling them to raise incomes of their families. The initiative almost doubled the average household income of an SE. Moreover, the company also invested in training the entrepreneurs and empowering them with sales tools like mobiles, bicycles, etc.

In general, a rural woman from poor economic background (in some cases member from a self-help group [SHG]) was selected as an SE, commonly referred as 'Shakti Amma.' She received stocks from HUL's rural distributor. After being trained by the company, the SE then sold those goods directly to consumers and retailers in the village.

Shakti, which started with 17 women in one state, currently provides livelihood-enhancing opportunities to over 65,000 SEs who distribute HUL products in more than 165,000 villages and reach over four million rural households. As per Unilever Sustainable Living Plan, Unilever will increase the number of SEs that it recruits, trains and employs from 45,000 in 2010 to 75,000 in 2015 globally. Historical data show that a majority of Shakti Ammas are earning more than INR 1,000 a month. This is a significant proportion when compared to the per capita income of their state, especially for the poorer states.

The programme was extended in 2010 to include 'Shaktimaans' who were typically the husbands or brothers of the Shakti Ammas. Shaktimaans complemented the Shakti ammas. They sold HUL products on bicycles to surrounding villages, covering a larger area than Shakti Ammas could do on foot.

HUL's project Shakti became the model to reach out to rural consumers in developing and emerging markets and enabled Unilever to tap opportunity at the BoP. The project was customised and adapted in several South-East Asian, African and Latin American markets like Bangladesh, Sri Lanka and Vietnam. In Bangladesh and Sri Lanka, it was promoted as project Joyeeta and Saubaghya respectively.

Social Entrepreneurship

Hockerts (2007) describes social entrepreneurship as the "discovery and sustainable exploitation of opportunities to create public goods." An example of supporting social entrepreneurship is seen in the efforts of Syngenta Foundation India (SFI) Ltd.

The foundation aims to create value for resource-poor small farmers in developing countries through innovations in sustainable agriculture and the activation of value chains. It focuses on smallholders, productivity and markets.

By extending science-based know-how, facilitating access to quality inputs, and linking smallholders to markets in profitable ways, it aims to transform small farmers into professional growers. This adds value for rural communities, and sustainably improves food security.

Smallholders produce part of their own food needs, and a surplus that helps feed their countries and supply international markets. With the right kinds of agricultural technologies and supporting services such as extension, credit and micro-insurance, smallholders could increase their production significantly and sustainably. In the process, they would improve their own food security and that of their communities and countries. 'Inclusive' agricultural growth would be promoted, the fundamental basis for equitable economic development.

The SFI focuses on productivity and the inclusion of farmers in remunerative value chains. With establishing pilot projects, the foundation also puts major emphasis on successful scale-up.

In India, Syngenta found that farming by smallholders was increasingly becoming unviable due to shrinking size of holding, farmers' inability to access and adopt productivity-enhancing technology, and to market their surplus produce for economic gain. Consequently, they were getting marginalised and compelled to migrate in search of alternative means of livelihood. The approach and priorities of SFI contained varied processes in helping low-income farmers to face challenges. Increasing income opportunities of smallholder farmers by raising productivity and improving access to market in a sustainable way, following the practice of collective marketing by producers using improved handling, logistics and marketing skills and enhancing the quality of produce that would bring about greater profitability were the value added methods which improved livelihood security of smallholder farmers.

SFI joined hands with reputed corporate like Field Fresh in Mokhada, near Jawhar, and with PepsiCo in Bishnupur, Bankura, to connect farmers' groups from its project areas so that they could directly sell their produce to these corporate. By tying up with these companies and learning their special production techniques for vegetables, okra and hot pepper for Field Fresh, and potatoes, for PepsiCo, these farmers' group were able to get better rates and were also protected against the hazards of fluctuating prices which were common for such perishable commodities.

SFI's partner in Jawhar, BAIF[1] promoted Amarai Cooperative Society for facilitating market linkage and value addition activities for mango and cashew grown by its members. The cooperative had around 2,000 members. Strengthening rural supply chain, preparing producers for high-value markets and empowering farming communities, seed treatment, soil and water management, post-harvest management, networking with agencies, and managing incomes had enhanced farm productivity in a number of ways, thereby largely benefiting the smallholder farmers.

In 2009-10, SFI entered into the second phase during which it spread its activities to new areas and used its tested skills for productivity enhancement of food crops to reach greater number of farmers. It also replicated, with success field demonstration, promotion of high value vegetable cultivation and other tested initiatives in these new areas. In the last two years, these interventions resulted in improved livelihood security of additional 15,000 smallholder farmers. In order to reduce the production and marketing risks of over-dependence on just one kind of crop, a large number of farmers in the SFI-PRADAN project area adopted

1. BAIF: The BAIF Development Research Foundation was formerly registered as Bharatiya Agro Industries Foundation. Now, it is known by its acronym BAIF.

diversified cropping patterns and benefited from it. SFI schemes led to the creation of a new group of Agri Entrepreneurs.

Eco-Innovation

Eco innovations are ecological innovations, which would guarantee 'environmentally benign growth' (Hockerts and Morsing, 2008).

Tata Chemicals Ltd. (TCL) provides an example of such innovations in the Indian context. The company used a novel approach to solve environmental problems at its soda ash facility at Mithapur. Through its project, it reclaimed 22 of its 30 acres of waste dumps near its site at Mithapur, Gujarat. This reduced the dust generation that was affecting local inhabitants. The local community had sought to solve this problem by spraying with seawater for more than 20 years, thereby making the soil quality poor. TCL engaged TERI, Delhi, which identified the most suitable plants and developed a microorganism inoculation to help them extract nutrients from the soil. At the same time, TCL developed and introduced patented filtration technology to prevent the disposal of soda ash effluent into settling ponds for the future.

Concluding Remarks

The paper attempts to answer the question: can CSIs be integrated into the CSR agenda. The extant literature review suggests that Indian companies tend to look at CSR and innovations as two distinct, mutually exclusive phenomena. In line with recent research, we suggest that there exists high complementarity between the two. The case studies pertaining to the Indian context demonstrate that CSIs of various kinds are being practised in recent times. However, such innovations can be more effective when developed within an open business model context, as also involving multiple stakeholders. The paper suggests a theoretical framework to use open business models to integrate CSIs with CSR agenda.

While an extensive study of company websites, followed by qualitative case studies may shed more light on the CSR-driven innovations, as also the limits of open business models in such contexts, the paper points to directions for further research.

Adoption of such integrated social innovations solutions may help India improve its rankings in both the Innovation and Competitiveness Indices, as also is a valuable source of national competitive advantage.

References

Balasubramanian, N.K., D. Kimber and F. Siemensma (2005). "Emerging Opportunities or Traditions Reinforced? An Analysis of the Attitudes towards CSR and Trends of Thinking about CSR in India", *The Journal of Corporate Citizenship* 17: 79-92 (Spring).

Banerjee, S.B. (2007). *Corporate Social Responsibility. The Good the Bad and the Ugly* Cheltenham: Edward Elgar.

Beavis, S. (n.d.). "Puma: Business and the Environment—Counting the Cost", *The Guardian*. Available from: *http://www.theguardian.com/sustainable-business/best-practice-exchange/puma-impact-environment-counting-cost* (15 October 2014).

Bhattacharya, J. (2007). *Corporate Social Responsibility: Ethical and Strategic Choice*. Delhi: Asian Books Pvt. Ltd.

Brown, K. (2001). *Corporate Social Responsibility, Perceptions of Indian Business*. Report by the Centre for Social Markets, Available from: *www.Csmworld.org/public/pdf/social_respons.pdf* (23 September 2014).

Carroll, A.B. (1979). "A Three-dimensional Model of Corporate Social Performance", *Academy of Management Review* 4(4): 497-505.

Chesbrough, H.W. (2003). "The Era of Open Innovation", *MIT Sloan Management Review* 44(3): 35-41.

Chesbrough, H.W., W. Vanhaverbeke and J. West (eds.) (2006). *Open Innovation: Researching a New Paradigm*. New York: Oxford University Press.

Christensen, C.M. (1997). *The Innovators Dilemma, When New Technologies Cause Great Firms to Fail*. Boston: Harvard University Business Press.

Freeman, R.E. (1984). *Strategic Management: A Stakeholder Approach*. Boston: Pitman.

Hockerts, K. (2007). "Managerial Perceptions of the Business Case for Corporate Social Responsibility", CBS Center for Corporate Social Responsibility, Available from: *http://openarchive.cbs.dk/handle/10398/7117* (28 September 2014).

Hockerts, H. and M. Morsing (2008). "A Literature Review on Corporate Social Responsibility in the Innovation Process", Copenhagen Business School (CBS), Centre for Corporate Social Responsibility, pp.1-28.

Holmes, S. and P. Smart (2009). "Exploring Open Innovation Practice in Firm-non-profit Engagements: A Corporate Social Responsibility Perspective", *R&D Management* 39(4): 394-409.

IndianNGOs.com (2002). "CSR Profiles of Indian Corporates". Available from: *http://www.indianngos.com/corporate/indian.html* (24 September 2014)

Jayashankar, M., C. Paul and S. Bhat (2013). "CSR Report Card: Where Companies Stand", *Forbes India*, March 18. Available from: *http://forbesindia.com/article/real-issue/csr-report-card-where-companies-stand/34893/1* (2 October 2014).

Kanter, R.M. (1999). "From Spare Change to Real Change: The Social Sector as a Beta Site for Business Innovation", *Harvard Business Review*77: 123-32.

Kumar, R., D.F. Murphy and V. Balsari (2001). *Altered Images: The 2001 State of Corporate Social Responsibility in India Poll*. New Delhi: TERI-India.

Kim, W.C. and R. Mauborgne (2005). *Blue Ocean Strategy: How to Create Uncontested Market Space and Make Competition Irrelevant*. Boston: Harvard University Business Press.

Kotler, P. and N. Lee (2005). Corporate Social Responsibility—Doing the Most Good for Your Company and Your Cause. Hoboken, New Jersey: Wiley and Sons, Inc.

Kumar, R. (2004). "The State of CSR in India 2004. Acknowledging Progress Prioritizing Action". CSRCSR. Background Paper. New Delhi: National Seminar on Corporate Social Responsibility.

McWilliams, A. and D. Siegel (2001). "Corporate Social Responsibility: A Theory of the Firm Perspective", *Academy of Management Review* 26(1): 117-27.

NSE/NIFTY (2003). "Proposal 84: Corporate Social Responsibility of NSE NIFTY Companies Content Implementation Strategies and Impact". *NSE Research Papers*. Mumbai: National Stock Exchange.

O'Sullivan, M.A. (2000). "The Innovative Enterprise and Corporate Governance", *Cambridge Journal of Economics* 24: 393-416.

Partners in Change (2003). *Indian Market Research Bureau Survey: The State of CSR*. Available from: *www.picindia.org* (24 September 2014).

Porter, M. (1980). *Competitive Strategy*. NY: Free Press.

Syngenta Foundation (2011). *Annual Report 2010-11.*

United Nations Development Programme (UNDP) (2002). Corporate Social Responsibility survey, UNDP/India British Council/CII/PricewaterhouseCooper Report, Available from: *www1.britishcouncil.org/India-rights-csrsurvey-report-2002.pdf* (2 October 2014).

World Business Council for Sustainable Development (WBCSD) (2005). Meeting Changing Expectations: Corporate Social Responsibility. Available from: *http://www.wbcsd.org/DocRoot/hbdf19Txhmk3kDxBQDWW/CSRmeeting.pdf* (1 October, 2014).

World Commission on Environment and Development (WCED) (1987). "Our Common Future", Report of the World Commission on Environment and Development. Oxford: Oxford University Press.

World Economic Forum. The Global Competitiveness Report 2014-15. Available from: *http://www.weforum.org/reports/global-competitiveness-report-2014-2015* (29 September 2014).

Documents and Website:

CII-Social Code for Business. Available from: *http://www.cii.inmenu_content.php? menu id=626* (24 September 2014)

Corporate Social Responsibility Survey 2002 India. Available from: *http://www.indiapartnershipforum.org/csrs2002.htm* (22 September 2014).

CSR Handbook (2005). Bombay: Bombay Chamber of Commerce and Industry.

Global Innovation Index (2014). Available from: *https://www.globalinnovationindex.org/userfiles/file/reportpdf/gii-2014-v5.pdf* (21 September 2014).

Hindustan Unilever Ltd. Available from: *http://www.hul.co.in/sustainable-living-2014/casestudies/Casecategory/Project-Shakti.aspx* (30 September 2014).

Joint Roadmap: Towards Zero Discharge of Hazardous Chemicals 2011. Available from: *http://nikeinc.com/system/assets/5408/111118_JointRoadmap_original.pdf?1321567189* (15 October 2014).

Karmayog CSR Ratings (2009). Available from: *www.karmayog.org/csr2009/ index.htm* (24 September 2014).

Syngenta Foundation. Available from: *http://www.syngentafoundation.org/index.cfm?pageID=30* (1 October 2014).

"The Global Competitiveness Report Characterizes India as a Factor-driven Economy. The Basis for National Competitiveness in such Economies is the Abundance of Labor and Natural Resources, which Drives Down Wages", *http://www.weforum.org/reports/globalcompetitiveness-report-2014-2015* (accessed 29 September 2014).

Tata Chemicals Ltd. Available from: *http://www.tatachemicals.com/media/releases/201309sept/ 20130926_icc_award.html#.VDDtkkuR3wI* (2 October 2014).

http://www.mca.gov.in/Ministry/pdf/CompaniesActNotification2_2014.pdf

9

ROOPINDER OBEROI

Creating Shared Value for Leveraging Full Spectrum Corporate Social Responsibility

An Emergent Deepening in Syntax of Responsible Capitalism

Objectives of the Study

The objective of the paper is to understand the interlaced beliefs that led to the increase in interest in shared value and which enables us to explore the shift in the whole field of business in a complex social-creative process that persuades, transforms, re-imagines and alters the outlook of the 'business in the space of society' wherein business is intrinsically grounded and contextualised.

This study is exploratory in nature, as it aims to offer both theoretical and empirical milieu for the transformation process of a company's non-market strategy from corporate social responsibility (CSR) to creating shared value (CSV). In the last section of the paper, empirical mapping of companies that have adopted a systematic and intentional approach to creating economic and social value shall be provided as an evidence of spurred innovation and novelty across the business community.

Reimagining Corporate Responsibility by Unfastening the Social and Economic Latent Value

The world today is grappling with enormous social, economic and environmental challenges. Organisations across sectors—public, non-profit, multilateral and private—are working to address issues ranging from poverty and malnutrition to social inequality and climate change. Yet social these problems remain obdurate on a massive scale, particularly for the four billion around the world with incomes well below the poverty line (BPL). The challenges facing poor or vulnerable populations require innovative, sustainable and large-scale solutions. Bill Gates speaking at the Corporate Social Responsibility ("CSR") Arms at the World Economic Forum in Davos Switzerland in 2008 said: "The world is not getting better fast enough, and it's not getting better for everyone as more people can make a profit, or gain recognition, doing work that eases the world's inequities." Porter and Kramer (2011) called in for creative capitalism and asserted in strong expression "Capitalism is under siege and business is caught in a vicious circle. So, indisputably all have come to concur that a more refined form of capitalism is indispensable—one imbued with a social purpose."

The corporate responsibility debate is not new. However, first decade of the 21st century brought with it the crucial catalysts for an enduring phase of hastened transformation in corporate responsibility lexicon combined with steadfast belief that business needs to do more for society. Corporates continue to face global backlash following a global recession. There was outrage over chief executive officers' (CEOs') vast pay packages, the gnawing certainty that executives cooked the books leading to discrediting of corporate post-economic crisis. Corporations were extensively looked upon as covetous and uncaring. Current events have also called into question the overall concept of global economic growth that was triumphantly hailed as the only alternative over the past several decades. Ideologically hegemonic positing of liberalisation, privatisation and globalisation, was all clubbed in concert as the 'formula for world prosperity.' This domineering *mantra* as a solution for the malaise in the world stands discredited today. The International Monetary Fund (IMF), the World Bank and the World Trade Organization (WTO) are all under rising fire. Global glaring disparities and inequalities are paramount concerns. Furthermore, many indicators are pointing to the fact that between the early 1990s and 2007, global unemployment actually rose by 30 per cent, and the income gap between richer and poorer households increased, affecting low-income groups disproportionately. Not only developing countries are suffering from poverty but poverty rates for 2010 rose higher than 22 per cent of the population in five European countries (Greece, Portugal, Italy, Spain and the United Kingdom) (European Commission, 2011).

Given the clout of multinational corporations (MNCs) to reallocate resources and production across borders, many have also suggested that they encourage a global 'race to the bottom' by chasing subsidies, incentives and lower costs wherever they might lead, at the expense of national and community interests. Wayne Visser argued that the global financial crisis represents 'a multi-level failure of responsibility—from the individual and corporate level to the finance sector and entire capitalist system' (Visser, 2010). Many others disparage the environmental consequences associated with material-intensive industries associated with global capitalism to the rest of the developing world (London and Hart, 2010). Thus the current global financial crisis made matters worse and exposed the deep cracks in the hyper-globalisation model. The fundamental question that has came to fore is: can business and society work collectively to advance each other's prosperity? No company works in a vacuum consequently, inter-reliant interrelationships develop involving business and the community within which it operates. The foremost concern then is to maximise the nature and extent of mutually beneficial interrelationships.

Since, 'business as usual' has come under tremendous scrutiny. Not only the anti-globalisation lobby groups but also conformists are ever more uncomfortable with increased corporate power and influence. Companies are widely perceived to be prospering at the cost of the broader community. The capitalist predisposition to externalise the cost on to society and environment needs instrument to prevent this proclivity. The ebbed confidence in business has knocked in at the business competitiveness and sapped financial growth. Research on how to undo the existing trust deficit in free market enterprise has resulted in the fresh precepts ranging from notions of capitalism (Barnes, 2006), to moral capitalism (Young, 2003) or humanistic management (Pirson and Lawrence, 2009), and many are suggesting that business needs to recast itself to meet the challenges of the 21st century. This is at the heart of creative capitalism debate. It's not just about doing more corporate philanthropy or asking companies to be more virtuous. It's about giving them a real incentive to apply their expertise in new ways, making it possible to earn a return while serving the people who have been left out. Synchronisation of these (contra) variables has become a formidable challenge for several theorists.

The fundamental shift from the 'for-profit' model to one that's 'for-purpose (and profits)' was heralded by management theorist like Peter Drucker, who opined that "every social and global issue is a business opportunity just waiting for the right kind of inventive entrepreneurship, the right kind of investment, the right kind of collective action" (Hollender *et al.*, 2010). There are numerous other writers who made noteworthy contributions to the body of knowledge in this broad area, such as Jed Emerson's blended value, Stuart Hart's mutual benefit, C.K. Prahalad and Hart's bottom of the pyramid, John Elkington's work along with Andrew Savitz and Karl Weber's work on sustainability and the triple bottom line, David Schwerin's and John Mackey's work on conscious capitalism, and many, many others. Leading companies have lately applying pioneering variety of social innovation by coalescing three fundamental ideas: the concept of shared value creation, the theory of the fortune at the bottom of the pyramid (BoP), and a corporate social entrepreneurship approach by which they penetrate low-income markets by serving to resolve global challenges at the same time generating profits. Recently, for-profit companies, engaging in strategic CSR, have chosen to implement new hybrid business models that are part of the broader trend of studies in the corporate social entrepreneurship school of thought (Austin *et al.*, 2005). Moreover, Kanter (1999) uses the term "corporate social innovation" (CSI) to assert that firms should use social issues as learning laboratories to identify unmet needs and to develop solutions. CSI is an important approach for companies that decide to reach the low-income market (Mahlouji and Anaraki, 2009). Prahalad argues that markets at the bottom of the economic pyramid are fundamentally new sources of growth for MNCs. Growth can be extremely rapid, because these markets are in the earliest stage of development. Sethi (2002) argues that, particularly in emerging markets, corporate responsible initiatives contribute to a company's social 'licence to operate.' Research also shows that CSR can create intangible assets that help companies reduce the liability of foreignness and gain competitive advantages over rivals (Gardberg and Fornbrun, 2006). According to Simanis and Hart (2008), it is imperative that companies move rapidly to a 'second-generation' of corporate BoP strategies that go beyond mere deep listening and extend into a deep dialogue with the poor that will result in a shared commitment born out of a mutual learning experience. Large companies are uniquely positioned to leverage their size and business models to address social problems sustainably and at scale. Corporations can serve as impact enterprises by creating shared value, using their core businesses to generate economic value through social progress. The second-generation BoP strategy "requires an embedded process of co-invention and co-creation that brings corporations into close, personal business partnerships with BoP communities." Distribution channel strategies are based on the concept of a shared business commitment that entails value co-creation and stresses the importance of involving local partners and sharing a vision and sense of responsibility (Michelini, 2012).

The shared value principle likewise becomes more influential when companies decide to expand their businesses to developing countries and target the low-income market, where the link between corporations and society grows stronger (Jamali, 2010; Matten and Crane, 2005). On the one hand, these countries/markets signify an excellent business opportunity, and on the other hand, these countries/markets are characterised by sizeable social problems. Thus, corporate business strategy and corporate social responsibility should engender profit, as well as social value as compared to other saturated markets (Michelini and Fiorentino, 2012). Recently at the World Economic Forum in Davos, Bill Gates also specified the birth of a "creative capitalism" wherein "more people can make a profit, or gain recognition, doing work that eases the world's inequities." A 2007 report by McKinsey stated that more than 90 per cent of the CEOs are engaging to push environmental and social strategies into their operations than five years ago. *The Economist,* in an earlier article, ridiculed corporate responsibility as a ''do-Gooding sideshow,'' however in 2008 changed its stance and wrote that ''CR is booming'' and ''few big companies can now afford to ignore it" (Hollender *et al.*, 2010). The M&S ticker demonstrates that CSR is booming. Whether through electronic screens, posters or glossy reports, big companies want to tell the world about their good citizenship. They are pushing out the message on their websites and in advertising campaigns. Nowadays, many businesses are being criticised for engaging in unrelated CSR activities for the sake of window dressing (Bhattacharyya *et al.*, 2008; Porter and Kramer, 2006). *The Economist* in its special report on CSR in 2008 stated:

> Starting in the 1980s, with environmental disasters such as the explosion at the Bhopal pesticide factory and the Exxon Valdez oil spill, industry after industry has suffered blows to its reputation. Big pharma was hit by its refusal to make antiretroviral drugs available cheaply for HIV/AIDS sufferers in developing countries. In the clothing industry, companies like Nike and Gap came under attack for use of child labour. Food companies face a backlash over growing obesity'.

And "Don't be evil" as a corporate motto offers no immunity: Google was one of several American technology titans hauled before Congress to be grilled about their behaviour in China. Companies typically allocate about 1 per cent of pre-tax profits to worthy causes because giving something back to the community seems "the right thing to do." But many companies now feel that arm's-length philanthropy—simply writing cheques to charities—is no longer enough. Shareholders want to know that their money is being put to good use, and employees want to be actively involved in good works (*The Economist*, 2008).

Value Constellation and Inclusivity as a Panorama for Responsible Corporates

Undeniably, the much propounded inclusive business model of shared value stands on the conception of the "value constellation." Some corporations have lately developed pioneering structure of social innovation by amalgamating three fundamentals—the theory of shared value creation, the premise of the fortune at the

BoP, and a corporate social entrepreneurship approach—through which they penetrate market by serving to get to the bottom of global challenges while concurrently making profits. This model is characterised by a strong and inextricable link with the three bottom lines. It is further than the extended value chain. The full canvas of ecosystem embraces the structural environment, the regulators, the supporting organisations and other actors, such as competitors and neighbouring communities. The correlation between the company and the ecosystem is founded on a reciprocal dependence (co-dependence), and the company must evolve mutually with the actors in the environment (co-evolution) (Marquez *et al.*, 2010). Wayne Vissers terms this enhanced position as Systemic CSR or CSR 2.0 which focuses its activities on identifying and tackling the root causes of our present unsustainability and irresponsibility, typically through innovating business models, revolutionising their processes, products and services and lobbying for progressive national and international policies. This new CSR 2.0 is based on five principles of creativity, scalability, responsiveness, locality and circularity and forms the basis for a new DNA model of responsible business, built around the four elements of value creation, good governance, societal contribution and environmental integrity. Companies that embrace the CSR 2.0 will be those that collaboratively find innovative ways to tackle global challenges and will be consequently rewarded in the marketplace. The idea of profit is getting disaggregated and not all profit is considered equal. This idea was for long lost in the narrow, short-term focus of financial bottom line in much of management thinking. A profit involving a social purpose represents a higher form of capitalism—one that will enable society to advance more rapidly and it also allows companies to develop all the more. The result is a constructive cycle of company and community prosperity, which leads to profits that endure (Porter and Kramer, 2011).

Stuart Hart's framework for sustainable value creation includes pollution prevention, clean tech, BoP, and product stewardship, all of which overlap but are not the same as the levels of CSV. Prahalad and Hart's path-breaking work on business with the BoP can also be an aspect of CSV; however, as Hart and Kash Rangan have separately written, BoP approach only creates sustainable value when they benefit the communities they serve, and not all BoP initiatives do so. The publication of the two articles, "The Fortune at the Bottom of the Pyramid," in *Strategy + Business* (January 2002) by Stuart Hart, and "Serve the World's Poor, Profitably" in the *Harvard Business Review* (September 2002) by Allen Hammond, made possible the process of extensive debate within corporations. The social business venture category also includes the inclusive business model. This kind of social enterprise seeks to contribute towards poverty alleviation by including lower-income communities (LIC) within its value chain while not losing sight of the ultimate goal of business, which is to generate profits (WBCSD, 2008). Prahalad and Hammond (2002) wrote

> by virtue of their numbers, the poor represent a significant latent purchasing power that must be unlocked. For example, all too often, the poor tend to reside in high-cost ecosystems even within developing countries. In the shanty town of Dharavi, outside Mumbai, India, the poor pay a premium for everything from rice to credit. Compare the cost of everyday items of consumption between Dharavi and Warden Road, a higher income neighbourhood in Mumbai. The poverty penalty in Dharavi can be as high as 5 to 25 times what the rich pay for the same services. Research indicates that this poverty penalty is universal, although the magnitude differs by country. The poverty penalty is the result of local monopolies, inadequate access, poor distribution, and strong traditional intermediaries. Large-scale private-sector businesses can "unlock this poverty penalty.

Indeed, inclusive businesses connect supply (producers) with demand (consumers) and the local dimension with the global, thereby unleashing positive self-reinforcing processes of economic wealth creation and social empowerment in developing countries. Thus, even though these theories may have a component of shared value, the equivalence between their theoretical precepts and CSV maybe far stretched.

Companies acknowledge the need to synergise social and environmental efforts. They have recognised that applying their energies to work out solutions for unremitting problems found in the social sector powerfully fuels the business development. For example investing in education will take care of tomorrow's supply of knowledgeable workers. Reduced joblessness affects the consumption capacity of people. In reality, a new paradigm of CSV establishes inextricable link between private enterprises and the public interest and goods that generates profitable and sustainable transformations for both sides. Thus, the central idea being put forward is that CSR strategies should generate profit, as well as social value for them to be scalable and enduring (Michelini and Fiorentino, 2012).

Following Porter and Kramer's premise, corporations investing particularly in developing countries have a choice of CSR strategy. These corporations can trim down the dangers caused by their value chain. Secondly, they can prefer a philanthropic strategy that develops the key areas of their competitive framework. Finally, they may choose to generate a shared value approach where the social aspect of their scheme can be converted into component of the value proposition. In recent times, corporations, engaging in CSR, have preferred to put into operation new hybrid business models that are element of the broader development of study in the corporate social entrepreneurship school of thought (Austin *et al.*, 2005). The changing responsibility of the corporation in society is consistent with companies engaging not only with environmental and social issues that are significant for their future financial performance, but also in fact engaging with issues that are short of direct materialality for their prospective financial performance (Eccles and Serafeim, 2013). Serafeim (2014) shows that a firm's value creation process is dependent on six capitals: natural, human, financial, physical, intellectual and social. Scholars suggest that enterprises are rewriting the rules of traditional business conduct (Elkington and Hartigan, 2008; Porter and Kramer, 2011). The renewed equilibrium between financial and social value creation can facilitate corporations to re-establish confidence, allow them to stay economical and add to their legitimacy.

Decrypting Porter and Kramer Shared Value Construct

Porter and Kramer first touched upon CSV in 2009, followed up with their 2011 *Harvard Business Review* article "Creating Shared Value: How to Reinvent Capitalism and Unleash a Wave of Innovation and Growth." At this point, there were already some companies, such as Nestlé and Unilever, who had been effectively integrating and implementing this approach in their business models. In fact, we may presuppose it was the impact of this differentiated approach at Nestlé and other CSV-focused companies that led to the research and development (R&D) of the concept of creating shared value. Given the modest empirical account of this model, there is not vast exploration on CSV construct, thus the contemporary perceptive of the conception is significantly based on the seminal work of Porter and Kramer. CSV focuses on how to mobilise capitalism for social change is a sharp departure from earlier thinking about corporate social responsibility. It is not about balancing stakeholders or behaving ethically, but rather seeing social problems as representations of business opportunities yet to be met. In rising to this challenge, corporations have discovered innovative products and services with reach far beyond the intended initial target market; they have established distribution networks that reach new customers; they have created significant improvements in productivity and cost effectiveness; and they have unlocked profits and growth by improving the competitive context within which they operate.

Expressing to some extent analogous apprehensions towards the existing capitalist model, Porter and Kramer (2011) argue that the capitalist system is plummeting in its legitimacy among citizens all over the world which necessitates revising the eminent logic underlying the traditional business models. Almost in the same breath they claim that capitalism is however an unparalleled vehicle for meeting human needs, improving efficiency, creating jobs and building wealth. A constricted notion of capitalism has disallowed business from harnessing its full potential to meet society's broader challenges. Correspondingly, Porter himself articulated that "my work aims not to be descriptive but normative" (Argyres and McGahan, 2002), and they assumed that CSV add together to "the next evolution in capitalism" and "major transformation of business thinking" (Porter and Kramer, 2011). CSV embodies a broader conception of Adam Smith's invisible hand. At its elemental level, the competitiveness of a corporation and the health of the communities around it are intimately entwined. A business desires a flourishing community, not only to generate demand for its commodities but also to make available crucial public assets and an accommodating setting. A community needs thriving businesses to supply jobs and wealth creation opportunities for its citizens. This mutuality means that public policies that destabilise the efficiency and competitiveness of industry are self-defeating. Thus, Porter constructed the CSV framework with the ingrained purpose of constructing a normative framework for the resolution of societal challenges which calls upon a radical alteration in the current business arrangement.

CSV concept is a new-fangled vision on corporate social responsibility. It is pursued in conjunction with the philosophy of "create value for all" (co-value construction) with the consciousness that by undertaking business with the BoP, firms generate the prospective for the augmentation of innovative business at the same time as they advance deprived people's living standards. Turning the pursuit of shared value opportunities into a regular activity requires defining a clear social purpose, publicising it internally and externally, and embedding it in core processes such as strategic planning and budgeting. This establishes a culture that unleashes the best in employees and helps mobilise external partners that have similar goals. Consequently, this business model "can give people the confidence and strength to escape poverty using their own means" (UNDP, 2008). Porter demonstrates the distinction between customary yet commendable CSR and the integrated, value-oriented CSV through the notion of fair trade. Fair trade is a label provided by Fair Trade Labelling Organisations (FLO) which requires that farmers be paid a minimum amount per pound of coffee (Carroll and Shabana, 2010). It is, in other words, a redistributive approach to make certain the minimum income of poor farmers. CSV on the other hand, spreads out the total pool of economic and social value by convalescing techniques and reinforcement the local cluster of supporting suppliers and other institutions in order to lift up farmers' efficiency, yields, product quality and sustainability. Porter and Kramer draw from studies of cocoa farmers in the Côte d'Ivoire, as it was found that while fair trade can add to farmers' incomes by 10 per cent to 20 per cent and, shared value investments can increase their incomes by more than 300 per cent and (Porter and Kramer, 2011).

The functioning of CSV is to structure a process of putting cooperatively economic and non-economic rationales for shared commitment into corporate organisation. This task entails an innate conviction in the continuation of the business case for CSR. In fact, according to Porter and Kramer (2011) "Businesses must reconnect company success with social progress. Shared value is not social responsibility, philanthropy, or even sustainability but a new-fangled technique to realise economic success." The evolving innovative capitalism employs enhanced ways to develop products, serve markets and build productive enterprises. According to Brown and Knudsen (2012) in many global corporations, CSR has been and often continues to be an ancillary function. Organising CSR as a component of integrated strategy is particularly important for the firm expanding overseas (Kostova and Zaheer 1999). Porter and Kramer (2006) explain that strategic CR can achieve 'win-wins' for the firm and for society when it is persistent on nurturing market surroundings. In fresh markets, there is frequently a great demand for infrastructure, establishment and human capital to make possible business opportunities. Porter and Kramer (2011) improved strategic CSR with CSV, resulting in a firm capitalising on their core competitiveness rather than from their collateral competence. Porter and Kramer's instrumental approach to CSV calls for extremely unambiguous actions in each context where the firm operates, dependent upon the existing infrastructure and institutional support for its activities (Brown and Knudsen, 2012). This suggests that CSR should be tailored to neighbourhood setting much like product markets strategies are custom-made when there are tough regulatory variance and/or consumer preferences across markets. The literature suggests that norms and values in a national business context can shape CR policies when these values are embraced by key and influential stakeholders (Brown and Knudsen, 2012).

The critical indication of differentiation between CSV and CSR (see Table 9.1) is that in the former, activities are not only able to provide societal values by contributing to the communities they belong to, but also they are able to obtain substantial economic benefits that enhance their own competence and competiveness (Spitzeck and Chapman, 2012). When companies do not understand or rigorously track the interdependency between social and business results, they overlook vital opportunities for innovation, growth and social impact at scale. Yunus *et al.* (2010) identified four components of a social business model for creating shared value: (a) the value proposition (the stakeholders and the product/service), (b) the social profit equation (the social profit and the environmental profit), (c) the value constellation (the internal value chain and the external value chain), and (d) the economic profit equation (the sales revenues, the cost structure and the capital employed). By contrasting the economic and social value generated by the enterprise, it is feasible to recognise the social impact of such an approach. The comparison discovers whether a company is more social or profit oriented (a market-based mission *versus* a social-

Table 9.1

Difference between CSR and CSV

CSR	*CSV*
• Value: doing good	• Value: economic and societal benefits relative to cost
• Citizenship, philanthropy, sustainability	• Joint company and community value creation
• Discretionary or in response to external pressure	• Integral to competing
• Separate from profit maximisation	• Integral to profit maximisation
• Agenda is determined by external reporting and personal preferences	• Agenda is company specific and internally generated
• Impact limited by corporate footprint and CSR budget	• Realigns the entire company budget

Source: Porter and Kramer (2011).

based mission) (Yunus *et al.,* 2010; Massetti, 2008). This social business model refers to joint ventures that aspire to resolve a social problem by using business methods, including the production and sale of products and/or services. These business activities should be undertaken in a way that is at least self-sustaining, and if some economic surplus is generated, it should be used to improve the level of attainment of social objectives (Yunus, 2008; 2010).

In short, CSV is supposed to focus on social predicaments or worsening, such as wasted energy and raw materials or expensive calamity, frequently affect the internal overheads for businesses (Porter and Kramer, 2011). At that moment then it necessitates a more refined structure of entrepreneurship, one that is permeated with a social purpose. However, that underlying principle should initiate not out of altruistic concern but out of a reflective approval and perceptive of market competition plus economic value creation. This synchronisation will make corporates inherently responsible. These new brand of corporations are being defined as 'integrated enterprises' or 'hybrid enterprises,' and they are competent to produce altered form of social improvement. Hybrid enterprises or CSV rebooted enterprises are "straddling the boundary between the for-profit business world and the social mission-driven public and not for profit organisations" (Hockerts, 2006). Thus, code of shared value creation cuts across the conventional segregation amid the responsibilities of business and those of government or civil society. From society's perspective, it does not matter what types of organisations created the value. What matters is that benefits are delivered by those organisations or combinations of organisations that are best positioned to achieve the most impact for the least cost (Porter and Kramer, 2011). Finding ways to boost up efficiency is likewise valuable whether in the service of commercial or societal objectives. In short, the principle of value creation should guide the use of resources across all areas of societal concern (Porter and Kramer, 2011). CSV forms the 'hybrid' signifier that can cover many diverse initiatives, oriented as an approach that can change welfare and social problems in the interfaces of the non-profit, public, voluntary, philanthropic and private sectors.

Michael Porter defined the success of both societal and business benefit as the "sweet spot" (Figure 9.1). If the activities of the company are exceedingly advantageous for society, but there is negative profit for the company, then the board executives and the investors will most likely be discontented. If, conversely, a community involvement programme produces in a soaring business advantage but no substantial community gain, the external stakeholders will still remain disappointed. They may consider companies actions as 'spin' or 'green washing,' and might view the corporation as utilising a community cause for its own growth. The 'sweet spot' is about attaining the equilibrium with the intention that everyone perceives they are component of a 'win-win' situation. Keeping this symmetry in consideration is significant when defining the companies' tangible strategy (Lakin and Scheubel, 2010).

Figure 9.1

Combined Social and Business Benefits

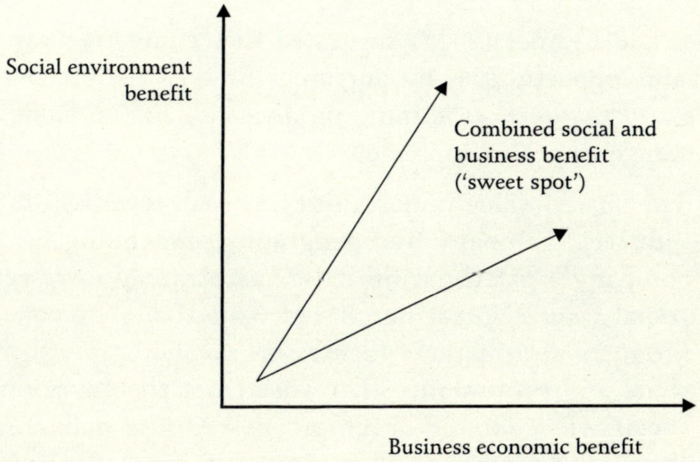

Source: Lakin and Scheubel (2010).

According to Porter and Kramer to plan and implement successful shared value strategies, business leaders should have premeditated goals about what they look forward to accomplish, search for noteworthy business contribution, and employ a portfolio approach when taking into account investments and opportunity costs. CSV constitutes the link between 'competitive advantage' and 'CSR.' To capitalise on the level of shared value created, business leaders can build up strategies that accomplish the following:

- Reflect thoughtful decisions about expected business and social goals, resulting in aligned resources, more effective operations, and reduced likelihood of unintended consequences of activities.
- Make a substantial business contribution, commanding more managerial attention and resources than small or sub-scale programmes.
- Constitute one component of a diversified business portfolio that delivers various rates of return over different time horizons, giving companies greater flexibility when considering potential activities.

Porter asserts that CSV can be applied to every major business decision by creating "concrete and tailored metrics for each business unit in each of the three areas" (Porter and Kramer, 2011).

Porter and Kramer (2011) suggested that companies can create shared value opportunities by pursuing three levels: preconceiving products and markets, redefining productivity in the value chain, and enabling cluster development.

- The shared value opportunities at each level will differ by industry, company and geography, depending on how a company's particular business and strategy intersect with social issues. Creating shared value from preconceiving products and markets focuses on revenue growth, market share and profitability that arise from the environmental, social, or economic development benefits delivered by a company's products and services.
- Creating shared value from redefining productivity in the value chain focuses on improvements in internal operations that improve cost, input access, quality and productivity achieved through environmental improvements, better resource utilisation, investment in employees, supplier capability and other areas.

- Creating shared value from enabling local cluster development derives from improving the external environment for the company through community investments and strengthening local suppliers, local institutions and local infrastructure in ways that also enhance business productivity.

Measuring shared value aims to track the progress and results of tailored shared value strategies. For each shared value opportunity, companies identify and track both social and business results; their parallel goals are to address a social problem and improve business performance. Stakeholders within government, civil society, philanthropic organisations, and private businesses can catalyse shared value by:

- Setting context: Shaping the environment within which companies conduct business.
- Providing information and insight: Conducting market research or offering expertise on populations, sectors or issues where companies may have limited experience.
- Supporting implementation: Directly supporting the development or execution of shared value strategies and helping to fill gaps in a company's implementation capabilities.
- Providing funding and other incentives: Providing resources to incubate launch, or scale shared value strategies and foster measurement approaches that facilitate accountability for achieving shared value goals.

In short, through CSV, a company is able to achieve superior performance by developing a unique area of focus and approach, aligning its operations to the strategy, and finally by defining concrete goals in its chosen fields to serve as the basis of evaluation.

Pioneers' and Pathfinder in Creating Shared Value: Linking Epistemology to Empirical

Despite the widespread embrace of the shared value concept, the tools to put this concept into practice are still in its infancy. The CSR literature is substantially scattered with case studies of responsible and sustainable projects. The difficulty is that so few of them ever go to scale of falling truly in the category of CSV. It is more or less as if, once the sound-bites and PR-plaudits have achieved their objectives, no further action is required. They become shining pilot projects and best practice examples. The sustainability struggle in the form of climate change or poverty is at such an enormous scale, and is so pressing, that piecemeal CSR solutions cannot be equivalent to it. It is, in essence an attempt to perform holistic, detail and context-oriented analyses of case studies over time in order to infer generic conclusions. The aim is to "to draw some broad generalisations out of a set of the cases over time" (Porter in Argyres and McGahan, 2002).

On 8 December 2010, executives from 10 major corporations gathered at Goldman Sachs's New York City headquarters to discuss how their companies were implementing shared value. They were brought together by FSG (Facilitation Services Group), the Stanford Social Innovation Review and the Committee Encouraging Corporate Philanthropy (CECP). Some of the companies such as Cisco Systems, Hewlett-Packard and IBM have been taking a shared value approach for some time. Other companies such as Western Union, Alcoa and InterContinental Hotels Group are new to the approach. But all of the participants which also included Goldman Sachs, Dow Chemical, Medtronic and PG&E are enthusiastic about the results and prospects for the future.

There are, on the other hand, instances like that of Wal-Mart's former CEO, Lee Scott, after his post-Hurricane Katrina Damascus occurrence decided that all cotton products in Wal-Mart will be organic and all fish Marine Stewardship Council (MSC)-certified in future. This can be perceived as commencement of CSR 2.0-type scalability. Adidas Group aligned with Nobel Laureate Muhammad Yunus's micro-finance organisation, Grameen Bank to manufacture a low-cost shoe for the poor in Bangladesh. The idea was "The shoes will be cheap and affordable for the poor, besides it will protect people from diseases," said Yunus. This programme is a wonderful case in point of the share value principle both for Adidas and for the Grameen Bank (Klein, 2011). Similarly, Procter & Gamble's new clothes rinse product for the rural poor lessens by two-third the amount of water required to rinse clothes after washing with detergent. It saves an enormous amount of time as well water. Other cases could be Toyota's laudable but premium-priced hybrid Prius for the rich and eco-conscious with Tata's $2,500 Nano, a cheap and eco-friendly car for the masses. The one is an incremental solution with long-term potential; the other is scalable solution with immediate impact. These cases illustrate that in a complex, interconnected world, companies (and their critics) will have to develop refined local contexts and discover the suitable local response, without forsaking universal principles.

It is also promising through partnerships to leverage traditional knowledge bases to produce more sustainable and, in some cases, finer products for consumption by affluent customers. Anita Roddick, CEO of the Body Shop International PLC, demonstrated the power of this strategy in the early 1990s through her company's "trade, not aid" programme of sourcing local raw material and products from indigenous people. More recently, the Starbucks Corporation, in cooperation with Conservation International, has pioneered a programme to source coffee directly from farmers in the Chiapas region of Mexico. These farms grow coffee organically using shade-grown practices, which preserves songbird habitat and prevent soil loss. Starbucks markets the product to US consumers as a high-quality, premium coffee; the Mexican farmers benefit economically from the sourcing arrangement, which eliminates middlemen from the business model. This direct relationship also improves the local farmers' understanding and knowledge of the market at the top of the pyramid and its customer expectations, making a steady transition from the informal to the formal economy possible.

Some other leading companies are making noteworthy advancement in building large-scale social enterprises. Corporations such as Nestlé, Unilever and Danone are repositioning themselves as nutrition and health companies. Carmakers companies like Nissan and Toyota are redefining their purpose as providing low-emissions mobility. And technology and telecommunications firms such as Intel and Verizon have made improving education and health care and making cities more liveable their central missions (Pfitzer *et al.*, 2013). In other cases, a leader can draw on a different legacy to direct the organisation toward a social purpose. Dow's launch of canola and sunflower seeds didn't emerge by chance from a rogue R&D initiative. It came from the combination of a strong tradition of innovation and leaders' recognition that many global social issues represent technological challenges as well as market opportunities (Pfitzer *et al.*, 2013). The ITC e-Choupal story illustrates how farmers with access to the Internet and thereby access to prices of commodities around the world can increase their incomes by 5-10 per cent. These farmers can decide when and how much to sell based on their understanding of the likely price movements for their products. Modern technology not only allows them to realise better prices, but also to improve their logistics. The aggregation of food grains allows for efficiencies for both the farmer and the buyer (Prahalad, 2005).

Then there are the revolutionary parts of more conventional corporate giants like eBay and IBM, who are applying their powerful resources to solving some of society's most vexing problems. Perhaps the quintessential example of such a business is the micro credit model introduced by Muhammad Yunus and the Grameen Bank. Yunus and Jollis (1999), in the aftermath of a devastating famine in Bangladesh, set up the Grameen Bank and it went from one $74 loan in 1974 to a $2.5 billion enterprise, spawning more than 3,000 similar microcredit institutions in 50 countries reaching over 133 million clients; this is a lesson in scalability and value creation. Another example of such a venture is Appropriate Technologies for Enterprise Creation (now KickStart), founded by Martin Fisher in 1991. Beginning as a non-profit company, KickStart has helped to create thousands of jobs in Kenya and other parts of East Africa, where more than half the population lives on less than $1 per day, by developing enabling technologies and working with local entrepreneurs to launch businesses using those technologies. Profits from the new small-scale businesses enable thousands of poor families to escape poverty, educate their children, afford health care and plan their futures. KickStart has helped to create 35,000 new micro enterprises in East Africa, with a total of $36 million per year in new profits. Revenues generated by these enterprises equal more than 0.5 per cent of Kenya's GDP (gross domestic product).

In 2007, Novartis India launched Arogya Parivar (Hindi for 'Healthy Family'), a programme designed to increase access to medicine in rural India. The company uses its generics manufacturer, Sandoz, to produce drugs at low cost and provides smaller package sizes to make products more affordable. In a parallel effort, Arogya Parivar 'health educators' work closely with village leaders and local non-governmental organisations (NGOs) to educate residents of rural communities about the benefits of healthy lifestyles, raising awareness and simultaneously creating demand for effective medicine. To ensure continuity of supply to local pharmacies, Novartis established distribution networks that were capable of supplying even the most remote locations. In addition to preconceiving its products and markets, Novartis is also strengthening its competitive context by working with international and local financial institutions to make infrastructure loans available to rural health care practitioners. Such loans allow local health practitioners to set up facilities, increasing the number of patients who can seek quality health care services and thus the market for medicine (Borgonovi *et al.*, 2011).

Hindustan Unilever Ltd. (HUL) demonstrates the ways that companies that explicitly seek to solve social problems using their core businesses can create impact beyond what is possible through philanthropy alone. HUL recognised that by preconceiving the market for its hygiene products, it could reduce the national incidence of diarrhea, which kills more than 500,000 Indian children every year. In 2002, the company partnered with local government leaders to launch the Lifebuoy Swasthya Chetna programme, a widespread campaign to promote improved hygiene and reduce diarrhea-related deaths in rural India. The campaign was instrumental in increasing awareness about the importance of hand washing among the rural poor and has reached 135 million Indians to date. The effort has also had a tremendous economic effect, helping the Lifebuoy brand secure an 18.4 per cent share of the Indian soap market and earning a place as one of the country's most trusted brands (Borgonovi *et al.*, 2011).

One another mega experiment, Project Shakti at Hindustan Lever Ltd. (HLL) in India, is a case in point. HLL created a direct distribution network in hard-to-reach locales (markets without distribution coverage through traditional distributors and dealers). HLL selected entrepreneurial women from these villages and trained them to become distributors, providing education, advice and access to products to their villages. These village women entrepreneurs, called Shakti Amma ('empowered mother'), have unique knowledge about what the village needs and which products are in demand. They earn between ₹3,000 and 7,000 per month ($60-$150) and therefore create a new capacity to consume for themselves and their families. More important, these entrepreneurial women are increasingly becoming the educators and access points for the rural BoP consumers in their communities.

This approach is not new. Avon is one of the largest cosmetics operations in Brazil and has used a similar approach by leveraging more than 800,000 'Avon ladies' as distributors to reach even the most remote regions of Amazonia (Prahalad, 2005).

Similarly, women in self-help groups (SHGs) working with ICICI Bank in India also have had their dignity restored. As a group, they decide which borrowers and projects will receive loans. This involvement of women in leadership development and in learning about finances and bank operations has given them a new sense of personal worth. The single-serve revolution has created a revolutionary level of choice for consumers at the BoP. For example, the 'switching costs' for the consumer are negligible because she can buy a sachet of shampoo or detergent or pickles; if she is not satisfied with her purchase she can switch brands the next day. Firms must continuously innovate and upgrade their products to keep customers interested in their brands, thereby improving quality and reducing costs.

Coca-Cola's Coletivo initiative in Brazil creates shared value by increasing the employability of low-income youth while strengthening the company's retail distribution channels and brand strength to increase local product sales. Coca-Cola has integrated shared value strategy and measurement steps and uses data and insights to unlock new value creation. In 2008, after six months of studying the needs of Brazil's growing lower middle class population, Coca-Cola identified skills development among low-income youth as a core social issue for strategic focus. The company now operates 135 Coletivos across Brazil, each with an average of 500 students, and plans to be running 170 by the end of 2012 (*FSG Report*, 2013).

InterContinental Hotels Group (IHG) tested dozens of options for reducing energy, water and waste to lower its environmental footprint while also driving down hotel operating costs. It launched its Green Engage programme when the company assessed its environmental footprint and realised that energy represented its second largest cost. IHG also identified water and waste as environmental and social issues with significant shared value potential. Green Engage started in 2009 by testing dozens of options for reducing energy use, water consumption and waste disposal in pilot hotels. These included new cooling/warming systems, solar panels and automatic computer shutdown applications. The objective was to provide a detailed ranking of all possible shared value opportunities in terms of returns to IHG as well as its franchises. Areas with high environmental impact and return were clearly distinguishable from other areas popular with the general public, such as solar energy, which yielded fewer reductions in emissions or economic value (*FSG Report*, 2013).

Nestlé trains and assists smallholder farmers to foster rural development while ensuring a reliable supply of high-quality raw materials. As the world's largest food and beverage company, Nestlé depends on a reliable supply of good quality raw materials, which in some cases are produced by smallholder farmers in low-income communities. Nestlé started to implement a rural development strategy, recognising that farmers earning decent incomes in thriving communities would be able to supply more and better agricultural goods. Nestlé employs over 1,100 agricultural staff and works with an additional 10,600 support staff across the world to train farmers, provide them with better technology and assist farm communities in local development projects. Nestlé has worked directly with more than 8,000 farmers in Rajasthan. The company's rural officers monitor progress through regular farm visits and they track specific indicators such as herd size and cattle health. Nestlé also measures the increased volume of milk it sources, which in this region has grown 13 per cent per year since 2008. As Nestlé's agronomists gain a deeper understanding of the performance of individual farmers, they are able to better allocate their efforts to those farmers who have the most improvement potential and can therefore increase the shared value created (Borgonovi *et al.*, 2011).

Concluding Observations

CSV is, no doubt, a seductive proposition, and one that has received massive consideration in the business community and among management scholars and educators. In the article by Crane *et al.* (2013) titled "Contesting the Value of Creating Shared Value" seek out to analyse and critically appraise the concept of shared value, both in terms of its stated aims to re-legitimise business, to redefine "the purpose of the corporation," to "reshape capitalism," and to "supersede corporate social responsibility in guiding the investments of corporations in their communities" and in terms of its overall contribution to understanding the social role and responsibilities of corporations. They suggest that the concept makes some significant progress towards enhancing attention to the social dimensions of business and may act as a spur for better practice. However, they point towards some uneasiness in the concept. They believe that Porter and Kramer CSV bears number of limitations that will grind down in the least actual opportunity for the deep transformation expected at by the authors. They emphasise that CSV is clichéd, it discounts inherent tensions between social and economic goals, it is naïve about the challenges of business compliance, and it is based on a shallow conception of the role of the corporation in society. Thus, while they concede several valuable facets of shared value, they eventually discern that it is a reactionary rather than transformational response to the crisis of capitalism. Therefore, CSV is not a resolution to capitalism's trouble but an indicator of an approach to supervision that is itself rife to the contemporary aggravation of the capitalist system (Crane *et al.,* 2013). In a similar vein, *The Economist* noted that CSV bore resemblance to Emerson's "blended value" concept "in which firms seek simultaneously to pursue profit and social and environmental targets" as well as having "an overlap" with Hart's

Capitalism at the Crossroads. Thus Porter and Kramer tend to abridge the convolution of social and environmental issues leading to possible misrepresentation of the appropriate investments and outcomes. Operating with a CSV approach, corporations might be predisposed to spend assets in advancing the impression that composite inconveniences have been changed into win-win status for all stakeholders, whereas in actuality predicament of systemic unfairness has not been resolved and the poverty of marginalised stakeholders might yet have enlarged as a result of the lopsided engagement of the corporation. As such given the intricacy of social and environmental struggles, Porter and Kramer unsuspecting study of CSV as novel starting place for profit may in reality compel corporations to provide in for uncomplicated problems and decoupled communication strategies than in cracking into deep seated societal issues.

The illustrations of Walmart and Nike are referred to as the case in point for having made significant investments in CSR. Walmart's sustainability programme is lauded for what it has accomplished in terms of reduced emissions and changes in consumer habits. But critics point that notwithstanding how many energy efficient light bulbs it sells, Walmart's core business model is to extract the lowest possible costs in the supply chain and this will curb the ability to realise any substantial social gain. For company like Nike, the dilemma is comparable. Nike spends a lot in codes of conduct and inspection for labour standards in its supply chain. Nevertheless, this scheme reflects inconsistency with its core business form that rewards lowest possible costs in purchasing. In both the Walmart and Nike illustrations, we can articulate that there 'win-wins' strategy and creating value for society have really been insufficient. The overall hammering in public faith suffered by corporations situates them in jeopardy of losing the legitimacy to function that society grants them, and social and environmental issues warn them that of the depleting state of the very resources that corporations rely upon. These mammoth issues can be tackled by the partaking of corporations themselves (Brown and Knudsen, 2012). Moreover, if the purpose of the shared value concept is above all to salvage capitalism from its social critics, in that case many will be unconvinced of what this innovative and much applauded concept of CSV will accomplish, and does it then in actuality appear to be any dissimilar to unadventurous CSR. If the intention is to make substantive inroads on the social and economic issues, does the much acclaimed shared value proposal set in motion enduring alteration in company's entrenched *modus operendi*? Hitherto, these enquiries do not trim down in importance to vast potential in the construct.

Reference

Argyres, Nicholas and McGahan (2002). "An Interview with Michael Porter", *Academy of Management Executive* 15(2): 43-53.

Austin, J., H. Leonard, E. Reficco and J. Wei-Skillem (2005). "Social Entrepreneurship: It's for Corporations, too", in A. Nicholls (ed.) (2005), *Social Entrepreneurship: New Paradigms of Sustainable Social Change*. Oxford: Oxford University Press.

Austin, J. and E. Reficco (2009). "Corporate Social Entrepreneurship", *Working Paper* 09-101, Boston, MA: Harvard Business School.

Austin, J., P. Marques and E. Reficco (2007). "Building New Value Chains with Low Income Sectors in Latin America", in V. Rangan, J. Quelch, G. Herrero and B. Barton (eds.) (2007), *Business Solutions for the Global Poor: Creating Social and Economic Value*. San Francisco, CA: Jossey-Bass.

Barnes, Peter (2006). *Capitalism 3.0-A Guide to Reclaiming the Commons*. San Francisco: Berrett-Koehler Publishers.

Bhattacharyya, Som Sekhar, Arunditya Sahay, Ashok Pratap Arora and Abha Chaturvedi (2008). "A Toolkit for Designing Firm Level Strategic Corporate Social Responsibility (CSR) Initiatives", *Social Responsibility Journal* 4(3): 265–82.

Brown, Dana and Jette Steen Knudsen (2012). *Managing CSR Globally and Locally: Lessons from a CSR Leader Business and Politics*, Available at SSRN: *http://ssrn.com/abstract=2139215*. (accessed on 15 October 2014).

Carroll, B. Archie and M. Kareem Shabana (2010). "The Business Case for Corporate Social Responsibility: A Review of Concepts, Research and Practice", *International Journal of Management Reviews*. Blackwell Publishing Ltd and British Academy of Management.

Crane, A., D. Matten and D. Moon (2004). "Stakeholder as Citizens? Rethinking Rights, Participation and Democracy", *Journal of Business Ethics* 53: 107-22.

Crane, Andrew, Guido Palazzo, Laura J. Spence and Dirk Matten (2013). "Contesting the Value of the Shared Value Concept", *California Management Review* 56/2, Winter 2014, Forthcoming. Available at SSRN: *http://ssrn.com/abstract=2368387* (accessed on 12 October 2014).

Crane, Palazzo, Spence and Matten (2014). *Contesting the Value of "Creating Shared Value"*, Berkeley: University of California, Vol. 56 (2), Winter 2014.

Drucker, P. (1993). *The Practice of Management*. New York: Collins.

Elkington, J. (1998). *Cannibals with Forks: The Triple Bottom Line of 21st Century Business*. Gabriola Island: New Society.

Elkington, J. and P. Hartigan (2008), *The Power of Unreasonable People: How Social Entrepreneurs Create Markets that Change the World*. Boston, MA: Harvard Business School Press.

Ennes, Meghan (2014). What's the Value of Shared Value? Available *http://sharedvalue.org/groups/shared-value-initiative-community/what%E2%80%99s-value-shared-value* (accessed on 17 October 2014).

Epstein, M. and K. Yuthas (2010). "Mission Impossible: Diffusion and Drift in the Microfinance Industry, Sustainability Accounting", *Management and Policy Journal* 1/2: 201-221.

European Commission (2011). *Patterns of Poverty and Social Exclusion in Europe*. Available at *www.europarl.europa.eu/.../2011/.../COM_SEC(2011)1618(PAR8)_EN.do* (accessed on 11 October 2014)

Gardberg and Fornbrun (2006). "Corporate Citizenship: Creating Intangible Assets across Institutional Environments", *Academy of Management Review* 31(2): 329–46.

Gates, Bill (2008). *Making Capitalism More Creative. http://perencanamuda.wordpress.com/2008/10/07/making-capitalism-more-creative/* (accessed on 15 October 2014).

Hart, S.L. (2005). *Capitalism at the Crossroads: The Unlimited Business Opportunities in Solving the World's Most Difficult Problems*. Pearson Prentice Hall.

Hockerts, K. (2006). "Entrepreneurial Opportunity in Social Purpose Business Ventures", in J. Mair, J. Robinson and K. Hockerts (eds.), *Social Entrepreneurship.* New York: Palgrave Macmillan. pp.142-54.

Hollender, J., B. Breen and P. Senge (2010). *The Responsibility Revolution: How the Next Generation of Businesses Will Win*. Jossey-Bass.

Jamali, D. and R. Mirshak (2007). "Corporate Social Responsibility (CSR): Theory and Practice in a Developing Country Context", *Journal of Business Ethics* 72(3): 243-62.

Jamali, D. and T. Keshishian (2009). "Uneasy Alliances: Lessons Learned from Partnerships between Businesses and NGOs in the Context of CSR", *Journal of Business Ethics* 84(2): 277–95.

Kanter, R.M. (1999). "From Spare Change to Real Change", *Harvard Business Review*, Boston May–June: 122–32.

Klein, Paul (2011). *Three Great Examples of Shared Value in Action. http://www.forbes.com/sites/csr/2011/06/14/three-great-examples-of-shared-value-in-action/(*accessed on 17 October 2014).

Kostova, T. and S. Zaheer (1999). "Organizational Legitimacy Under Conditions of Complexity: The Case of the Multinational Enterprise", *Academy of Management Review* 24(1): 64–81.

Kramer, Mark and John Kania (2006). "Changing the Game Leading Corporations Switch from Defense to Offense in Solving Global Problems", *Stanford Social Innovation Review*, Spring.

Kramer, Cooch and Stearns (2003). *Doing More with fewer, FSG Perspectives on Corporate Philanthropy*. Available at *www.fsg.org* (accessed on 12 October 2014).

Lakin, Nick and Veronica Scheubel (2010). *Corporate Community Involvement: The Definitive Guide*. Greenleaf Publishing Ltd.

London, Ted and Stuart L. Hart (2010). *Next Generation Business Strategies for the Base of the Pyramid.* London: FT Press.

Mahlouji, Hossein and Kalbasi Anaraki (2009). "Corporate Social Responsibility towards Social Responsible Innovation: A Dynamic Capability Approach", *International Review of Business Research Papers* 5(6): 185-94, November.

Mair, Johanna, (2005). *Social Entrepreneurship Creating Economic and Social Value.* Available at SSRN: *http://ssrn.com/abstract=975107* (Accessed on 17 October 2014).

Márquez, A. and C. Fombrun (2005). "Measuring Corporate Social Responsibility", *Corporate Reputation Review* 7(4): 304-08.

Massetti, B.L. (2008). "The Social Entrepreneurship Matrix-tipping Point for Economic Change". E: C. 10 (3): 1-8.

Matten, D. and A. Crane (2005). "Corporate Citizenship: Toward an Extended Theoretical Conceptualisation", *Academy of Management Review* 30(1): 166-79.

Michelini, Laura (2012). "Social Innovation and New Business Models", *Springer Briefs in Business*: 1-18.

Michelini, L. and D. Fiorentino (2012). "New Business Models for Creating Shared Value", *Social Responsibility Journal* 8(4) :561-77.

Organisation for Economic Co-operation and Development (OECD) (2011). *Perspectives on Global Development. Social Cohesion in a Shifting World. http://www.oecd.org/site/0,3407, en_21571361_49041236_1_1_1_1_1,00.html.*

Pfitzer, Marc., Valerie Bockstette and Mike Stamp (2013). "Innovating for Shared Value", *Harvard Business Review*, 3. Available at *hbr.org/2013/09/innovating-for-shared-value/ar/1.* (accessed on 14 October 2014).

Pirson, Michael (2010). "Social Entrepreneurship—A Model for Sustainable Value Creation". Fordham University Schools of Business Research Paper No. 2010-011. Available at SSRN: *http://ssrn.com/abstract=1535146/* (Accessed on 19 October 2014).

———. (2011). "Social Entrepreneurs as the Paragons of Shared Value Creation? A Critical Perspective", Fordham University Schools of Business Research Paper No. 2011-001. Available at SSRN: *http://ssrn.com/abstract=1753908/*(accessed on 16 October 2014).

Porter, M.E., and M.R. Kramer (2002). "The Competitive Advantage of Corporate Philanthropy", *Harvard Business Review* 80 (December): 5–16.

———. (2006). "Strategy and Society: The Link between Competitive Advantage and Corporate Social Responsibility", *Harvard Business Review* 84(12): 78–92.

———. (2011). "The Big Idea: Creating Shared Value", *Harvard Business Review* January-February (1): 1-17.

Porter, Hills, Pfitzer, Patscheke, and Hawkins (2013). *Measuring Shared Value: How to Unlock Value by Linking Social and Business Results*. Available at *www.fsg.org.* (Accessed on 10 October 2014).

Prahalad, C.K. (2005). *The Fortune at the Bottom of the Pyramid: Eradicating Poverty with Profits*. Philadelphia: Wharton Business Publishing.

Prahalad, C.K. and A. Hammond (2002). "Serving the World's Poor, Profitably", *Harvard Business Review* 80(9): 48-57.

Prahalad, C.K. and S.L. Hart (2002). "The Fortune at the Bottom of the Pyramid", *Strategy and Business* 26(1): 1-14.

Serafeim, George (2014). "Integrated Reporting and Investor Clientele", *Harvard Business School Accounting & Management Unit Working Paper* No. 14-69. January 14. Available at SSRN: *http://ssrn.com/abstract=2378899 or http://dx.doi.org/10.2139/ssrn.2378899*

———. (2013). *The Role of the Corporation in Society: An Alternative View and Opportunities for Future Research*. Available at SSRN: *http://ssrn.com/abstract=2270579* (accessed on 14 October 2014).

Sethi, S.P. (1975). "Dimensions of Corporate Social Performance: An Analytic Framework", *California Management Review* XVII: 58–64.

Simanis, E. and S. Hart (2008). "Beyond Selling to the Poor: Building Business Intimacy through Embedded Innovation", *Working Paper.* Johnson School of Management. Available at: *http://erb.umich.edu/Research/*

Spitzeck, H. and S. Chapman (2012). "Academic Paper: Creating Shared Value as a Differentiation Strategy—The Example of BASF in Brazil", *Corporate Governance* 12(4): 499-513.

Steyaert, C. and D. Hjorth (eds.) (2003a). *New Movements in Entrepreneurship*. Cheltenham, UK and Northampton, MA, USA: Edward Elgar.

———. (2006). *Entrepreneurship as Social Change*. Cheltenham, UK and Northampton, MA, USA: Edward Elgar.

The Economist (2008). *Just Good Business—Special Report: Corporate Social Responsibility. http://www.economist.com/node/10491077* (accessed on 17 October 2014).

UNDP (2008). *Creating Value for All—Strategies for Doing Business with Poor*. New York, USA. *http://www.undp.org/gimlaunch*. Accessed on 15 October 2014.

Veronica, Borgonovi, S. Meier, M. Sharda and L. Vaidyanathan (2011). *Creating Shared Value in India*.FSG. Available at *www.fsg.org* (accessed on 12 October 2014).

Visser, W. (2008). *CSR 2.0: The New Era of Corporate Sustainability and Responsibility.* CSR Inspiration Series No. 1. Published online by CSR International: *www.csrinternational.org*.

———. (2010). "CSR 2.0 and the New DNA of Business", *Journal of Business Systems, Governance and Ethics* 5(3): 7.

———. (2011). *The Age of Responsibility: CSR 2.0 and the New DNA of Business*. London: Wiley.

———. (2012). "The Future of CSR: Towards Transformative CSR, or CSR 2.0", Kaleidoscope Futures Paper Series, No. 1. (accessed on 12 October 2014).

Young, Stephen (2003). *Moral Capitalism: Reconciling Private Interest with the Public Good.* San Francisco: Berrett-Koehler Publishers.

Yunus, M. (2008). *A World without Poverty: Social Business and the Future of Capitalism.* New York: Public Affairs.

———. (2010). "Building Social Business". *Public Affairs*, New York, NY.

Yunus, M. and A. Jolis (1999). *Banker to the Poor: Micro-Lending and the Battle Against World Poverty.* New York: Public Affairs.

Yunus, M., B. Moingeon and L. Lehmann-Ortega (2010). "Building Social Business Model: Lessons from the Grameen Experience", *Long Range Planning* 43(2/3): 308-25.

10

MANOSMITA MAHAPATRA
SUBHRANSU PANDA

Ethical Business for Sustainable Development

A New Paradigm of Corporate Social Power in Global Governance

Introduction

Corporates are found to play a significant role in sustainable development of society. Business role at global level has become increasingly important over the last decade as largest corporations control 25 per cent of world's economic output. Corporate social responsibility (CSR) is defined as the sustainable development efforts undertaken by corporates emphasising the social concern of society apart from it being economic and profit oriented. Being an economic entity, corporates earlier had only a philanthropic approach for their contribution to societal development. But with the advent of globalisation, the criteria of development have been shifted from economic growth perspective to social dimension of development. The role of CSR in promoting development is recognised (Jenkins, 2005), and hence the corporates display of social responsibility has become widespread over the past two decades (Vogel, 2006) giving corporates the rights to be socially and politically powerful. Corporate social power can be understood as the corporate power and responsibility are matter of public concern (Parkinson, 1993), where corporations have decisive impact on outcome of employment, social inequity and host of other issues.

World Business Council for sustainable development considers CSR as engine for the social dimension of fulfilling the responsibility towards stakeholders as good citizens and defines CSR as "business commitment to contribute to sustainable economic development, working with employees, their families, local community and society at large to improve their quality of life." In this context, a link in CSR and sustainable development is brought in as corporations have increasingly social, environmental and ethical impacts upon the livelihood of people and societies for development (Moon, 2004). In India, corporates through their strategic measures are found to overcome the governmental gaps that put a negative effect on the society regarding the disappointing effects of companies like in mining industries. Through this, the role and impact of corporates as actors is recognised as influential participants for the society at least in developing countries (Campbell, 2012).Therefore, the legitimacy of the corporate is well recognised and the social power of corporate is emphasised even by the Johannesburg Declaration on sustainable development which asserts the need for corporate accountability and the duty of the private sector to contribute to the evolution of equitable and sustainable communities and societies [United Nations Economic Commission for Africa (UNECA) and African Union (AU), 2010].

Aim of the Paper

It is seen that CSR as an organisational practice can be more clearly understood from a political economy approach depicting corporate social power rather than solely from economy or moral explanation. The role of business in sustainable development of society has been depicted in the paper, taking examples of companies specially operating in eastern part of India (Odisha, Jharkhand and Chhattisgarh). Earlier the corporate philanthropy practice was encouraged which was often a donor-recipient relationship (Austin, 2000), but later on corporate involvement of community as a stakeholder has been widely recognised. Very little research has explicitly used a sustainable livelihood approach to explore relationships between the private sector and its stakeholders (Hobley and Shields, 2001). The present paper attempts an exploration of the societal development initiative undertaken by Tata Steel and SAIL where CSR plays a pivotal role in sustainable development for the community. The methodology adopted in this study is of general review nature and belongs to the category of exploratory study based on the secondary sources of data. Content analysis has been used to analyse the impact assessment through the annual reports of the concerned companies. The objectives undertaken for the study are:

- To examine the CSR of companies such as Tata Steel and SAIL, towards community sustainable development.
- To identify the Institutional means of the corporate ensured for community development and their impact on society depicted through corporate social performance (CSP) theory.

Structural Domains for Sustainability

In relation to failure of developmental projects by government, Garvey and Newell (2005) argued that community 'powerlessness' on a number of level, the diversity of community livelihood action, intra-community dynamics, and the nature of relationship between communities and external actors who claim to represent them all contribute to the necessity of understanding the community for a strategic development mechanisms. In this way, the companies are found to dominate the society by involving in socially responsible actions bringing a relationship of trust between business and society, controlling political economic structure of society.

Moreover, the socially responsible business practices strengthen corporate accountability of empowering people in the communities and practicing corporate citizenship, where a company integrates social concern and improves the quality of life of local community by making initiatives contributing to human development of stakeholders both within and outside the corporation. Such social services towards stakeholders are categorised by Clarkson (1995) as implicit and explicit CSR. Implicit CSR is welfare of employees and thus CSR within the company, whereas explicit would focus on development of society which is CSR outside the company. The present paper would focus on the explicit CSR initiatives where companies involved in social context carryout socially responsible behaviour and social initiatives are often implemented informally as a response to local expectation and demands (Morsing, 2005). In this backdrop, the paper highlights the corporate social community sustainable development of Tata Steel and SAIL giving emphasis on three aspects which are the reason of backwardness in development i.e., capacity building and entrepreneurship, maternal health and hygiene, and addressing community concerned priority issues.

Both the steel companies follow a strategic business community development approach. The strategy used by Tata Steel is Tata Steel Rural Development Society (TSRDS) and the strategy used by SAIL is Triple Bottom Line (TBL). TSRDS is established in 1979 involving in various social development progrmmes aimed at helping the rural communities living around Tata Steel's operational units. TSRDS covered 32 villages around Jamshedpur in its first year of operation; today it covers 600 villages in the state of Jharkhand, Odisha and Chhattisgarh. For the sustenance and development of the community, the focus of Tata Steel is to build the community capacity through training programme, engaging the community as partners in project implementation, agencies involvement for village developmental programmes. They help for sustainable livelihood by agriculture intervention, maternal and infant survival, environmental protection by renewable energy and plantation, and education for underprivileged children.

The TBL of SAIL contributes to a more sustainable society and to its entire stakeholder by providing social initiatives to a number of villages covered under its operation area in Jharkhand, Odisha and Chhattisgarh with special focus on economic, social and environmental issues. It is seen that the plants are established in economically backward regions with high presence of scheduled caste/scheduled tribe (SC/ST) population. SAIL practises implicit CSR by giving employment to 17,592 SCs, 14,662 STs and 9,758 other backward caste (OBC) in 2010. They engage local people as temporary recruitment cell in the company for their socio-economic improvement. Disadvantaged people get an opportunity to take different type of services. This brings local unemployment a kind of development entrepreneurship. The company is implementing provisions of the Disability Act and has employed about 750 persons suffering from various disabilities.

Capacity Building and Entrepreneurship

The efforts taken by Tata Steel in Jeypore District of Odisha is through the popular self-help group (SHG) called as Tejaswini. Tejaswini provide detail training to women on the finer aspects of various kinds of machinery like bulldozers, mechanical shovels, dumpers, tractors and forkits, and light commercial vehicles. There is an access to the leadership qualities, where a five-month long competition was organised in Kalinganagar and the women are engaged in income generating activities like poultry farming, gardening, stone carving, saura painting and setting of small industries like phenyl and pickle making. It is seen that TSRDS has helped in credit linkage of SHG and marketing of products inside and outside market. There has been an increase in the number of women in non-agricultural activities from 5 in the pre-displacement period to 200 in 2010. Pragati SHG in Kendujhar District started small business like bricklines, pottery, poultry, public distribution system and mushroom farming. It has impacted as traditional job of leaflet making products were not sold in right price because of lack of finishing touch, but with the training and machine, it has become good business. By getting support for farming, there has been an increase in farming mostly in spinach and all other kinds of seasonal vegetables.

The CSR efforts of SAIL have helped formation of famous SHG Mahila Samithi for empowering women. It was formed in 1957 and is a ladies group for community welfare. It has 4,000 members and 15 affiliations with nation-level organisation. It involves women from weaker sections. The activities of the SHG includes income through manufacture of hand gloves, soaps, masala, canteens, spices, towels, gunny bags and community welfare programmes like sewing, embroidery centre, crèches and kinder garden; psychological support to ill-treated tribal women, tree plantation; and workshop on rights of women, banking, information technology (IT). There are others who have been trained in trades like embroidery, masonry, carpentry, cycle and hand pump repairing. Moreover, 48 villages have undergone training in mushroom, embroidery and food processing in Rourkela. It has impacted skill in garment making and enables them to take up employment with garment companies.

Rourkela steel plant tied up with Society for Rural Industrialisation (SRI) to train villagers in skill-based activities and various trades that have helped many to start their own enterprise or join any professional organisation.

Maternal Health and Hygiene

For the mother and child health care, the approach of Tata Steel towards maternal health is both project based and also preventive-curative health services. Projects like AASTHA and SAATHI exists in Odisha and projects like MANSI, KAVACH and RISHTA in Jharkhand. The project AASTHA is delivering reproductive and child health services, MANSI aims to reduce maternal and child mortality and morbidity. Both the projects RISHTA and KAVACH of Jharkhand aim at improving the sexual and reproductive health along with adolescent well-being and in creating awareness of HIV respectively. SAATHI covers 20 districts in Odisha aiming to set up a 10-bed community care centres for people living with HIV/AIDs.

All these projects are found to reduce maternal mortality and morbidity, improving the health status of rural poor and sexual well-being. More than lakh of patients are found to be benefited from each project. The company established Tata Steel Family Initiatives Foundation which is a non-profit organisation promoted by Tata Steel addressing reproductive health concern. Under the Tata Steel Family Initiatives Foundation (TSFIF), the number of couples protected in 2010-11 is given Table 10.1. And Table 10.2 shows the health care initiatives taken by the company.

Table 10.1

Number of Couples Protected in 2010-11 under TSFIF

Activity	*Achievement*
Antenatal check-up	3782
Post-natal check-up	2693
Immunisation	2115
Laparoscopic Tubectomy	6281
Non-scalpel Vasectomy	340

Source: Documents of Knowledge, Centre of TSFIF.

Table 10.2

Preventive and Curative Initiatives of Tata Steel

Initiatives (Number of Persons)	*Impact Year (2010-11)*	*Impact Year (2011-12)*	*Impact Year (2012-13)*
Primary Health Care	2,13,208	2,89,517	3,70,000
Family Planning Services	8783	6633	7189
Immunisation	9914	12717	14006
Antenatal Check-up Care	12,931	11,629	12,000
HIV Awareness coverage	35,659	3,10,000	3,10,000
Eye Care Services	1818	3000	2890

Source: Secondary information from the department of TSRDS.

Health awareness of SAIL shows a concern for healthy environment by its wide network of medical and health services and health camps. SAIL's efforts have resulted in access to improved health infrastructure for 26.7 million people. It has helped in promoting health care services related to reproductive child health programme, safe motherhood and child survival, family planning, universal immunisation programme against measles, malaria, tuberculosis, diabetes, open heart surgery, neurosurgery, kidney transplant, treatment of HIV/AIDs, and fertility. Around 2,200 health camps were organised in 2008-09 where free health check-ups and treatments have been provided. Similarly, 475 medical camps were held in 2007-08 benefiting 5 lakh people. SAIL opened a free medical unit for the poor in Odisha called NIVEDITA providing treatments by general physician for gynecology, surgery and paediatrics.

Addressing Priority Issues

Tata Steel has provisions for education development as distribution of books, creating awareness to school students regarding local language and early child education centre. Various *balwadis* for educational development have also been opened by TSRDS to encourage the dropouts. There has been establishment of Kalinga Institute of Social Science for tribal education. The initiatives by TSRDS include camp school, non-formal education, financial support to needy children and adult literacy programme.

The adult literacy programmes show that around 2,555 women were made functional literate, effecting a change in the way they manage their SHG meeting as well as the confidence with which they interact with various local authorities' different forums. The company enrolled 159 tribal children to residential schools, 545 children formal schools and 252 in *ashram* schools.

Tata Steel attempts to empower the socially excluded group by contributing towards their upward social mobility. The company focuses upon facilitating education, supporting livelihood especially non-farm-based activities and generating employment. For such purposes, the company has created a non-profit organisation called Tribal Cultural Society (TCS) in 1993. The company has contributed ₹14,250,000 in 2005-06 and ₹17,500,000 in 2006-07 towards TCS. In order to mitigate the tribal problems of basic economic assistance, the company has provided community health and hygiene, civic amenities and educational programme. It promotes tribal music, tribal languages and tribal sports. There are also skill-based training programmes for the encouragement and promotion of sustainable livelihood and income. It has supported a total of 22 SHGs in and around Jamshedpur and provided training on account keeping and catering, and traditional training.

The company has promoted agriculture development through TSRDS. It has provided them with good quality seeds and fertilisers and community-based water management groups are also formed. There has been increase in productivity of paddy from 0.5-0.6 tonne/acre in 2004-05 to around 1.8 tonnes/acre in the 2008-09. The Waste-Land Development Programme (WDP) of TSRDS improves the green cover and productivity of land and promotes horticultural plantations as livelihood opportunity. For agriculture development in Jharkhand, 64 water bodies have been created, 12,000 acres were covered by cashew and mango plantation benefiting around 4,300 households. Moreever, the development of ponds and irrigation structures improved irrigation potential of 850 acres of land. For the sustenance of farmers in Jharkhand, TSRDS has not left an opportunity to create a demonstration-cum-training centre (KOLEBIRA Centre), which has been established to maintain supply chain system, nursery development, marketing and monitoring value addition through SHGs.

SAIL has taken an initiative to enable a global economic environment and environmental sustainability. SAIL communities offer quality education at subsidised fees and free education for SC\ST. Special schools for BPL (below poverty line) families cater to 1,400 children providing mid-day meals, uniform dress, text books and accessories. The location of schools are within 1-2 km of target population for easy access. It provides basic infrastructure for schools, availability of trained teachers especially for IT-based higher learning. It has helped in eliminating gender disparity at all levels of education maintaining 1:1 girls-boys ratio. SAIL has provided people with water resources within 20 km radius of the plant location. There were more than 4,500 water sources including tubewells, pipelines, borewells, ponds, etc. Lack of proper water sanitation has been considered often as a reason for disease. In 2009, 1,050 number of water infrastructure were created. Many villages lack transport facilities thereby bringing a barrier to social mobility and integration. Good road connectivity has been made as an attempt to the stakeholders through CSR.

SAIL has been involved in construction of 67 km of (*pucca*) roads during the year 2008-09 providing access across 38 villages. It has developed more than 75 km of roads in its mines that are located in dense forest. For recreation, it has developed several recreation sports academics at 6 plant locations, focusing on sports like football and hockey. They provide scholarship to 491 students for sports academics. In order to nourish the socio-cultural fabric, the company has provided sustainability to tribal folk, tribal festivals, folk arts, preserving heritage structure, organising cultural events and concerts for tribes. All these efforts taken by Tata Steel and SAIL for community development has a corresponding effect on societal sustainable development. Such impact on society has been analysed through theoretical approach under integrative theory which mainly focuses on integration of social demands through issue management, public responsibility, stakeholder management and corporate performance.

Theoretical Approach

The corporate social initiatives for sustainable development have helped the multinationals to achieve unprecedented economic and political power. These social means of control are also legitimised through transparency and corporate accountability. If a firm does not use its social power, it will lose its position in society because other groups will occupy it, especially when society demands responsibility (Davis and Blomstorm, 1971). Due to such demand from business, Garriga and Mele (2004) have highlighted from the work of Carroll (1979) the model of "corporate performance" depicting issues involved under CSR and philosophy of response to social issues. Moreover, Wood (1991) argues that CSP is more comprehensive than CSR model since it involves the identification of domains of an organisation's social responsibility, the development of processes to evaluate stakeholder demand and the implementation of programmes to manage social issues. Wood (1991) considered that CSP includes (a) principles of CSR, (b) processes of corporate social responsiveness and (c) outcomes of corporate behaviour.

In the present paper, the CSP theory is understood through the societal impact of the initiatives undertaken by Tata Steel and SAIL for the community sustainable development through CSR. The companies efforts are found to bring about a significant positive impact on the community as stakeholder. The principles of CSR provide an institutional approach towards community development where health, education and women empowerment have been focused on. The present paper applies CSP theory in order to explain the societal impact of the companies because the theory emphasised the process of corporate social responsiveness which shows increased demand of business involvement in society thereby promoting business community partnership to achieve significant social benefit (Austin, 2000) in tackling pressing social issues (Lee, 2011) and establishing the corporate to gain social power (Whitehouse, 2003). The third element of Wood's explanation of CSP highlights the outcome of corporate behaviour which mostly focuses on social impacts of the business actions through CSR. In this context, the CSP of Tata Steel and SAIL is presented in the conceptual framework model (Figure 10.1) for corporate social power.

Figure 10.1

Conceptual Model on Corporate Social Power

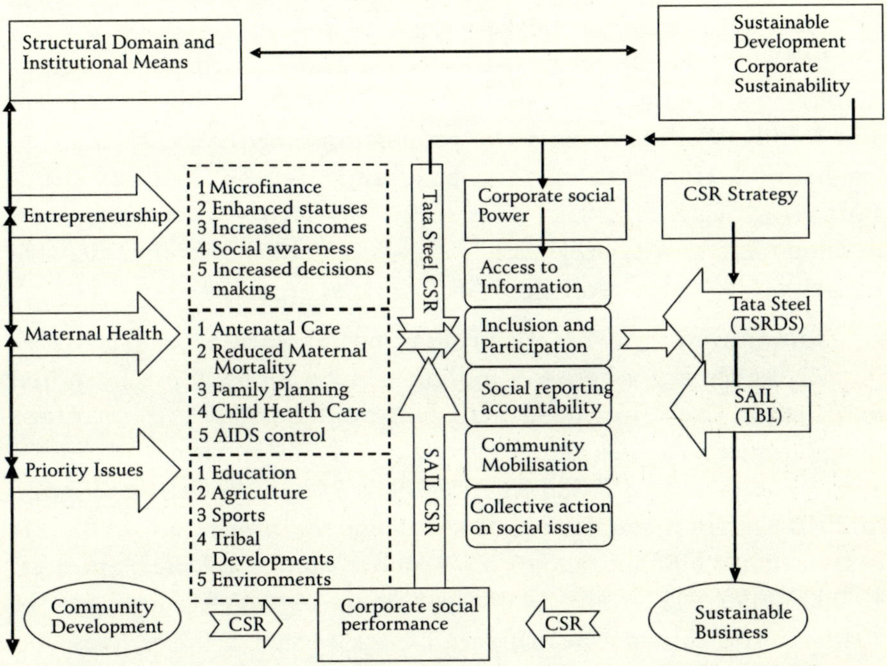

The CSP has brought about a significant change in the economic independence and sustainability of stakeholders. The TSRDS strategy of Tata Steel covers nine units under its area of operation for community development. The areas are Jamadoba, Noamundi, West Bokaro, Joda, Kalinganagar, Gopalpur, Bamnipal and Sukinda. The CSR strategy of SAIL covers areas such as Bhilai, Durgapur, Rourkela and Bokaro. The corporate sustainability services cover rural, urban, tribal and family health in case of both the companies for community development. With reference to rural and tribal development, special focus highlights on empowerment of women through SHGs and promotion of rural enterprises with preservation of ethnic identities respectively. The greatest community development impact on society is combating gender discrimination and promoting empowerment of women through income generation schemes and maternal health care. Such gender discrimination and oppression of women which is a greatest barrier to the development of nation can be easily seen by the recent National Family Health Survey (NFHS) data indicating inadequacy in pre-natal and post-natal maternal care and child health. The focus of Tata Steel is specifically towards this emerging problem of inadequate maternal health care services. It is because studies conducted in Jharkhand also support the fact that there is a lack of maternity and child health care for which the Department of Health and Family Welfare depicts the proportion of girls being admitted for malnutrition is more than boys and highest than any other states (Aguayo *et al.*, 2012). This requires an asset-based community development as a strategy for CSR will establish a comprehensive framework towards strategic CSR (Fisher *et al.*, 2009).

Community health care programme of Tata Steel has wider impact on society where 0.4 million people annually are benefited in Odisha. There has been zero maternal mortality, zero infant mortality, zero adolescent pregnancy and better family planning. TSFIF has benefited 5,786 in 2008-09, 4,843 in 2009-10 and 6,621 in 2010-11. Total couples protected under the project are 14,806. It is seen that 4,600 households are benefited under AASTHA project, 13,000 under RISTA and 14,450 people under KAVACH project. In 2012-13, the primary health care centre served 370,000 lives and also infant death reduced from 6.15 to 1.58 and percentage of neo-natal death from 5.9 to 1.15.

With regard to the health initiative of SAIL, it is noticed that rural people who did not have proper health infrastructure are benefited to a large extent. There has been an opportunity to have free medical treatment and medicines provided by five special health centres. SAIL organises more than 3,000 health camps every year. People are also benefited by special project Aksharya for providing free investigation to TB patients of underprivileged sections of society and project Chetna for treatment of sickle anaemia in Rourkela. Due to availability of good medical infrastructure, the infant mortality rate is 39.2 per thousand live birth which is much lower than the national average. A similar situation follows for maternal mortality rate. SAIL provides vaccination to nearly 100,000 beneficiaries each year, has reported average immunisation of 90 per cent along with 3,000 major surgeries are performed annually and 1.5 million per annum. In 2009, number of immunisation and health beneficiaries are 1,82,363 and 47,19,520 respectively. There are 61 primary health centres (PHCs) and 8 rural health centres (RHCs) have been created.

The financial independence of rural women has affected the self-esteem and have increased the family decision making power leading to their enhanced social status. The capacity building programme of Tata Steel and SAIL has made these rural women to be self-dependence from all perspectives. The experience of women over 737 SHGs and 9,181 members has demonstrated that a collective spirit and group dynamics enhances their bargaining power, brings about behavioural change, creates informal structure of support and help women make economic strides. The cumulative savings generated by the SHGs supported by TSRDS has now exceeded ₹3.24 crore. SAIL is tied up with society for rural industrialisation to train villagers in skill-based activities. There are others who are trained in trade like carpentry, diesel engine repairing, motor cycle repairing and water pump. In 2012-13, Tata Steel has supported 750 SHGs as well as trained 2,225 youths of which 597 were gainfully employed. The SHGs have improved in 2013 with 9,500 members over 727 SHGs in 2011-12 having 9,089 members. From the successfully employed trainees, 35 per cent belong to SCs and STs. The SHGs linked to entrepreneurship development earn an average income of about ₹28,000 per member per annum in 2012-13.

With regard to education, SAIL has a survival rate in primary school of 95.8 per cent. There were 24 adult education centre constructed in 2009 with a total 138 number of schools within township and 269 outside township. For the community development action of SAIL, 56,06,453 people benefited from road connectivity providing access to 38 villages. There were 12 new sports facilities created during 2009 benefiting 11,825 talented children. CSR of Tata Steel has helped in adults literacy programmes which made adults functionally literates. The people are benefited lot by various training programmes like community health providers, IT-based training and security guard training. The total achievement of adult literacy in 2007-08 was 58 per cent, in 2008-09 was 77 per cent and in 2009-10 was 88 per cent.

In 2012-13, it is seen that under CSR of Tata Steel, 2,477 scholarships were awarded to students from local communities, and more than 49,000 school children were served mid-day meals. Around 8,000 tribal youth in Jharkhand and Odisha were reintroduced to their traditional language and script. The number of adult literate women in 2012-13 was 13,000 compared to 5,600 and 2555 in 2011-12 and 2010-11 respectively. Number of girls attending camp schools was doubled in 2012-13 compared to 2011-12. More than 2,400 students from SC and ST were awarded scholarships for education. Moreover, 278 had basic adult literacy classes and 243 advance literacy classes.

In 2012-13, there has been agriculture and infrastructure development helping 400 acres of farms under better paddy crops and 200 acres under *rabi* crops in Jamadoba in Jharkhand. To improve sustainable livelihood, the company helped in enhancing the productivity of land through scientific agriculture of 4192 acres in 2012-13 compared to 3966 acres in 2011-12. CSR of Tata Steel has formed bio toilets where 230 villages assessed for Human Development Indices (HDIs) in the same year. For irrigation infrastructure and drinking water, Tata Steel continued to install borewells for rural households of 250 houses, while deep borewells were installed in 89 villages benefiting thousands of households and also 100 lift irrigation systems in 2012-13. There had been 372 hand tube wells constructed in 2012-13 compared to 241 in 2011-12. More than 1,800 solar lights were installed in Jharkhand and Odisha and safe drinking water reached 350 villages.

In 2013-14, health projects MANSI of Tata Steel has brought a positive impact by a drop in infant mortality rate by 26.5 per cent and neonatal mortality rate by 32.7 per cent. Jyoti Fellowships awarded to nearly 3,000 meritorious students from SC and ST in Jharkhand and Odisha. The company trained 93 tribal girls as nurses from the naxalite-affected region of Jharkhand. In 2013-14, 1,800 youths were trained through a range of skill development programme. Nearly, 10,000 youths learned tribal scripts for Ho, Santhali and Oraon languages. Under the solar street lights project, nearly 2,300 lights were installed in villages of Jharkhand and Odisha in 2013-14. The social performance and community development impact on society of SAIL has been highlighted in Table 10.3.

Table 10.3

Community Development Impact of SAIL

Indicators	*Years*	
Health Services	*2011-12*	*2012-13*
Number of primary health centres	54	53
Number of RCH	4	7
Number of beneficiaries of health during the year	44,05,928	21,03,726
Immunisation coverage	1,14,891	98,235
Sterilisation coverage	12,027	8,069
Women Development		
Number of women engaged in SHG	1664	1141
Number of women employed	5234	5213
Other priority issues		
Girl-boy ratio in education	1.14:1	1.36:1
Adult education centre	7	7
Number of schools within township	137	148
Number of schools outside township	346	492
Number of water infrastructure	796	1329
Number of villages impacted for road connectivity	86	96
Total number of beneficiary for road during the year	1,02,000	55,575

Source: Documents and reports of the company.

Conclusion

There has been significant social transformation in the health, education and economic condition of rural dwellers through CSR efforts. Tata Steel and SAIL, the two steel companies in India, are found to bring about a tremendous change in the neglected areas in terms of livelihood generation thereby empowering the rural women and excluded population. In response to the political indifference and under-investment by governmental efforts in the neglected areas, CSR is seen to have a greater positive impact on the sustainability of society by such developmental activities. Hence, sustainability and citizenship of the companies are the social agents who emphasise social behaviours contributing to social change and turning the economic entities (business) to new paradigm of being socially and politically powerful.

Reference

Aguayo, V.M., S. Jocob, N. Badgaiyan, P. Chandra, A. Kumar and K. Singh (2012). "Providing Care for Children with Severe Acute Malnutrition in India: New Evidence from Thailand", *Public Health Nutrition* 32(1): 97-112.

Austin, J. (2000). *The Collaboration Challenge*. San Francisso, CA: Jossey-Boss.

Campbell, Bonnie (2012). "Corporate Social Responsibility and development in Africa; Redefining the Roles and Responsibilities of Public and Private Actors in the Mining Sector", *Resources Policy* 37: 138-43.

Carroll, A.B. (1979). "A Three-Dimensional Conceptual Model of Corporate Performance", *Academy of Management Review* 4(4): 497-505.

Clarkson, M. (1995). "A Stakeholder Frame Work for Analysing and Evaluating Coporate Social Responsibility", *The Academy of Management Review* 16(2): 132-47.

Davis, K. and R.L. Blomstorm (1971). *Business, Society and Environment. Social Power and Social Response*, 2nd edition. New York: McGraw-Hill.

Fisher, K., J. Geenen, M. Jurcevic, K. Mcclintock and G. Davis (2009). "Applying Assets-based Community Development as a Strategy for CSR: A Canadian Perspective on a Win-Win for Stakeholders and SMEs", *Business Ethics: A European Review* 18(1): 66-82.

Garriga, E. and D. Mele (2004). "Corporate Social Responsibility Theories: Mapping the Territory", *Journal of Business Ethics* 53: 51-71.

Garvey, N. and P. Newell (2005). "Corporate Accountability to the Poor? Assesing the Effectiveness of Community-based Strategy", *Development in Practice* 15(3): 389-404.

Hobley M. and D. Shields (2001). "Governance and Institutional structures", Paper presented to the DFID Seminar on *Governance and Sustainable Livelihoods*. Birmingham.

Jenkins, R. (2005). "Globalisation, Corporate Social Responsibility and Poverty". *International Affiars* 81(3): 525-40.

Lee, L. (2011). "Business-community Partnership: Understanding the Nature of Partnership", *Corporate Governance* 11(1): 29-40.

Moon, J. (2004). "Government as Driver of Corporate Social Responsibility. The UK in Comparative Perspective", *ICCSR Research Paper Series* in 20-2004. The University of Nottingham, pp.1-27.

Morsing, M. (2005). "Inclusive Labour Market Strategies", in A. Habisch, J. Jonker, M. Wenger and R. Schmidpeter (eds.), *Corporate Social Responsibility across Europe*. Berlin: Springer. pp.23-35.

Parkinson, J. (1993). *Corporate Power and Responsibility: Issues in the Theory of Company Law*. Oxford: Oxford University Press.

UNCEA (United Nations Economic Commission for Africa) and AU (African Union) (2010). *Minerals and Africa's Development: A Report of the International Study Group on Africa's Mining Regimes*, second draft. August.

Vogel, D. (2006). *The Market for Virtue*. Washington, DC: Brookings Institute.

Whitehouse, Lisa (2003). "Corporate Social Responsibility, Corporate Citizenship and the Global Compact: A New Approach to Regulating Corporate Social Power", *Global Social Policy* 3(3): 299-318.

Wood, D.J. (1991). "Corporate Social Performance Revisited", *Academy of Management Review* 16: 691-718.

11

SWETA SAURABH

Awareness of Corporate Social Responsibility Activities through Internal Communication Practices

Introduction

Previous studies have often indicated about the importance of corporate social responsibility (CSR) in organisations. Aguinis, and Glavas (2012) very aptly pointed out that CSR activities enhances employees attitude, behaviour and also productivity in the workplace. CSR activities also contribute to company's profitability and it becomes emerging issue for the practitioners in understanding 'how' to implement CSR initiatives in a workplace rather than debating upon the practice of CSR. Morsing *et al.* (2008) put forward the view that employees are the important contributor to CSR activities. Collier and Esteban (2007) also supported this by expressing that employees are the ambassadors of the organisation and they are the ones communicating organisational values to external stakeholders.

It is also evident from past studies (Michael, 1995; Hashim, 2002; Monge, 2007) that organisations have begun to realise that employee communication is critical to business success. Communication is an essential requirement for this new breed of employee relations, and if employees are not well informed and motivated, the quality of an organisation's relationship with other public might be affected. Woodruffe (1995) opined that internal communication acts as treating employees with immense value through the practices of communication to attain organisational objectives. It basically establishes clear linkages and internal relations among employees to strengthen the organisation. In today's changing business environment, it is important to have a strong employee communication network so as to manage the organisational goals.

Being well-informed about organisational issues provides employees with empowering job resources, allowing them to contribute to the organisational goals. This could, consequently, lead to a greater attachment to the organisation. Verhoeven (2013) discussed that employee' perceptions regarding organisational communication may also influence their emotional attachment to the organisation.

It is evident that the CSR in every organisation is gaining prominence in India, with policies and strategies being developed in a variety of ways. Hopkins (2006) stated that some companies champion their own CSR departments, others prefer to distribute the responsibility across the business, but there are also those who work closely with non-governmental organisations (NGOs) in an attempt to increase transparency. It has very much become a way for organisations to give support to both external and internal stakeholder groups. Studies (Dawkins, 2005; Sen *et al.*, 2006; Brammer *et al.*, 2007; Birth *et al.*, 2008; Morsing *et al.*, 2008) have shown that although organisations may engage in the CSR activity, employees may not always be aware of these activities. This in result may compromise the potential beneficial effects of the initiatives. Therefore, it becomes important for the organisations to strengthen the internal communication practices so that it may help in member identification in CSR activities. As CSR activities are hardly ever observed directly, it can only affect employees to the extent that the policies regarding the activities are communicated. It is only through internal communication practices that employees may become aware of the CSR activities that an organisation engages in.

Keeping the above studies in mind, the paper aims to map out how internal communication practices in the organisation enhance the employees CSR awareness and implementation.

Literature Review

Internal Communication Practices

Since communication is the basis of human interaction, the process of communication is central to any organisation. Academicians believe that a positive communication environment contributes to organisational effectiveness. Saurabh (2014) defined internal communication as the exchange of information both informal and formal between management and employees within the organisation. Internal communication practices may include downward, upward or horizontal communication and may be started by anyone within an organisation. However, it remains the responsibility of the management to take into account that effective and efficient organisational communication is in place for the employees to get timely, relevant and important information. Spike and Lesser (1995) stated that communication is regarded as an important issue in the successful implementation of any policy in the organisation. It is used as a tool for announcing, explaining and preparing people for the implementation of new policies.

Further, Woodruffe (1995) opined that internal communication acts as treating employees with immense value through the practices of communication in an organisation to attain organisational objectives. It basically establishes clear linkages and internal relations among employees to strengthen the organisation. In today's changing business environment, it is important to have a strong employee communication network so as to manage the organisational goals. Multiple information floats in the organisation, and it becomes important for the employees to have a fair amount of information about the same. Michael (1995) points out that the information on strategies, plans, missions and goals should reach the employees on time to ensure the effectiveness of internal communication in an organisation.

Corporate Social Responsibility

Although many definitions of CSR are identified in the literature, Kotler and Lee (2005) defined CSR as a discretionary business practices and contributions of corporate resources intended to improve societal well-being. Based on the report of Towers (2009), CSR is the third most important driver of employee engagement. Mohin (2012) stated that Forbes has cited the use of CSR as a means to enhance employee performance as a major trend. Aguilera *et al.* (2007) and Mackey *et al.* (2007) defined CSR as voluntary actions by firms which enhance social or environmental conditions.

Carroll (1979; 1999) also offers an insight on CSR and suggests that when businesses engage in CSR activities, the company participates in four discrete categories of activities:

1. economic,
2. legal,
3. ethical, and
4. discretionary/philanthropic.

Support for this notion of CSR is evident in the work by Ismail (2009) as he discussed the common roles of CSR. The study discussed that the CSR has many roles like necessitating ethical business process; creating closer ties between corporations and community; helping in transfer of technology; helps in protection of human rights, labour and environment; alleviate poverty; and helps in getting talents. Ismail (2009) was of the view that organisation with a reputation about CSR may take advantage of their status in strengthening their appeal for potential employees.

Grant *et al.* (2008) demonstrated in the study that employees' affective commitment will not only increase from receiving support, but also from giving support in the form of charitable foundation.

Internal Communication and CSR

The organisation whether it is big or small could not exist without communication. Internal communication keeps employees informed about the organisation's business and vision, and helps every individual in the organisation to work together with a common purpose. Williams (2013) opined that organisations that manage change effectively and that have effective communications are 2.5 times as likely to outperform their peers in financial performance.

The study also notes that the best internal communication are essential for business intelligence, fostering knowledge processes, and delivering value well beyond simple message delivery.

Hargie *et al.* (1993) observed that communication is a crucial variable determining the success of an organisation. Gruing (1992) expressed that internal communication is so entwined with the process of organising and with organisational structure, environment, power and culture that many theorists of organisational communication argue that organisations would not exist without communication. And when it comes to CSR communication, many studies (Deegan and Gordon, 1996; Deegan and Rankin, 1999; Brown and Deegan, 1998; Hooghiemstra, 2000) have taken place and have emphasised on providing information that legitimises an organisation's behaviour by trying to influence stakeholders' and society's image of the company at large. Previous studies have demonstrated a relationship between employees' loyalty and their company's CSR (Bevan and Wilmott, 2002). Joyner and Payne (2002) discussed that employees working in an ethical and socially responsible organisation are found to be more committed towards the organisation.

Weldon *et al.* (2013) stated the importance of identifying and measuring the employee-focused CSR activities in an organisation. Turker (2009) referred internal CSR practices as employee-oriented CSR activities which are directly related to the physical and psychological working environment of employees concerning their health and well-being in the organisation.

Research Problem

Earlier studies have indicated that practice of internal communication within an organisation is very important to produce a cohesive corporate identity by increasing employees' knowledge about the overall philosophy of the CSR in an organisation (Aguilera *et al.*, 2007; Mackey *et al.*, 2007; Weldon *et al.* 2013; Grant *et al.* 2008). These studies have largely focused on the relationship between CSR and employees commitment, satisfaction and productivity. The concern about how to create awareness about CSR initiatives in a workplace still remains unattended to.

Research Focus

Previous studies have mainly focused on the macro level of analysis of CSR issues concerning basically regarding corporate communication, employee engagement, external stakeholder's opinions and the like; the present paper on the other hand rests on the micro level study. The paper gives an attempt to analyse the importance of internal communication practices in an organisation and its effect on the implementation of CSR activities. This leads to the following research question: Whether employees' engagement with CSR implementation can be predicted based on internal communication practices in an organisation?

Hypothesis

H0: Internal communication practices do not exhibit a higher involvement of employees in CSR activities.

H1: Internal communication practices exhibit a higher involvement of employees in CSR activities.

Methodology

The method used for this study is basically a quantitative examination of data collected from the retail store.

General Background of Research

The general research approach shall be described as a descriptive cross-sectional survey. The data for the study are primary data and analysis is exploratory. The study is based on an empirical survey of 60 employees of one carefully and conveniently selected retail store in Ghaziabad, India. The employees were selected randomly from the store. Sixty self-developed and self-administered questionnaires were used to solicit information on the internal communication practices affecting CSR activities of employees.

Sample of Research

The sample for the selection of organisation was conveniently selected from the directory of retail stores in Ghaziabad. However, it was made sure that the sample chosen was not just another organisation, rather it should cater to the responsibility towards society.

With regard to survey of the employees, 60 questionnaires formed the basis of the sample size. Randomly the store level employees were selected to fill the questionnaire. However, 48 questionnaires were properly filled and returned representing 80 per cent which was significant for the study. Bruce and Bonjean (1969) based their study on the sample size of 64 employees. No considerations were taken in terms of gender and age, however the study made sure that the sample size covered all the personnel placed in store.

Research Instrument and Procedure

The instrument used to assess employees perceptions of the organisation's internal communication practices was derived from Goldhaber and Rogers' (1979) and Downs and Adrian (2004), Communication Audit Survey (CAS). Koning and Jong (2007) opined that the International Communication Association (ICA) audit questionnaire is a well-known questionnaire which is used for measuring internal communication and is considered very comprehensive in scope. In its original form, the CAS consists of eight sub-scales: receiving information from others; sending information to others; follow-up on information sent; sources of information; timeliness of information received; organisational communication relationship; organisational outcomes; and channels of communication.

Many changes were made to fit the questionnaire according to the study. Sub-scales like 'receiving information from others; sources of information; and channels of communication' were used and other sub-scales were eliminated from the study questionnaire, as the information on this was not required from the study population.

Questionnaire on CSR-induced intrinsic attributions from the study by Du *et al*. (2007) and Ellen *et al*. (2006) were also incorporated as it was required for the study population.

The standardised instrument comprised of closed ended questions and enabled the participants to offer their candid opinions on information regarding the internal communication process in the organisation. The questions were measured using a seven-point Likert scale ranging from 1 to 7: 1=strongly disagree; 2=disagree; 3=disagree somewhat; 4=undecided; 5=agree somewhat; 6=agree; 7=strongly agree. None of the questions were reversed-scored.

Data Analysis

The data collected for this study were analysed using Statistical Package for the Social Sciences (SPSS) version 22.0 to provide descriptive analysis for the test of regression.

Regression analysis is a statistical tool for the investigation of relationship between variables. Usually, the investigator seeks to ascertain the causal effect of one variable upon another. The researcher also typically assesses the 'statistical significance' of the estimated relationships, i.e., the degree of confidence that the true relationship is close to the estimated relationship. The study has used linear-multiple regression as it is a technique that allows additional factors to enter the analysis separately so that the effect of each can be estimated. It is valuable for quantifying the impact of various simultaneous influences upon a single dependent variable.

The model may be written as:

$$Y = b_1X_1 + b_2X_2 + \dots + A$$

where Y is the dependent variable (involvement of employees in CSR activities) the study is trying to predict; X_1, X_2 and so on are the independent variables we are using to predict it; b_1, b_2 and so on are the coefficients or multipliers that describe the size of the effect the independent variables having on the dependent variable Y, and A is the value that Y is predicted to have when all the independent variables are equal to zero.

Result of Analysis

Table 11.1

Model Summary

Model	R	R^2	Adjusted R^2	Std. Error of the Estimate
1	.613a	.375	.161	.801

Table 11.1 provides the R and R^2 values. The R value represents the simple correlation and is 0.613 (the 'R' column), which indicates a high degree of correlation. The R^2 value (the 'R^2' column) indicates how much of the total variation in the dependent variable, involvement of employees in CSR activities, can be explained by the independent variables. In this case, 37.5 per cent can be explained, which is not bad, but the higher the better.

Table 11.2

ANOVA[a]

Model		*Sum of Squares*	*Df*	*Mean Square*	*F*	*Sig.*
	Regression	13.475	12	1.123	1.751	.097[b]
1	Residual	22.441	35	.641		
	Total	35.917	47			

Note: a. Dependent variable: employees involvement.

b. Predictors: (constant), written CSR policy, telephonic communication, community service, information about organisational policies, socially responsible company, workshop on CSR, superior gives info, morally obliged, audiovisual, face to face, info. from co-workers, info. about service.

Table 11.2 shows ANOVA (analysis of variance). The multiple regression model with all the predictors produced $R^2=0.375$, $F(12, 35)=1.751$, $p>0.001$. Here, the F-test outcome has a value 0.097 which is greater than 0.05, so we can say that the study fails to reject the null hypothesis and the research has observed a sample that is plausible assuming the null is true.

Table 11.3

Correlation Analysis of a Studied Variable

Model		Unstandardised Coefficients		Standardised Coefficients	T	Sig
		B	Std. Error	Beta		
1	(Constant)	6.433	2.237		2.876	.007
	Company socially responsible	.038	.156	.039	.246	.807
	Morally obliged	-.061	.155	-.060	-.395	.695
	Give to community	-.281	.141	-.323	-1.985	.055
	Info about orgl policies	.224	.235	.242	.954	.347
	Info about service	.039	.249	.041	.158	.876
	Info from co-workers	-.199	.170	-.207	-1.168	.251
	Superior gives info	-.096	.152	-.105	-.635	.529
	Face to face	-.049	.019	-.402	-2.559	.015
	Telephone	.163	.168	.149	.974	.337
	Audiovisual	.152	.167	.143	.912	.368
	Work shop on CSR	-.067	.081	-.123	-.829	.413
	Written CSR policy	.144	.109	.201	1.321	.195

Note: a. Dependent variable: employees involvement.

As can be seen in Table 11.3, the variables have a significant negative weight (opposite in sign from its correlation with the criterion), and the variables having positive weight were also found not to be of significant strong nature denoting that the variables like sharing information about organisational policies with employees; having good telephonic channel of communication; having good audio-visual communication process in the organisation; and having a written CSR policy of the organisation with a copy to employees do play a significant role in involving employees in the CSR activities of the organisation. However, with other predictors depicting negative values, it is seen that either the predictors has no effect, or its effect is so small that it is considered unimportant.

Shuttleworth (2008) stated that accepting the null hypothesis does not mean that it is true. It is still a hypothesis, and must conform to the principle of falsifiability.

Discussion

The attempt is first of its kind to understand the importance of communication practices in the organisation in involving the employees to become socially aware about the place they work in. CSR being an important issue in any organisation should encompass the internal stakeholders especially the retail sales employees who works in a boundary-spanning environment, and continuously interacts with the external environment. The paper has opened a discussion forum not only for theorists but also for practitioners as how to include the employees through the process of internal communication to create an awareness about CSR to the society at large.

Limitations and Future Scope

Since the present study was to understand the significance of communication practices and its impact on involvement of employees in CSR activities of the organisation,[1] the sample was intentionally chosen that of retail sales employees that naturally limits its size and accountability regarding the subject matter, which may act as the limitation.

Another limitation may be that it is very important that a questionnaire is valid and reliable in the population you wished to measure. Here, although the questionnaire used were standardised, it was not piloted for retail sales employees.

Future research on employee involvement in CSR activities shall encompass the more direct indicator like that of communication satisfaction, job satisfaction, employee engagement and the like.

1. The name of the organisation is kept confidential on its request.

References

Aguilera, R., D.E. Rupp, C.A. Williams and J. Ganapathi (2007). "Putting the 's' Back in Corporate Social Responsibility: A Multilevel Theory of Social Change in Organizations", *Academy of Management Review* 32(3): 836-63.

Aguinis, H. and A. Glavas (2012). "What We Know and Don't Know about Corporate Social Responsibility: A Review and Research Agenda", *Journal of Management* 38(4): 932-68.

Bevan, S. and M. Wilmott (2002). *The Ethical Employee*. London: The Future Foundation.

Birth, G., L. Illia, F. Laurati and A. Zamparini (2008). "Communicating CSR: Practices among Switzerland's Top 300 Companies", *Corporate Communication: An International Journal* 13(2): 182-96.

Brammer, S., A. Millington and B. Rayton (2007). "The Contribution of Corporate Social Responsibility to Organizational Commitment", *International Journal of Human Resource Management* 18(10): 1701-19.

Brown, N. and C. Deegan (1998). "The Public Disclosure of Environmental Performance Information: A Dual Test of Media Agenda Setting Theory and Legitimacy Theory", *Accounting & Business Research* 29: 21-41.

Bruce, G.D. and C.M. Bonjean (1969). "Self-Actualisation among Retail Sales Personnel", *Journal of Retailing*, Elsevier Science Publishing Company, Inc. p. 73.

Carroll, A.B. (1979). "A Three-dimensional Conceptual Model of Corporate Performance", *Academy of Management Review* 4(4): 497-505.

Carroll, A.B. (1999). "Corporate Social Responsibility: Evolution of a Definitional Construct", *Business and Society* 38(3): 268-96.

Collier, J. and R. Esteban (2007). "Corporate Social Responsibility and Employee Commitment", *Business Ethics: A European Review* 16(1): 19-33.

Dawkins, J. (2005). "Corporate Responsibility: The Communication Challenge", *Journal of Communication Management* 9(2): 108-19.

Deegan, C. and B. Gordon (1996). "A Study of the Environmental Disclosure Policies of Australian Corporations", *Accounting and Business Research* 26(3): 187-99.

Deegan, C. and M. Rankin (1999). "The Environment Reporting Expectations GAP: Australian Evidence", *The British Accounting Review* 31: 313-46.

Downs, C.W. and A.D. Adrian (2004). *Assessing Organizational Communication: Strategic Communication Audits*. New York: Guilford Press.

Du, S., C.B. Bhattacharya and S. Sen (2007). "Reaping Relational Rewards from Corporate Social Responsibility: The Role of Competitive Positioning", *International Journal of Research in Marketing* 24(3): 224-41.

Ellen, Pam Scholder, Deborah J. Webb and Lois A. Mohr (2006). "Building Corporate Associations: Consumer Attributions for Corporate Social Responsibility Programs?", *Journal of the Academy of Marketing Science* 34 (2): 147-57.

Grant, Adam M., Andrew Molinsky, Joshua Margolis, Melissa Kamin and William Schiano (2008), "The Performer's Reactions to Procedural Injustice: When Prosocial Identity Reduces Prosocial Behavior", *Journal of Applied Social Psychology* 39(2): 319-49.

Goldhaber, G. and D. Rogers (1979). *Auditing Organisational Communication Systems: The ICA Communication Audit*. Kendall/Hunt.

Grunig, J. (1992). *Excellence in Public Relations and Communication Management*. Hillsdale, NJ: Lawrence Erlbaum Associates, pp. 531-76.

Hargie, C., D. Tourish and O. Hargie (1993). "Managers Communicating: An Investigation of Core Situations and Difficulties within Educational Organizations", *International Journal of Educational Management* 8 (6): 23-28.

Hashim, A. (2002). "Kepentingan Organisasi Dan Komunikasi Di Malaysia", *Jurnal Komunikasi dan Perniagaan* 17(4): 5-13.

Hooghiemstra, R. (2000). "Corporate Communication and Impression Management: New Perspective why Companies Engage in Corporate Social Responsible Reporting", *Journal of Business Ethics* 27(1/2): 55-68.

Hopkins, M. (2006). "What is Corporate Social Responsibility all About?", *Journal of Public Affairs* 6: 298-306.

Hoeven, Claartje L. ter and Joost W.M. Verhoeven (2013). "Sharing is Caring", *Corporate Communications: An International Journal* 18(2): 264-79. Permanent link to this document: *http://dx.doi.org/10.1108/13563281311319526*

Ismail (2009). "Corporate Social Responsibility and its Role in Community Development: An International Perspective Maimunah Ismail", *The Journal of International Social Research* 2(9).

Joyner, B. and D. Payne (2002). "Evolution and Implementation: A Study of Values, Business, Ethics and Corporate Social Responsibility", *Journal of Business Ethics* 41: 297-311.

Koning, K.Z. and M. Jong (2007). "Evaluating the Communication Satisfaction Questionnaire as a Communication Audit Tool," *Management Communication Quarterly* 20(3): 261-82. doi:10.1177/0893318906295680.

Mackey, A., T.B. Mackey and J.B. Barney (2007). "Corporate Social Responsibility and Firm Performance: Investor Relations and Corporate Strategies", *Academy of Management Review* 32(3): 817-35.

Michael, C. (1995). "From Nice to Necessity". *Communication World*, 20-22. Retrieved October 16, 2004, from ProQuest database.

Mohin, T. (2012). *Resilient Responsibility: Three Ways AMD Maintains CSR Commitment in Tough Times.* Retrieved November 16, 2014 from Academic Search Premier database.

Monge, C. (2007). "Internal Marketing and Organisational Behavior: a Partnership in Developing Employee Conscious at Every Level", *Journal of Business Research* 20(1): 63-70.

Morsing, M., M. Schultz and K.U. Nielsen (2008). "The 'Catch 22' of Communicating CSR: Findings from a Danish Study", *Journal of Marketing Communications* 14(2): 97-111.

Sen, Sankar, C.B. Bhattacharya and Daniel Korschun (2006). "The Role of Corporate Social Responsibility in Strengthening Multiple Stakeholder Relationships: A Field Experiment", *Journal of the Academy of Marketing Science* 34 (2): 158-66.

Shuttleworth, Martyn (Sep 21, 2008). *Falsifiability*. (Accessed Oct 07, 2014) from Explorable.com: *https://explorable.com/falsifiability*

Saurabh, S. (2014). "Measuring Salesforce Productivity—A Study of the Retail Sales Employees", *AIMA Journal for Management and Research* (AJMR) 8(2/4). May.

Spiker, B.K. and E. Lesser (1995). "We Have Met the Enemy...", *The Journal of Business Strategy* 16(2): 17-21

Towers, Perrin (2009). Corporate Social Responsibility: It's no Longer an Option. Available at *http://www.towersperrin.com/tp/showdctmdoc.jsp* (accessed on 12 Sep. 2014).

Turker, D. (2009). "Measuring Corporate Social Responsibility", *Journal of Business Ethics* 85: 411-27.

Woodruffe, H. (1995). *Services Marketing*. London: Pitman Publishing.

12

KRITHIKA RAM

Inclusiveness as a Tool for Corporate Social Responsibility

A Perspective

Introduction

Corporate social responsibility (CSR) is often confused with philanthropy. While the practice of corporate philanthropy is not something alien, the concept of CSR is new. Of course, just as in case of corporate philanthropy CSR is also about 'giving and sharing,' but is not just limited to that alone. CSR includes other important elements *viz.*, responsibility, accountability, sustainability and most importantly inclusiveness.

Although each of these elements is important in its own way, the component of inclusiveness has not received much of importance while CSR is put to practice. This could be the result of poor understanding of CSR and the resulting blind philanthropy, which involves mindless signing of cheques or showering cash donations, without trying to understand the need of the beneficiary. On the other hand, any corporate who is serious about a transparent and sustainable CSR initiative, pays attention to the element of 'inclusiveness.'

Inclusiveness in CSR: What it Means

The word 'inclusive' has the following meaning according to the Merriam-Webster Dictionary:

- covering or including everything,
- open to everyone: not limited to certain people, and

- including the stated limits and everything in between.

In context of CSR, inclusiveness would mean:

- Considering the welfare, interest and needs of all the stakeholders viz. employees, clients, shareholders, consumers, government agencies, civil society and the local community (without any discrimination whatsoever).
- Engaging all stakeholders in the development process.
- Sharing the fruits of development equally with all stakeholders.
- Keeping each stakeholder informed of the corporate's progress as well as shortfalls.

Hence, it is clear that inclusiveness in itself covers the aspects of responsibility, accountability and Sustainability. For example, by consulting stakeholders before initiating a project, and ensuring participation of stakeholders in the process of development, a company is taking care of sustainability. While sharing, the fruits of development and reporting the progress are positive signs of transparency and accountability.

Ensuring Inclusiveness in CSR

Inclusiveness at Community Level

Any development initiative that does not include the interest and needs of all the sections of the community is bound to be a failure. Need assessment is the first step in ensuring inclusiveness at the level of community. It is a rather rampant practice that either due to lack of time or expertise, a large chunk of corporates conveniently skips the need assessment process before CSR projects. Even if they do it, the findings are full of discrepancies due to poor methodologies involved. In worst cases, the need assessment is just eyewash and the findings are hardly taken seriously. There are only a handful of corporates who take need assessment seriously, as their ultimate objective is to set up a successful CSR model, which gives sustainable benefit for the community.

Need assessment: Need assessment process is something that cannot be overlooked, as it is the very foundation on which community-based CSR initiatives need to be built. Following are the features of a meticulously planned and executed inclusive need assessment:

- Having a clear idea of the target area and population before planning the assessment. Especially getting to know its socio-cultural aspects well.
- Inclusion of all socio-economic and cultural sections of the community.
- Scientific tools of assessment, which are designed keeping in mind the nature of the target population and their limitations.
- Avoid creating false ideas in the mind of the target population about the corporate's social development project being designed for them. It is rather safe to not reveal anything about the underlying plan for them. This will rule out unrealistic expectations among the beneficiaries.
- Is not influenced by the powerful and influential in the community who are trying to show only 'what they want to,' whereby the real issues take a backseat.

Planning: The very next step after the need assessment is to plan out the CSR initiatives. Here again it is important that the outcome of the need assessment is shared with the target community and the projects are planned according to what they think they need the most. This way the corporate can avoid thrusting its own ideas on them and be more democratic in its approach. Activities planned in consultation with them will create a lot of enthusiasm and a sense of belongingness, both of which are crucial for the success of the projects.

Execution: Once planned, it is important that the execution of the projects is done through the involvement of the community members. This will serve all the following purposes:

- A person from the target population working in his/her own area's development project will know the positives and negatives of his/her community and will therefore be able to deal with the hitches in a better manner compared to an outsider.

- Penetration into the community will be better.
- Seeing his/her own community member working on a CSR project will create atmosphere of trust and positivity, as they will be able to relate better.
- It makes more sense to give priority to the community members in the new employment opportunities generated in the CSR initiatives, rather than bring an outsider.
- Involvement of community will bring transparency.
- Handing over of the project to the community will become much easier.

There is absolutely no doubt that inclusiveness has been the most important factor behind the success of many CSR projects, one fine example being the CSR initiatives of TVS Group which has created wonders through community participation.

Inclusiveness at Employee Level

It is being increasingly stressed that CSR needs to be "embedded into the DNA of the company." Therefore, will it be enough to have just a CSR policy, impressive set of objectives and a long list of thrust areas? Not really! Then what is it that would make it complete? Well, the answer is 'inclusiveness.'

In a majority of companies CSR-related discussions are held among a set of topmost executives *viz.*, the directors, chairman, chief executive officer (CEO), chief operating officer (COO), vice president (VP) and maybe at the most, the heads of various business verticals. There are very few companies who regularly communicate CSR-related information to the employees and involve them. Many companies either release it as news once in a while or worst still they publish it in some report meant for the external stakeholders. The end result in the latter two cases is an employee population, which do not even know what CSR stands for.

The true spirit of inclusiveness at the employees' level lies in their engagement, which involves:

- Consulting the employees (taking into consideration the interest and ideas of even the bottom-most cadre) while framing the CSR policie—who knows there might be someone within your own company who could contribute invaluable ideas.
- Finding ways of engaging employees in the planning and implementation of CSR initiatives—Employee volunteering over weekends or even giving a day off for the same.
- Reporting regularly to the employees and taking their feedback every now and then.

The end result of such inclusive CSR decision-making within the company would not only improve the quality of the CSR initiatives, but will also serve as a motivation for employees and will help retain them, while attracting new ones. This will also keep the top management on toes and make them consciously work towards improving the quality of CSR engagements, never letting it stagnate. Including employees in CSR and making it an integral part of a company's culture also ensures that whichever employee takes over from his/her superior continues the projects further. This is crucial for community-related CSR initiatives that need constant evaluation and quality improvement. Many CSR projects have died a premature death due to change of leadership in the organisation.

Figure 12.1

Inclusiveness and Stakeholders in CSR

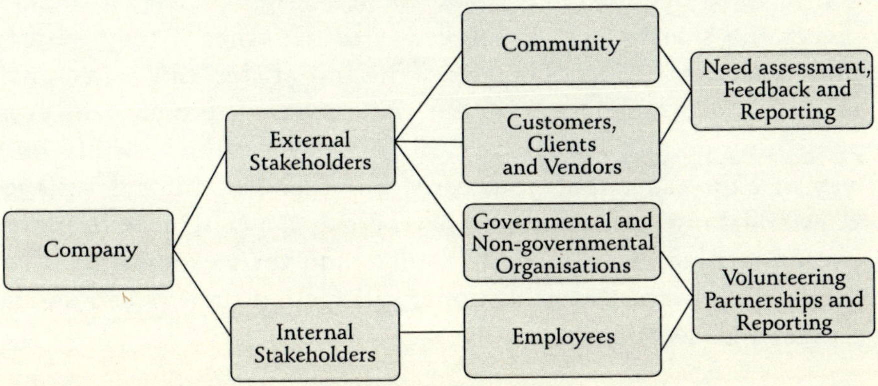

Inclusiveness is the only way of embedding CSR into the company's DNA, which in turn will go a long way in ensuring sustainable CSR practices both within and outside the companies.

Inclusiveness at the Level of Customers, Vendors and Clients

It is being increasingly observed that a company's social responsibility is also being judged on the basis of the way they are engaging the customers, clients and shareholders in their CSR initiatives. There is no doubt that the quality, accountability and transparency in business are the topmost priorities, but there is something more that could be done to make these important stakeholders a part of the CSR system.

It is crucial to understand the level of seriousness among companies in inclusion of the above-mentioned stakeholders. There are only a handful of companies who publish regular reports and take feedbacks and suggestions on their CSR initiatives. There are few others who go a step further and have special projects and programme for these stakeholders e.g., the P&G's Shiksha campaign whereby customers are encouraged to buy their products so that a small percentage could be contributed towards education of underprivileged children.

A large category of companies are still hesitant to engage these stakeholders either because they themselves lack clarity on CSR or due to the fear as to whether it would cause too much of interference in their day-to-day functioning. However, it is important for these companies to understand that in future, they will have to open up and think about engaging their customers, clients and shareholders in some way or the other, if they wish to enjoy their patronage. Therefore, the initial step can be as small as getting customer feedback on the quality of products or even publishing details about the CSR initiatives, which would be a way of expressing that you 'care.' For example, Infosys believes in establishing strong vendor partnerships, whereby it conducts vendor satisfaction surveys to understand their expectations. For the customers, they have customer satisfaction surveys and annual customer leadership meets.

Inclusiveness at the Level of Government

The first step to ensuring inclusion of government in a company's CSR is by adhering to the laws of the land and being transparent about the business practices. This is a way of showing that as responsible citizen of the country, the company is 'with the government.' Any CSR initiative taken up ignoring the laws of the land is futile.

We need to remember that we cannot and must not set up parallel systems to the one which already exist in the country. Yes, in all good spirit, a corporate could be putting in its best to enhance the socio-economic status of a community, but it is definitely not wise to work independent of the government agencies. The reason is simple. Government agencies have a better penetration and experience compared to the corporate agencies. Also, there could be certain programmes or initiatives of the government, which could be used wisely to supplement any CSR project rather than replicating the same. This will serve dual purpose:

- Firstly, we need not 're-invent the wheel' and therefore the project cost can be cut significantly. For example, some of government's rural community development programmes have a scope for cutting the labour cost through the means of *shramdaan* from the local community.
- Secondly, it will be more sustainable. For example, using the mode of Total Sanitation Campaign (TSC) would be a much better way of addressing the sanitation issue in a village rather than spending huge amounts on building toilets. The reason being: the comprehensive nature of the TSC project, which has elements of local participation, awareness creation, regular monitoring and upkeep.

A better approach in this case would be:

- To explore and study what policies and programmes government has announced or is running in the target area.
- To see if it would match or supplement any of the planned projects.

- To understand how successful it has been or why it has failed to work.
- To connect to the respective agencies to see how the company could supplement the project. For example, in case of a TSC, probably a part of the 10 per cent contribution that needs to come from the community can be contributed by the company.
- To help the community run the project by through regular monitoring and interactions and touch base with government agencies wherever required.

It is a known fact that follow-up with government agencies does need a lot of patience and perseverance. But success stories in many communities tell us that the wait is worth it. For example,Tata Power's village sanitation programme at Tunda village, Gujarat, in tie up with the Ministry of Drinking Water and Sanitation, Government of India (GoI), is one classic example of a successful corporate-government partnership model.

Inclusiveness at the Level of Non-governmental Organisations

Today's world is grappling with various socio-economic issues, all of which cannot be solved by the government alone. The non-governmental organisations (NGOs) play a crucial role in not just bringing forth these crucial issues, but also creating awareness in the society and ensuring that they are address appropriately. They also try doing their bit for the world by offering their skills and expertise using the local resources.

Given the kind of importance NGOs enjoy in today's world, it is crucial to include them as partners in CSR. NGOs possess certain set of skills required for running social intervention programmes. Also, they are closer to the grass-roots compared to the corporates or even the government agencies and have a better penetration. Their humane appeal makes them more approachable to the community and they are well aware of the ground realities. Therefore, it is ideal to partner with NGOs for community-related CSR projects rather than implementing it ourselves. This will save a lot of time and also help us channelise our resources in a much better manner.

Some reputed NGOs doing commendable work either slow down or cease to exist due to lack of funds. Identifying such NGOs based on the CSR projects and funding them to run the same would not only take care of the finances of the NGO but will also help us in implementation of the project in a more effective manner.

Many corporates today engage in what is called 'supporting an NGO' as a part of their CSR. How is 'support' different from 'inclusion'? Support majorly involves providing financial support or sometimes skill-based help to the NGO. While the skill-based support is a sign of true responsibility, pure financial support (without elements of the latter in some form) is not only wasteful but is also dangerous as it encourages the NGO to not only expect more and more, but also makes the corporate complacent. There is also a very high scope for misuse of money by the beneficiary NGO, which defeats the whole purpose of doing CSR. Mere writing off cheques for 80G or for advertisement is nothing but a colossal wastage of the precious CSR fund. Skill-based support on the other hand is valuable as it strengthens the NGO and helps it grow. Since skill-based support typically involves employee volunteering, it takes care of employee inclusion and is therefore the most recommended form of support.

'Inclusion' of NGO in CSR is one step higher than 'support.' While in 'support,' the NGO plays the major role and the corporate only supplements it, in 'inclusion,' the corporate plays a lead role whereby the NGO is included in the CSR initiative. The best approach here is:

- Identifying NGOs based on corporate's thrust areas for CSR intervention.
- Having a scorecard system to choose the best NGO to work with.
- Discussing the project with the NGO(s) and laying down clear terms and condition regarding implementation, evaluation, reporting and financials.
- Regular and clear communication on the side of the corporate and checking work progress with the NGO.

- Systematic and prompt reporting at the NGO side.
- Ensuring that the partnership with the NGO is time-bound, so that the corporate can move out of the project once the NGO is able enough to handle it on its own.

Inclusion calls for more accountability and transparency on the part of both the corporate and the NGO. The planning and implementation is a joint exercise and the initiatives are time-bound. The only requirement here is that of open communication and strict monitoring and evaluation to ensure that there is no scope for malpractices at either end. There is a larger scope for sustainability since the NGOs are the agents of the society and hence have the welfare of the community on top of in their mind. However, the inclusion of NGOs is equally challenging given the fact that many of them are unaware of corporate systems and therefore may need a lot of orientation on the corporate style of working. With open communication and plenty of support, this partnership can create wonders. For example, as a part of Dell's Youth Learning initiative, Dell India in partnership with Agastya International Foundation runs i-Mobile Labs in Noida and Coimbatore, to improve the creativity of school children in their science classroom. The Dell i-Mobile Labs use 17 different innovative sessions of information and communication technology (ICT)-based learning through face-to-face classroom methods, enhanced student-teacher interaction models and computer-mediated activities.

Conclusion

Inclusiveness has to be reexamined under the microscope of positivity, rather than skepticism. While on one hand it does demand for a lot of transparency and accountability on the part of the company, on the other hand it helps the company set up a sustainable CSR model where every stakeholder has a role to play. Despite its own set of challenges, inclusiveness is a blessing in disguise which will not only ensure that the company effectively implements the CSR initiatives but will also deter the company from engaging in harmful and unethical business practices. Most importantly the concept of inclusiveness encourages a corporate to view the stakeholders as 'partners in development' rather than plain 'beneficiaries'.

References

CSR Rules (2014). Ministry of Corporate Affairs, Govt. of India *http://www.mca.gov.in/Ministry/pdf/CompaniesActNotification2_2014.pdf* (accessed on 26 September 2014)

Merriam Webster Dictionary. *http://www.merriam-webster.com/dictionary/inclusive*

Srinivasan Services Trust Annual Report 2012-13. http://www.tvssst.org/resources/SST-Report-2012-2013.pdf (accessed on 25 September 2014)

P&G's Social Responsibility Programs in India, *http://www.pg.com/en_IN/sustainability/social_responsibility/social-responsibility-programs-in-india.shtml* (Accessed on 25 September, 2014)

Infosys Sustainability Report 2008-09, http://www.infosys.com/sustainability/reports/2008-09 (accessed on 25 September 2014)

Tata Power, *http://www.tatapower.com/sustainability/clean-and-healthy-village.html*

Business Wire India Thursday, 18 October 2012, *http://businesswireindia.com/news/news-details/dell-i-mobile-lab-travels-gudivanka-village-andhra-pradesh/33088* (accessed on 29 September 2014)

13

A. SRIDHAR RAJ

Monetising Corporate Social Responsibility Activities of Employees

Challenges and Opportunities

Introduction

Organisations carry out various activities as a part of their societal obligations and such activities are done in true sense of their obligation towards the betterment of the society. In fact, long before the advent of the triple bottom line approach, many organisations have been already focusing on people and planet apart from focusing on profits. However, the focus sharpened in the recent past with the rising awareness among the people and the government about the societal responsibilities of the business world. The feeling that the organisations derive their inputs from the society; hence need to replenish resources in one form or the other gained currency in the recent past, and the governments all over the world too became aware of the business world's responsibility in fulfilling societal roles and goals for the betterment of the society and its people.

Background of Philanthropic Activities

Although there are few murmurings about the obligation of societal responsibility on the business world as mandated by the New Companies Act 2013, a large section of the business world is favourable towards the idea of the corporate social responsibility (CSR) as gleaned from the media reports. Such an inclination is visible in the activities of the organisations where the employees are encouraged to participate in various social and economic activities aimed at ameliorating the living conditions of the people. That apart, during natural crises and disasters, the business world extends its support in reaching out to the people and offers them relief by distributing food and necessary clothing as happened in Jammu & Kashmir (J&K) floods.

The business world also extends support in building the nation through special funds which are aimed at the development of the country's infrastructure like roads, schools and hospitals. However, all such endeavours have been more in the nature of charity and philanthropy, and the funding and activities were more uneven in spread and scale leading to wastage of resources. The impact was cosmetic and transient and earlier existing conditions soon came to dominate the changes done as a part of CSR.

Long before the concept of CSR made its way into the management literature, the Tata Group under the visionary founders did seminal work towards the fulfilment of its social responsibility. The activities ranged from promotion of educational institutions of high quality to providing scholarships to the needy people of the society. In fact, the establishment of trusts to take care the societal responsibilities of the Tata Group speaks volumes about the leaders of the group and their inclination towards social responsibility. Similarly, the concept of trusteeship was promoted by GD Birla wherein the focus was on making the lives of the people better by teaching them the skills needed for better living.

Deloitte celebrates Impact Day, wherein the employees reach out to different types of needy people—children, aged, adolescent girls, etc., and the effort is to create an impact in their lives at least for a day. The employees are encouraged to shoulder the responsibility of impacting the lives of at least a few for one day so that the organisation as a whole contributes to the society and also to enable the employees to get sensitised to their social responsibility.

CSR: A New beginning

CSR is the new buzzword in the business world and has generated a lot of enthusiasm, of course skepticism too, among policy makers, business world and also the people. CSR is fondly described as the voluntary and willing responsibility of the business world towards the societal issues for the larger benefit of the society and its people. According to the United Nations Industrial Development Organization (UNIDO), "Corporate Social Responsibility is a management concept whereby companies integrate social and environmental concerns in their business operations and interactions with their stakeholders." The Government of India (GoI) has not defined what constitutes CSR but has attached CSR with certain activities mentioned in Table 13.1 of this paper, and the list of such activities is expanding with the passage of time. The European Commission has defined CSR as "the responsibility of enterprises for their impacts on society." Long before the term CSR became a buzzword, many progressive organisations have been performing various activities which are now called as CSR. While speaking about the social responsibilities of business, Drucker (1977) stated that, "It demands that business take responsibility for social problems, social issues, social and political goals and that it become the keeper of society's conscience and the solver of society's problems."

However, the crux is that there are a large number of organisations which focus on their societal responsibilities but such activities are more or less scattered and lack focus. It is in this context that the CSR as a part of the New Companies Act 2013 should be debated and discussed. The author himself overhead a discussion between two senior officers of a public sector company where they were discussing about the construction of toilets for schools. The discussion revolved around whether to renovate the toilets or to construct the new ones.

The idea behind CSR is not only about construction of school buildings or toilets or taking care of environment. The discussion under the new CSR programme needs to be more about the creation of awareness among people as part of an organisation towards society and environment. The question is whether the CSR can move beyond spending money under the New Companies Act 2013 and move towards a new direction.

Table 13.1

CSR Activities under the New Companies Act 2013

1.	Promotion of education
2.	Eradication of extreme poverty and hunger
3.	Gender equity and empowerment
4.	Reducing child mortality and improving maternal health
5.	Combating HIV-AIDS, malaria and other diseases
6.	Social business projects
7.	Environmental sustainability
8.	Employment enhancing vocational skills
9.	Contribution to Prime Minister's relief fund and other such state and central funds

Source: *Handbook on Corporate Social Responsibility in India* (CII).

Some of the activities closely resemble the Millennium Development Goals (MDG) enunciated by the United Nations and such activities are the responsibility of the government, not the business world. In spite of the fact that the government is solely responsible for some of the activities mentioned as a part of CSR, the business world has shouldered the responsibility of carrying out those activities. Although it is debatable whether such a shifting of the responsibility would augur well for the business world or not, as of now the CSR activities have become a part of the law. In the recent past, the government has conceded further ground to the business world as the donations to the 'Swachh Bharat Kosh' would be considered as spending under the CSR budget. It is in this context that monetisation of CSR activities of employees should be considered so as to create more awareness among the people, in and out of the business world.

Monetisation of CSR Activities

The Mukund Rajan Committee (Mukund Rajan is the Chief Ethics Officer of Tata Group) has come out with a formula to monetise the activities undertaken by the executives as a part of CSR. The argument is that the time spent by the executives in undertaking CSR activities should be equated in terms of money based on the category of the executive—junior level, middle level and senior level as shown in Table 13.2.

Table 13.2

Monetisation of Employee Activities under CSR

Category of Employee	*Years*	*Monetisation per Hour (₹)*
Junior	0 – 5	252
Middle Management	6 – 10	565
Senior Management	11 – 15	1205
VP/President/Directors/CXO	16 years and above	2711

Source: *Economic Times*, 11 September 2014.

The monetisation of CSR activities is a new idea in the field of CSR and organisations like Deloitte do not get monetary benefit from their activities as a part of Impact Day. (The debate whether MNCs are also covered by the CSR provisions of the New Companies Act 2013 is still continuing). The argument is that such CSR activities undertaken by the executives should be monetised and should be treated as part of CSR activities. This helps the companies to show such activities under CSR funding and also help the employees in playing a larger role in nation building activities of the country. It is a rarity that the executives from the corporate world with their wide expertise and experience contributing to the country's development, not in terms of money but in terms of their expertise and experiences. They provide a new impetus and dimension for the CSR activities and altogether take the entire concept and application of CSR to a new high. Some of the benefits of such monetisation of CSR activities include the following:

Employees become a party: The idea that the organisations need to spend some part of their profits towards CSR is noble and appreciable, but such spending is known only to the senior management which plays a major role in channelising the CSR activities. The limited awareness among the organisation is not fruitful for the society as the employees need to know what activities are being focused upon by their organisation and find out whether there exists some scope for them to add something to CSR. Therefore, opting for monetisation necessarily leads to spreading awareness among the employees and some employees would be interested to spend one day towards CSR activities. In the process, the organisation gets benefited and the employee also feels empowered as he/she is a party to the CSR activities.

Employee motivation: Employee motivation is one of the complex elements in the organisational world and how and when employees get motivated is still a deep mystery. However, there is small window wherein some employees intend to carry out some activities which can benefit the society. The employees in order to overcome the drudgery and monotony of their corporate activities may intend to take a break for rejuvenating themselves and this is where the monetisation of CSR activities may greatly help both the organisation and the employees.

New insights: The executives who have completed their education from different parts of the world and have worked in different organisations may provide new insights into the CSR activities. Apart from the construction and building of new buildings for schools, hospitals, etc., given an opportunity, they may provide new insights into the functioning of CSR activities and help the society in a better manner.

Expertise and experience: The executives undergo a rigorous life in the corporate world and in the process gain rich expertise and experience in their profession. In fact, the government needs to show its willingness to tap their talent which is unmatched in the government sector and government agencies. With their rich experience and expertise, the executives may help CSR in gaining more fruits and dividends.

Learning for government officers: The coming together of executives from the business world and the government officers is a unique one, and this coming together would provide new learning for the government officers, who otherwise are neck deep in files and mundane activities. The working together of government officers and the executives from the corporate world would at least provide fresh impetus and thrust for the government officers.

Challenges

Monetisation of the executive activities under CSR head is appreciable and very much doable, but there are numerous challenges which may mar such new path. The very idea that the corporate world would spare their executives for CSR activities is doubtful as they need the talent for their growth and profitability. Therefore, to what extent the business world would spare their high profile executives is a million dollar question to be answered. That apart, would the corporate world use this programme to offload its average performers? The tendency to retain the best talent is very high in the business world and there is a possibility that the programmes may be used provide rest place for the average performers.

Another question is whether keeping a track of thousands of employees as a part this initiative is difficult given the wide and varied nature of the tasks. That apart, how will the expert and experience of the executives be utilised by the government agencies, even if they are willing to work in the field? Another challenge for the organisations is how long employees need to work in to claim the benefits of CSR under the New Companies Act 2013. In case, the organisations raise the salary pay out for the employees so as show their increased spending on CSR activities, then who should bell the cat. Should the basic pay be used as a parameter for monetising the activities or the allowances too need to be considered is another question to be discussed?

Conclusion

The CSR activities have come to stay and the organisations need to spend the money on such activities as per the guidelines of the New Companies Act 2013. The question is how to increase the effectiveness and efficacy of such activities so that the mandate is not limited to spending money but also extends to creation of awareness among the employees of the spending organisations. The awareness about CSR coupled with monetisation of employee activities is the right way of spreading the message of CSR to the individual level and also increase the effectiveness of CSR spending.

Monetisation of CSR activities may be considered as an initial step towards creating more space for individual social responsibility activities in the days to come.

References

Drucker, Peter F. (1977). "Management", New York: Harper's College Press, p.261.

"Tata Groups' Chief Ethics Officer Mukund Rajan-led Task Force Proposes CSR Math for Corporate", *Economic Times*, 11 September 2014.

The Times of India (2014). "Donations to Swach Bharat, Clean Ganga now part of CSR", 28 October.

Websites:

http://ec.europa.eu/enterprise/policies/sustainable-business/corporate-social-responsibility/index_en.htm

www.unido.org/csr.html

SECTION III

Best Practices in Corporate Social Responsibility

14

M. JOTHI

Corporate Social Responsibility Practices and its Outcomes in Public and Private Undertakings in India*

Introduction

One does not need to look far to find the term 'corporate social responsibility' (CSR) in the literature today (Engle, 2007). In recent years, the concept of CSR is receiving spectacular attention both from business practitioners and academicians in different parts of the world (Dentchev, 2005; Potluri *et al.,* 2010). Business houses embedded the CSR practice under different names such as corporate citizenship, social responsibility, business social responsibility, social responsible investment and the like. However, a widely quoted definition by the World Business Council for Sustainable Development (WBCSD) states,

> Corporate Social Responsibility is the continuing commitment by a business to behave ethically and contribute to economic development while improving the quality of life of the workforce and their families as well as of the local community and society at large.

The father of modern CSR is H.R. Bowen. In 1953, he initially proposed the term CSR, suggesting that business should take into accordance the objectives and values of the society (Wartick and Cochran, 1985). Since the introduction of the term CSR in the 1950s and onwards, the concept has gained considerable acceptance and broader meaning (Carroll, 1989). However, it was in the United States (US) which experienced the growing interest in CSR in

---

* An explorative study based on selected undertakings in Tamil Nadu.

the 1960s and 1970s (Vogel, 2005). Initially the concept includes the responsibility to deliver social services such as pensions and medical care are primarily performed by corporate sector. Later the scope of CSR was widened in the 1980s towards environment and employees without compromising in making of good profits. The new global economy has further highlighted the importance of CSR in other developed countries of the world.

Corporate Social Responsibility Practices in India

India has a long rich history of close business involvement in social causes for national development. In India, CSR is known from ancient time as social duty or charity, which through different ages is changing its nature in broader aspect. From the origin of business, which leads towards excess wealth, social and environmental issues have deep roots in the history of business. In the post-Independence era, it was considered as charity and traditional philanthropy that was predominantly influenced by Gandhian Ethical economic model. The Ethical model was followed by Statist model of Nehru which emphasised on the state ownership and legal requirements to decide the corporate responsibilities. After 1970s, the Liberal model supported by Milton Friedman focused on adherence to law and creation of wealth and fulfilling CSR through taxation and private charitable choices (Tulasi Das and Reddy, 2014). The CSR performance of business organisations in the post-liberalisation era in India has been witnessed by the survey conducted by the NGO Karmayog. It has rated CSR performance of top 500 companies in India from 0 to 5. These ratings are based on the parameters like amount invested in the CSR activities, legal compliances, environmental compliances and Separate Sustainability reports of banks and so on. Table 14.1 shows the CSR ratings of largest 500 companies in India from 2007 to 2010.

Table 14.1 reveals the comparison of CSR ratings of largest 500 companies in India from the year 2007 to 2010. The table shows that the companies belongs to the ratings 1, 2, 3 and 4 has been increased from 93, 144, 38 and 4 respectively in the year 2007 to 148, 161, 66 and 12 respectively in the year 2010. Noticeably, companies having zero level rating were 221 in the 2007 which decreased to

113 in the year 2010. It is concluded that the CSR activities of the large-scale companies has been increased at noticeable level in India.

Table 14.1

Comparison of CSR Ratings of Largest 500 Indian Companies from 2007 to 2010

Karmayog CSR Ratings	*Number of Companies*			
	2007	*2008*	*2009*	*2010*
Level 0 (Lowest)	221	173	128	113
Level 1	93	118	147	148
Level 2	144	161	146	161
Level 3	38	38	66	66
Level 4	4	10	13	12
Level 5 (Highest)	0	0	0	0

Source: *www.karmayog.org.*

Legal Aspect of CSR in India

Even though Environmental Protection Act 1986 and Ministry of Corporate Affair's (MCA's) National Voluntary Guidelines (NVGs) 2009 provide necessary legal measures for CSR activities of the companies in India, India is the first country in the world to give legal shape to the CSR practices of companies. The provisions relating to the CSR are incorporated in the Companies Act 2013. Clauses 134 and 135 of the act specify that companies with net worth more than ₹500 crore or turnover more than ₹1,000 crore or net profit more than ₹5 crore are required to constitute a CSR committee to formulate CSR policy for the company. Companies are now obliged to spend a minimum of two per cent of average net profit earned during preceding three years before formulations of the policy (Singh and Agarwal, 2013). As per Schedule VII of the act, the activities relating to the following area may be included by companies in their CSR Policies:

- Eradicating extreme hunger and poverty.
- Promotion of education.
- Promoting gender equality and empowering women.
- Reducing child mortality and improving maternal health.

- Combating human immunodeficiency virus (HIV), acquired immune deficiency syndrome (AIDS), malaria and other diseases.
- Ensuring environmental sustainability.
- Employment enhancing vocational skills.
- Social business projects.
- Contribution to the Prime Minister's National Relief Fund or any other fund set up by the central government or the state governments for socio-economic development and relief and funds for the welfare of the SC, ST, OBC, minorities and women.
- Such other matters as may be prescribed.

Review of Literature

Das (2009) in his study called "Status and Direction of Corporate Social Responsibility in India Perspective: An Exploratory Study" has found that the social sector remained a neglected area as, despite a rise in their revenue earnings, the states are perennially in financial distress due to a more than proportionate increase in expenditure. This study also highlights the poor budgetary allocation for education, ineffective doctor-patient ratio, heavy interest payments/servicing debt and lesser governmental efforts to initiate the CSR as a most effective tool.

Jothi (2010) in his study titled "CSR: Can it Survive the Global Economic Recession?" has revealed the impact of Global Economic Recession on the CSR practices of companies in India. The impact of Global Economic Recession has been examined by classifying the CSR into philanthropic, strategic and the embedded CSR. The study concludes that how far will CSR be affected by the global financial crisis depends on how deep CSR runs within the organisation, whether it is philanthropic, strategic or embedded, rather than the degree of Global Economic Recession.

Jothi and Mathiraj (2011a), in their study titled "Competitiveness, Sustainability and CSR Initiatives of Commercial Banks of India—An Empirical Study of BSE Listed Commercial Banks", has distinguished the relationship between the competitiveness, sustainability and CSR practices of commercial banks in India, which reveals that the approach of CSR is perceived as an imperative pillar in the development process of commercial banks in India, since the CSR practices deals with the two crucial facets of commercial bank: the first is sustainability in the competitive market and the second facet is community development. Although the study has explored CSR initiatives as poor, good and excellent in respect of the two facets of CSR—sustainability and community involvement, it reveals that the majority of commercial banks in India has not been practising the community involvement while they do the business. Correspondingly, the majority of banks in India are having the CSR initiatives at poor level.

Jothi and Mathiraj (2011b), in their study titled "The Strategic Role of HRM in Corporate Social Responsibility Practices: An Overview" has revealed the following socially responsible human resource management (HRM) policies and practices:

- Formulation of ideal HR policies and practices to bring about the right number of people with the right attitude and skills in the right place at the right time.
- Recruitment of people with environmental concern, train people to be socially and economically concerned and develop them in a sustainable manner.
- Fixing the realistic standard to be achieved by the workforce in the organisation.
- Include and consider the employees group in the strategic decision-making process of the organisation.
- Act as a 'change agent' for promoting suitable organisational culture, employee commitment and superior performance management practices.
- Providing equal opportunities for the workforce in the organisation for their development hitherto concentrating on organisational development.

Jothi and Mathiraj (2013a), in their study titled "An Embedded Corporate Social Responsibility Matrix: A Way Ahead for Sustainable and Equitable Benefit for the Firm and the Society," have analysed the sustainability with the help of CSR into three different ways *viz.*, financial sustainability, environmental sustainability and social environmental sustainability, which provides the CSR matrix in order to achieve the sustainable and equitable benefits by the firm in the society. This study concludes by referring motto of the Rio + 20 (2nd UN Conference for Sustainable Development) that the concept of sustainable development and the urgent need to implement environmental friendly policies are more relevant today than ever before. Thus, the embedded CSR matrix can change the way business think, perceive and behave with respect to financial, environmental and social responsibility in order to achieve the sustainable benefit for firm and the society.

Jothi and Mathiraj (2013b), in their study titled "The Relationship between Social Performance (SP) and Financial Performance (FP) of Public Sector Banks (A Study Based on Selected Commercial Banks in India)," have correlated the relationship between CSR and corporate financial performance of public sector banks in India, which is based on a case study of State Bank of India (SBI). This study emphasises the fact that issues such as global warming and climate changes poses a greatest risk to the environment and can be quite damaging to the business models of companies. Only a scenario in which the quality of the environment and social systems synergise with business models, it can lead to sustainable development. This study also analyses the types of CSR initiatives such as external activities and internal CSR initiatives including supporting education, girl child adoption, assistance for natural calamities, supporting health care and green banking. This study has revealed that the CSR initiatives of public sector banks in India are growing well irrespective of their overall performance including financial performance in the industry.

Jothi (2013), in his study titled "Corporate Social Responsibility: Initiatives and Practices through Non-government Organisations in India," has classified the NGOs into directed NGOs, funded NGOs and established NGOs. The established NGOs include the philanthropic institutions, individuals, and government aided NGOs. These were in order to explore the role of NGOs in the CSR initiatives of selected corporates in India, which is based on the nine corporates that belong to different industries in India. This study concludes that business organisations irrespective of their nature of business—health care, manufacturing and information technology enabled service (ITES)—would like to achieve philanthropic CSR ambitions through their own established NGOs. Such kind of philanthropic activities include rural health care, education and environmental initiatives, women empowerment, infrastructure and disaster relief, primary health care and cultural programmes.

Statement of the Problem

Since the CSR practices in India are voluntary for all the business organisations till the end of March 2013, the latest Companies Act, 2013, ensures that the CSR practices are compulsory for certain companies subject to fulfilling certain conditions. Companies in India do not disclose their CSR activities in Companies Annual Reports (CARs) completely. Some companies are disclosing it partially and some others are not so. The practice of CSR disclosure by the companies is influenced by factors like nature of ownership of the company, nature of industry and the like (Hackston and Milne, 1996; Neu et al., 1998). Therefore, the researcher has made an attempt to explore the CSR practices theoretically and analyse its outcomes of the selected public and private undertakings in the study area.

Objectives

The study has the following specific objectives:

- To explore the CSR practices of select public and private sector undertakings in Tamil Nadu.
- To identify the outcomes of CSR practices of the selected public and private sector undertakings in Tamil Nadu.

Methodology

The study has based on largest 12 companies which consist of six public undertakings and six private undertakings in Tamil Nadu. The sample companies have been selected conveniently based on the *Economic Times* ratings of Top 500 Companies 2012 in India (ET Ratings 2012). The CSR practices of these companies have been explored from the websites of respective companies. The outcome of CSR practices has been analysed with the help of the data relating to the CSR practices of the respective companies in the study area.

CSR Practices of Selected Companies in Tamil Nadu

This study has included the following companies in order to explore the CSR practices of the public and private undertakings in Tamil Nadu.

- Neyveli Lignite Corporation Limited (NLC).
- Tamil Nadu Newsprint and Papers Limited (TNPL).
- Chennai Petroleum Corporation Limited (CPCL).
- Madras Fertilisers Ltd (MFL).
- Indian Bank (IB).
- Indian Overseas Bank (IOB).
- Apollo Hospitals Enterprise Ltd.
- Sakthi Sugars Limited.
- TVS Motor Company.
- E.I.D-Parry (India) Limited.
- Shriram Transport Finance Company Limited (STFCL).
- MRF Ltd.

Neyveli Lignite Corporation Limited (NLC)

NLC Ltd., a 'Navratna' Public Sector Enterprise, incorporated in the year 1956, is a pioneer among the public sector undertakings, which believes that "Community is not another entity but it is part and parcel of its very existence." NLC does not believe in profit alone as its prime objective but follows the policy of integrating people, planet and profit. Corporate sustainability vision addresses society, environment and economy for the success of the company and for the well-being of various stakeholders. Its philosophy on sustainability is to contribute for a greener and healthier planet and hand it over to the future generations. NLC has been practising

CSR in its best form for around six decades, well integrated with its day-to-day business and focused on people and the planet. NLC's operations are technology and projects driven with extensive land requirements. NLC is aware of the three dimensions of the CSR which are specific and conspicuous as natural corollary to its large scale mining and power station projects, namely:

- The production and supply of electricity at low cost with minimum impact on the environment.
- The community development by regular extra-business contributions to the society.

Focusing Areas of CSR

Although NLC has been following the National Voluntary Guidelines (NVGs) as principles of its business responsibility, the thrust areas are identified and documented in NLC's CSR policy. The company has a practice of investing one per cent of profit after tax (PAT) on the identified thrust areas for the previous three financial years. In 2013-14, the company has spent 1.80 per cent (₹26.30 crore) of PAT of the previous year 2012-13 on CSR activities. The details are given in Table 14.2.

Table 14.2

NLC's Focusing Areas of CSR

Sl. No.	*Focusing Area*	*Expenditure in 2013-14 (₹ in crore)*
1	Medical, Health, Sanitation and Family Welfare	6.14
2	Drinking Water Supply Facilities	1.24
3	Water Resource Augmentation, Irrigation and Food Control	1.59
4	Capacity Building/Skill Development	6.44
5	Education and Scholarship	3.18
6	Community Development	2.30
7	Formation of Link Road	0.35
8	Construction of School/Library/Laboratory	0.17
9	Sustainable Development Initiatives	1.62
10	Relief/Rehabilitation of areas Affected by disasters	2.78
11	Others	0.49

Source: Annual Report.

Tamil Nadu Newsprint and Papers Limited (TNPL)

TNPL was established by the Government of Tami Nadu during early 1980s to produce newsprint and printing and writing paper using bagasse, a sugar cane residue, as primary raw material. The company has constituted the Corporate Social Responsibility Committee after implementation of the Companies Act, 2013, consisting of five independent directors as members of the committee. The committee has formulated a CSR policy, which aims to promote economic, social, environmental and cultural growth of the community at large in an equitable and sustainable manner. The company's goal is to protect and nourish the interests of all its stakeholders and contribute to sustainable development. Ethics, values and transparency will underpin all its interactions within the community in which it operates. All its activities are of social aspirations and the nation's needs and these will be carried out with integrity, honesty, dignity and decorum.

Investment in CSR

The company has a practice of investing certain per cent of PAT on the identified thrust areas of CSR initiatives. It has invested three per cent of PAT (₹3.27 crore) for CSR activities for the year 2012-13, which is more than expected level as per the clause 135 of Companies Act, 2013. The focusing areas of CSR activities are:

- education,
- health,
- infrastructure,
- economic development,
- environment,
- culture and heritage, and
- other community welfare services,

Beneficiaries of CSR Activities

The company is consistently taking up various community welfare initiatives for the benefit of the people living in neighbouring villages. TNPL's CSR activity mainly covers Punjai Pugalur, Kagitha Aalai, Punjai Thottakkurichi, Punnam, Vettamangalam, Nanjai Pugalur, Thirukkaduthurai and Kombupalayam Panchayat areas situated around TNPL factory premises. In addition to the above, need-based activities are also be carried out in peripheral areas, which can be the locations in other districts within Tamil Nadu.

Chennai Petroleum Corporation Limited (CPCL)

CPCL, formerly known as Madras Refineries Limited (MRL), was formed as a joint venture in 1965 between the Government of India (GoI), AMOCO and National Iranian Oil Company (NIOC) having a share holding in the ratio of 74 per cent:13 per cent:13 per cent respectively. After getting many changes in its capital structure, presently IOC holds 51.89 per cent while NICO holds 15.40 per cent and rest is held by Unit Trust of India (UTI), Mutual Funds, insurance companies and banks.

Policy and Focusing areas of CSR

The CPCL aligns its organisational objectives and business goals with the social objectives in order to achieve inclusive sustainable growth. Being a responsible corporate citizen, the CPCL has implemented a number of CSR activities, benefiting many stakeholders. The focus areas of CSR activities are:

- skill development,
- education,
- health and hygiene facilities, and
- women empowerment.

Investment in CSR

During the year 2013-14, the company has spent an amount of 1.1 crore on various CSR activities for the benefit of community around its factory at Manali and Cauvery Basin (CBR), Nagapattinam, which include the following:

- Running four community health centres serving 50,000 people, conducted two general medical camps and one eye care camp in association with various hospitals.
- Merit scholarships to the students of rural educational institutions and Sponsorship of "Home Management for Visually Challenged Students" programme.
- Installation of one 10 KW grid connected Solar Photo Voltaic system at Polytechnic College, Manali, and sponsorship of sports meet for promoting sports among the school students.
- Provision of toilet and drinking water facilities for school students and for public.
- Provision of placement linked computer training programme for 100 beneficiaries, in association with M/s ITCOT, Chennai at Computer Sciences Corporation (CSC) Nagapattinam at a cost of ₹10 lakh. Of the 100 youths trained, around 72 have been gainfully employed.
- Mobile Science Lab Education Programme for the schools in Nagapattinam District conducted in association with M/s Agastya International Foundation, Bangalore, at a cost of ₹4.00 lakh benefiting around 15,000 school students.

Madras Fertilisers Ltd. (MFL)

The company was incorporated on 8 December 1966 as a joint venture between GoI and AMOCO India Incorporated of the US (AMOCO) in accordance with the Fertiliser Formation Agreement executed on 14 May 1966 with equity contributions of 51 per cent and 49 per cent respectively. Presently after the allotment of shares to the public, the shareholding pattern is: the GoI has 59.50 per cent, Naftiran Intergraded Co. Ltd. (affiliate of NIOC) has 25.77 per cent and the public has 14.73 per cent. MFL is engaged in the manufacture of ammonia, urea, complex fertilisers and biofertilisers.

MFL's activities include marketing of these fertilisers and trading in agro chemicals in accordance with the corporate objective.

CSR Practices of MFL

The CSR initiative of the MFL has tradition of conducting informative and educational programmes for the farmers and dealers as a part of social responsibility in upliftment of farming community. During 2011-12, 89 promotional programmes were conducted benefiting 25,190 farmers. MFL continued to have demos on biofertilisers, follow-up on soil tests results with farmers and participation in government exhibitions and the like.

Indian Bank (IB)

IB was established on 15th August 1907 as part of the Swadeshi movement and serving the nation with a team of over 19,429 employees in 2,250 branches as on 31 March 2014. It is the pioneer bank in introducing self-help groups (SHGs) and financial inclusion project in the country and won the Best Performer Award for Micro-Finance activities in Tamil Nadu and Union Territory of Puducherry from the National Bank for Agriculture and Rural Development (NABARD). The bank has been playing an important role in the rural India by means of its CSR initiatives.

Focusing Areas of CSR

The bank has spent an amount of ₹241.89 lakh (0.21% of PAT) on CSR activities for the year 2013-14, which include the following thrust areas:

- Green initiative to promote the green concept.
- Providing equipments towards clean and green city drive.
- Awareness among students created through competition on sustainable energy and powering sustainable growth.
- Bringing smiles by celebrating festivals with senior citizens at old age homes and children at orphanages.

- The bank has conducted voluntary blood donation camps and was awarded the Rolling Shield. The Bank maintains its number one position for the 26th consecutive year since 1988.

Indian Overseas Bank (IOB)

IOB was founded on 10 February 1937 with three branches simultaneously—at Karaikudi and Chennai in India and Rangoon in Burma (presently Myanmar), by Shri M.Ct.M. Chidambaram Chettyar, a pioneer in many fields: banking, insurance and industry with the twin objectives of specialising in foreign exchange business and overseas banking.

CSR Initiatives of IOB

The bank has involved in CSR activities directly as well as with the association of NGO called SakthiIndian Overseas Bank Chidambaram Chettyar Memorial Trust. Their major CSR projects include the IOB-Sampoorna Project—A Total Village Development Project and Educating Tribals scheme.

IOB-Sampoorna Project—A Total Village Development Project

IOB Sampoorna is an innovative rural development project aimed at total village development. IOB-Sampoorna is a unique project encompassing several livelihood initiatives in the villages to ensure all-inclusive growth of rural population. It comprises of credit and non-credit components such as financial inclusion, IT enabled banking operations with bio-metric smart cards under business correspondent model, tree planting and social forestry, cleaning water bodies, health care, skill training for youth in computer, rural business process outsourcing, promotion of non-conventional energy and rural tourism.

Educating Tribals

During the year 2013-14, the bank has sponsored 98 Ekal Vidyalaya School in association with M/s Friends of Tribals Society, an NGO to attack illiteracy at the grass-roots level through a unique concept *viz.*, "One teacher School" or Ekal Vidyalaya. The Bank in association with Max Academy implemented the project on uplifting educational standards of the under privileged children in five villages during the year 2013-14.

Sakthi-Indian Overseas Bank Chidambaram Chettyar Memorial Trust

The trust, set up jointly by the management of the bank, Indian Overseas Bank Officers Association and All India Overseas Bank Employees Union to perpetuate the memory of bank's founder Shri M.Ct.M. Chidambaram Chettyar, continued to provide entrepreneurial development training to women, thereby empowering them socially and financially to meet the challenges. During 2013-14, nine skill development programmes were conducted in various regions under aegis of Sakthi-IOB Chidambaram Chettyar Memorial Trust, wherein 245 women have been trained. The trust has so far conducted 71 entrepreneurship development programmes (EDP) and skill-based training programmes exclusively for women at various centres, benefiting 3,576 women.

Apollo Hospitals Enterprise Ltd.

Apollo Hospitals opened its doors in 1983 and ever since nurtured a goal which read as "Our mission is to bring health care of international standards within the reach of every individual. We are committed to the achievement and maintenance of excellence in education, research and health care for the benefit of humanity." Apart from the major social initiatives and programmes that Apollo Hospitals has initiated, every individual hospital in the group does its bit for the community it serves. Its CSR initiatives channelised through the NGO called Apollo Telemedicine Networking Foundation (ATNF) as well as directly which include:

- DISHA: Distance Health care Advancement Project.
- CURE: An Apollo Hospitals Cancer Care Initiative.
- SACHi: Saving a Child's Heart Initiative.

- Disaster Relief Programmes—floods, earthquake, tsunami and the like.
- Awareness campaigns.

Sakthi Sugars Limited

Sakthi Sugars Limited is one of the important members of the Sakthi Group contributing a large share of revenue to the group's turnover. In its pursuit for business excellence, the Sakthi Group, ever since its inception in 1921 at Pollachi, Coimbatore, has been staunchly inclined towards fulfilling its social commitments. As a dutiful corporate, Sakthi Group has set up 'The Mahalingam-Mariammal Manivizha Charitable Trust' in the year 1983 at the Kasturba Gandhi National Memorial Buildings, Coimbatore. Under the aegis of this trust, it is reaching out to more people every day, extending their help to destitute women, children and the socially neglected and downtrodden individuals. The foundation has involved in CSR activities in the following manner:

- Kasturba Gandhi Oral School for the Hearing Impaired, Varadarajapuram, Coimbatore.
- Kasturba Gandhi Memorial De-addiction and Rehabilitation and Research Centre, Coimbatore.
- Kasturba Gandhi Memorial Siddha Hospital and Research Institute, Varadarajapuram, Coimbatore.
- Mahatma Gandhi Museum.
- Suicide Prevention Counselling Centre.
- Sakthi Thiranalayam (Sakthi Skills Development Centre).
- Sakthi Higher Secondary School, Sivaganga.
- Sakthi Polytechnic College.
- Sakthi PURA (Providing Urban amenities in Rural Areas).

TVS Motor Company

TVS Motor Company is the third largest two-wheeler manufacturer in India and one among the top 10 in the world, with annual turnover of more than USD 1.4 billion in 2011-12. TVS Motor Company Ltd (TVS Motor), member of the TVS group, is the largest company of the group in terms of size and turnover. The company has constituted a Corporate Social Responsibility Committee during the year 2013. However, the CSR activities have already been textured into the company's value system through Srinivasan Services Trust (SST), established by the group companies in 1996 with the vision of building self-reliant rural community.

The Srinivasan Services Trust (SST)

The trust has played a pivotal role in changing lives of people in rural India by creating self-reliant communities that are models of sustainable development. At present, SST is working in 2,501 villages spread across Tamil Nadu, Karnataka, Maharashtra, Himachal Pradesh and Andhra Pradesh. Its major focus areas are: economic development, health care, quality education, environment and infrastructure. Its significant achievements are:

- Through partnership with the community, over 5,300 SHG were formed.
- Hundred per cent enrolment in schools, 0 per cent drop-outs, 93 per cent students pursue higher studies and over 60,145 adult women were made literate.
- Illiteracy amongst women reduced from 47 per cent to 12 per cent.
- 1,75,205 ha under afforestation.
- 12,938 ha covered for soil and water conservation.
- Proper solid and liquid waste management practices adopted in 1,418 villages.
- SHG members have a group saving of ₹25.57 crore.
- Over 1,47,136 of the families living in these villages have a monthly income of around ₹15,000 per family.
- 1,296 villages have access to safe drinking water.

- Enriching 2,501 villages across five states. Creating the most effective synergies for socio-economic development in India.

E.I.D-Parry (India) Limited

E.I.D. Parry has been synonymous with dynamism since 1788. It became a part of the Murugappa Group in 1981 and its businesses now cover a wide range of products including sugar, microalgal health supplements from Parry Nutraceuticals and bio products from Bio Products Division. E.I.D-Parry (India) Limited is part of the Tamil Nadu-based ₹225 billion Murugappa Group and the largest sugar producer in South India and is one of the top five sugar producers in the country.

Corporate Social Responsibility Initiatives

E.I.D-Parry, being a constituent of "The Murugappa Group" has upheld its ancient family tradition of earmarking and spending a portion of its income for social service in its business enterprise as well. E.I.D-Parry firmly believes that social responsibility is not just a ritual, but it is fulfilling one's *dharma*. Therefore, in all its philanthropic endeavours, the Murugappa Group reflects its spiritual conscience and not just corporate obligation.

Investment in CSR

E.I.D-Parry, through Murugappa Group, invests a portion of its wealth—one per cent of PAT—for the welfare of society since it went into business. In addition to this, it also conducts a lot of welfare measures for the needy residing in and around its various units.

The AMM Foundation

The AMM Foundation, earlier known as the AMM Charities Trust, an autonomous, charitable trust, is dedicated to community friendly initiative in the fields of education and health care. Founded in 1953, the trust embodies the family's concern for the underprivileged. The AMM Foundation's philanthropy is unique;

the giver's humility as well as concern for the beneficiary's dignity exemplifies its altruism. It manages a polytechnic college, four schools and four hospitals, each a benchmark in its area.

Shriram Transport Finance Company Limited (STFCL)

STFCL, as a India's largest player in commercial vehicle finance, was established in the year 1979. The company has a network of 620 branches and 515 rural centres. The company practices various social, environmental and economic responsibilities towards its stakeholders. The company has adopted all the nine principles provided by NVGs by the MCA as its CSR policy. These principles have been given in its website as Business Responsibility Statement.

MRF Ltd.

K.M. Mammen Mappillai started MRF's journey as a toy balloon manufacturing unit in a shed in Tiruvottiyur in Madras in 1946. Since then, the company has been growing well in different dimensions. The MRF Ltd. has consistently involved in CSR initiatives since the inception of 'The MRF Pace Foundation' in 1987. It was set up to make up for the fact that the Indian cricket team lacked quality pace bowlers. Combined with the Australian pace legend Dennis Lillee, it provided world-class training to potential bowlers, together with the understanding that it would be a long-term process requiring patience and commitment. Its major CSR initiatives include:

- Funding and developing the sports activities.
- Concentrating on educational developments of rural people.
- Concentrating on health care services to the local community.

CSR Practices and its Outcomes of Selected Companies in Tamil Nadu

It is observed during the study that none of the private undertakings in the study disclosed their CSR practices either in website or annual report, whereas in the case of public undertakings in the study area, a small number of companies—NLC and TNPL—are disclosing their CSR practices completely, some of them disclosing it partially—Chennai Petroleum Corporation Ltd., Madras Fertilisers Ltd.—and some of them not disclosing it completely—IB and IOB. In spite of this kind of CSR disclosure by the companies in the study area, the researcher has collected the data relating to CSR practices from different sources, compiled them and represented in the following manner as given in Table 14.3.

It is observed from Table 14.3 that most of the undertakings in the study area both public and private are focusing the CSR on women empowerment, education, community welfare, poverty eradication and health care, which have direct impact on the society. A few companies *viz.*, TVS Motor and E.I.D.-Parry (India) Ltd. are focusing on water, health care services and environmental activities, which have impact on the environmental protection. All the private undertakings except STFCL are involving in CSR practices indirectly with the assistance of their own NGOs, whereas STFCL is alone practising its CSR activities directly. In case of public undertakings, IOB has NGO for its CSR practices, the rest of the undertakings have involved directly. NGOs can act as an avenue to fulfil the CSR activities in India, the role played by NGOs to the corporate and the society is not quantifiably easy (Jothi, 2013). It is remarked that the rest of the companies can also adopt this strategy in order to have sustainable CSR practices thereby they may have the benefits of CSR practices for the long-run period. Further the CSR practices of these undertakings have link to their business directly for companies like IB, IOB, E.I.D.-Parry (India) Ltd. and the like, and indirectly for some companies like NLC, TNPL and the like. So it is observed that the CSR practices of companies are related to their nature of the business activities.

Findings of the Study

The study has reveals the following important findings:

- The CSR outcomes of all the public undertakings in the study are community development services—education, health care, rural development programme and the like.

Table 14.3

CSR Practices and its Outcomes of Selected Companies in Tamil Nadu

S. No	Company	Ownership	Industry	Focus Area	Business Linkage	Methodology Adopted	Outcome
1	Chennai Petroleum Corporation Ltd	Public	Refineries	Women Empowerment, Edn, Community Welfare	Indirect	Directly	Community services
2	Indian Bank	Public	Bank	Rural development, Poverty eradication, Sports	Direct	Directly	Community services
3	Indian Overseas Bank	Public	Bank	Women empowerments and Rural development	Direct	NGO–IOB-CCMTa	Community services
4	Madras Fertilisers Ltd.	Public	Fertilisers	Community welfare, Rural development Vocational	Indirect	Directly	Community services
5	Neyveli Lignite Corporation Ltd.	Public	Power generation	training Community Welfare, Education,	Indirect	Directly	Community services
6	Tamil Nadu Newsprint & Papers Ltd.	Public	Paper products	Health care Community Welfare, Education, Health	Indirect	Directly	Community services
7	Apollo Hospitals Enterprise Ltd	Private	Hospital	care Children, Healthcare, Community welfare	Direct	NGO-ATNFb	Community services
8	Sakthi Sugars Ltd	Private	Sugar	Community Welfare, Healthcare, Education	Indirect	NGO-MMCTc	Community services
9	TVS Motor Company Ltd.	Private	Automobile	Health, Education, Environment	Direct	NGO-Srinivasan Services Trust	Environmental protection
10	EID Parry (India) Ltd	Private	Sugar	Water, Rural develop, Environment	Direct	NGO-The MM Foundation	Environmental protection
11	MRF Ltd	Private	Auto Ancillary	Sports, Health care, Education	Indirect	NGO-MRF pace foundation	Community services
12	Shriram Transport Finance Co. Ltd	Private	Fin. Service	Education, Children, Community Welfare	Direct	Directly	Community services

Source: Compiled from primary and secondary data; IOB-CCMT-Sakthi-Indian Overseas Bank Chidambaram Chettyar Memorial Trust; ATNF–Apollo Telemedicine Networking Foundation; cMMCT-The Mahalingam–Mariammal Manivizha Charitable Trust

- The CSR outcomes of private undertakings in the study are the community development and environmental protection.
- The CSR activities of the select undertakings have both direct and indirect linkage with its business activities.
- Majority of the public undertakings have directly involved in CSR activities rather than through the NGOs.
- Majority of the private undertakings have involved in CSR activities with the help of its established NGOs.
- Among the PSU in the study area, the IOB has involved in CSR activities through its established NGO called Sakthi-Indian Overseas Bank Chidambaram Chettyar Memorial Trust.
- Among all the selected companies in the study area, the TNPL has invested highest amount of 3 per cent (₹3.27 crore) on PAT in CSR activities for the year 2012-13 which is followed by the NLC has invested 1.80 per cent (26.30 crore) on PAT in CSR activities for the year 2013-14.

Conclusion and Managerial Implications

Business houses in India are emerged into new avenue of CSR practices where the importance of social and environmental issue is recognised well. This study has the vital implication for the policy makers of both public and private undertakings in India particularly in the study area of Tamil Nadu that CSR has become the password not only to lock the competition, but also to open the opportunity in the global market provided when they realistically adopt the provisions of CSR included in the Companies Act, 2013.

References

Carroll, A.B. (1989). "Business & Society—Ethics & Stakeholder Management", Cincinnati, USA: South-Western Publishing Co.

Das, Sudhir Chandra (2009). "Status and Direction of Corporate Social Responsibility in India Perspective: An Exploratory Study", *Corporate Governance* 5(1): 34-47.

Dentchev, N. (2005). "Corporate Social Performance: As Business Strategy", *Journal of Business Ethics* 55(4): 395-419.

Engle, Rober L. (2007). "Corporate Social Responsibility in Host Countries: A Perspective from American Managers", *Corporate Social Responsibility and Environmental Management* 14: 16-27.

Hackston, D. and M.J. Milne (1996). "Some Determinants of Social and Environmental Disclosures in New Zealand Companies", *Accounting, Auditing & Accountability Journal* 9(1): 77-108.

Jamali, D. and R. Mishak (2007). "Corporate Social Responsibility (CSR): Theory and Practice in a Developing Country Context", *Journal of Business Ethics* 72: 362.

Jothi, M. (2010). "CSR: Can it Survive the Global Economic Recession?", *HRM Review* 10(7): 48-51.

———. (2013). "Corporate Social Responsibility: Initiatives and Practices through Non-government Organizations in India", *JIM QUEST Journal of Management and Technology* 9(1): 76-85.

Jothi, M. and S.P. Mathiraj (2011a). "Competitiveness, Sustainability and CSR Initiatives of Commercial Banks of India—An Empirical Study of BSE Listed Commercial Banks", *SONA Global Management Review* 5(2): 1-14.

———. (2011b). "The Strategic Role of HRM in Corporate Social Responsibility Practices: An Overview", *HRM Review* 11(9): 11-14.

———. (2013a). "An Embedded Corporate Social Responsibility Matrix: A Way Ahead for Sustainable and Equitable Benefit for the Firm and the Society", *International Journal of Research in Computer Application & Management* 3(6): 62-8.

———. (2013b). "The Relationship between Social Performance (SP) and Financial Performance (FP) of Public Sector Banks (A Study Based on Selected Commercial Banks in India)", *SONA Global Management Review* 7(2): 1-10.

Neu, D., H. Warsame and K. Pedwell (1998). "Managing Public Impressions: Environmental Disclosures in Annual Reports", *Accounting Organizations and Society* 23(3): 265-82.

Potluri, Rajasekhara Mouly, Yespayeva Batima and Kunev Madiyar (2010). "Corporate Social Responsibility: A Study of Kazakhstan Corporate Sector", *Social Responsibility Journal* 6(1): 33-44.

Singh, Ramendra and Sharad Agarwal (2013). "Does CSR Orientation Reflect Stakeholder Relationship Marketing Orientation? An Empirical Examination of Indian Banks", *Marketing Intelligence & Planning* 31(4): 405-20.

Tulasi Das, V. and Sreethar Reddy (2014). "Corporate Social Responsibility Awareness of Employees of Small Scale Industries: An Empirical Study", *Management Today: An International Journal of Management Studies* 4(3): 19-25.

Vogel, D. (2005). *The Market for Virtue: The Potential and Limits of Corporate Social Responsibility*. Harvard Business School.

Wartick, S.L. and P.L. Cochran (1985). "The Evolution of the Corporate Social Performance Model", *Academy of Management Review* 20(4): 758-69.

Wood, D.J. (1991). "Corporate Social Performance Revisited", Academy of Management Review 16(4): 691-718.

Websites:

http://www.nlcindia.com/index.php?file_name=investor_annual_report_1314 (accessed on 3 September 2014).

http://www.tnpl.com/CSRPOLICY.pdf (accessed on 3 September 2014).

http://www.cpcl.co.in/AnnualReports/CPCL%20Annual%20Report%202014.pdf (accessed on 31 August 2014).

http://madrasfert.nic.in/ (accessed on 3 August 2014).

http://www.indian-bank.com/annual_report.php (accessed on 5 August 2014).

http://www.eidparry.com/the-company/about-us.aspx (accessed on 3 September 2014).

http://stfc.in/home.aspx (accessed on 3 September 2014).

http://www.eidparry.com/the-company/about-us.aspx (accessed on 3 September 2014).

http://stfc.in/home.aspx (accessed on 3 September 2014).

15

H. URDHIN • K. PADACHI • K. SEETAH

Assessing Corporate Social Responsibility Practices of Mauritian Companies

Introduction

Over the last decades, corporate social responsibility (CSR) has been a subject of intense debate among academics and practitioners (Galbreath, 2009). Sims (2003) defined the term as "the continuing commitment by business to behaving ethically and contributing to economic development while improving the quality of life of the workforce and their families as well as of the community and society at large" that is CSR is a form of self-regulation integrated in business models that describes the role and responsibilities of organisations towards stakeholders. Through CSR, businesses attempt to contribute towards the welfare of society and become sustainable to fulfil the economic, social and environmental dimensions rather than only maximising profit. CSR focuses on different areas such as education, health, environment, community/livelihood development, arts and culture, and disaster relief.

Nowadays, most firms irrespective of their sector of activity or the country in which they operate are engaged in CSR, as it enables those organisations to maintain high moral and ethical standards while operating on both the local or international market. One of the main factors which have led to an increase in the need for CSR is the erosion of trust of stakeholders towards organisation due to corporate scandals involving reputable institution which even led to the financial crisis of 2007. Due to these financial scandals, the need for CSR has strengthened and it is positively accepted in the world business climate (Chen and Wang, 2011). Accordingly, the Deliotte

Report (2008) pointed out that CSR can help to restore trust in the corporate world. In addition, there is a greater need for CSR as the world is experiencing environmental degradations such as climatic changes and global warming, and the need to preserve the nature has become vital.

Overview of CSR in Mauritius

A few years back, the Government of Mauritius introduced the concept of CSR and initiated the Eradication of Absolute Poverty (EAP) programme in collaboration with the private sector. As from 2009, every profitable company is required to set up a CSR fund equivalent to 2 per cent of its profits chargeable to income tax, derived during the preceding year. The CSR fund may be used to implement approved programmes of the organisation, finance the project of an approved non-governmental organisation (NGO), implement an approved programme under the National Empowerment Foundation (NEF) and implement projects in collaboration with public sector organisations. With the objective to ensure that investments in CSR initiatives are carried in the most effective and efficient way, the government has initiated a list of approved NGOs as well as a list of programmes.

In line with Ragodoo (2009), the leading hundred companies of Mauritius do express a high level of commitment with regard to their social responsibilities. Approximately 80 per cent of them have established well-structured CSR programmes with the objective to choose and prioritise funding in the needy areas. CSR has become increasingly important and is integrating in the Mauritian business environment very rapidly. Referring to Gokulsing (2011), companies such as the Mauritius Commercial Bank (MCB), Barclays Bank, Hong Kong and Shanghai Bank (HSBC), CIEL Ltd., Airports of Mauritius Ltd. (AML), British American Investment Group, Medine Sugar Estate and Beachcomber Group had started adopting CSR strategies well before it became legally mandatory.

Problem Statement

Carroll (1991) highlighted that companies need to fulfil their economic, legal, ethical and philanthropic responsibilities in order to be good corporate citizens. On the other hand, in Carroll and Buchholtz (2009), it was highlighted that Milton Friedman argued that the responsibility of managers are to maximise the organisation's profit as well as the return of the shareholders and owners, and social issues are not the concerns of business people.

Dusuki (2008) claimed that "firms are engaged in CSR to secure their 'license to operate'" and on the contrary Porter and Kramer (2006) argued that strategic CSR activities should be so designed in a way that it improves the competitiveness of a firm or industry, but in developing countries, this logic of thinking needs to be altered. Bhattacharyya *et al.*, (2008) further argued that firms undertaking CSR initiatives can gain both tangible resources such as raw material, human resources, and increased profits as well intangible resources like reputation, brand name, goodwill and know-how.

Most of the previous studies on CSR have focused on developed countries and till now only a few researches have been conducted for developing countries such as Mauritius. Therefore, it is worth investigating on CSR practices in Mauritius as an attempt to bridge this gap and to contribute towards the literature in this field. Hence, this study assesses the CSR practices of non-listed banks and the companies officially listed on the Stock Exchange of Mauritius (SEM) to disclose the reasons motivating them to engage in CSR.

Study Objectives

Meyer and Fienberg (1992) contended that a successful study must have clearly defined objectives which must be ranked and reflect some form of priority. As CSR is becoming an important feature on the businesses in Mauritius, the ultimate aim of this study is to assess the CSR practices of non-listed banks and companies officially listed on the SEM. It aims at analysing the reasons encouraging firms to engage in CSR and how CSR is beneficial to these organisations.

More specifically, the objectives of this study are to:

- Identify and assess the involvement of stakeholders between companies listed on the SEM and non-listed banks.

- Explore the reasons which motivate listed companies and non-listed banks to engage themselves in CSR activities and how they benefit from these activities.
- Investigate whether there is a sectorial difference in the incentive to increase CSR activities and its possible implications.
- Identify the main focus of companies' CSR initiatives.

The rest of the paper is structured as follows. The second section reviews the relevant literature, covering the evolution of CSR, conceptual framework of CSR and benefits of CSR activities. The research methodology is elaborated under the third section and it gives support for the research instrument. The fourth section analyses and discusses the survey results and the fifth section concludes on the study.

Literature Review

Evolution of CSR

Over the years, there has been a continuing discussion regarding CSR and it is not a new concept (Gokulsing, 2011). Literature on CSR started in the 1950s with the publication of Bowen's book *Social Responsibilities of the Businessman* and authors are still showing more and more interest about this particular topic. Throughout the definitional history of CSR from the 1950s till date, Rahman (2011) identified 10 major dimensions which are the obligation to the society, stakeholders' involvement, improving the quality of life, economic development, ethical business practice law abiding, voluntariness, human rights, protection of environment, transparency and accountability.

Initially, CSR was viewed as the obligations of businesses towards the society that is managers had started to think that there is a society and they had some duties towards the society. The 1960s dealt with relationship between corporation and society, whereas in the 1970s, organisations put emphasis on corporate philanthropy as well as community relations with the objective to improve the quality of life of the society that is emphasis was laid on stakeholder's involvement, social interests and solve neighbourhood issues as well as economic, legal, ethical and discretionary responsibility. Consequently, in the 1980s, stress was laid on voluntariness, economically profitable, law abiding, ethical and socially supportive, economic, legal, ethical and voluntary or philanthropic. In addition, the definitions of the 1990s were mainly concerned with stakeholders' involvement, obligation to society, environmental stewardship, people, planet, and profit and finally recent explanations of the 21st century focus on integration of social and environmental concern, voluntariness, ethical behaviour, economic development, improving the quality of life of the citizens, human rights, labour rights, protection of environment, fight against corruption, transparency and accountability.

Hence, the main idea of CSR is that businesses should not only concentrate on the internal aspects of the organisations but should also take into consideration the external environment to which they are exposed, as their activities have impacts on the stakeholders and other external factors. Adopting the right CSR policies will enable firms to achieve their objectives by being ethical to the stakeholders.

Conceptual Framework of CSR

Carroll's CSR Conceptualisation

One of the most famous and widely accepted conceptualisation of CSR known as the Pyramid of CSR[1] was developed by Carroll (1979) which identified four categories of CSR namely, economic, legal, ethical and philanthropic. Carroll (1991) affirmed that even though these components were not mutually exclusive, it helped managers to see the various types of responsibilities. The concept of CSR had been widely supported by empirical researches and based on Carroll's CSR Pyramid, Hemphill (2004) summarised the four layers of CSR as to be profitable (economic), obey the law (legal), be ethical (ethics) and be a good corporate citizen in its relationship with stakeholders (philanthropic).

1. See Carroll (1991) and Carroll and Buchholtz (2011).

Figure 15.1

Carroll's CSR Pyramid

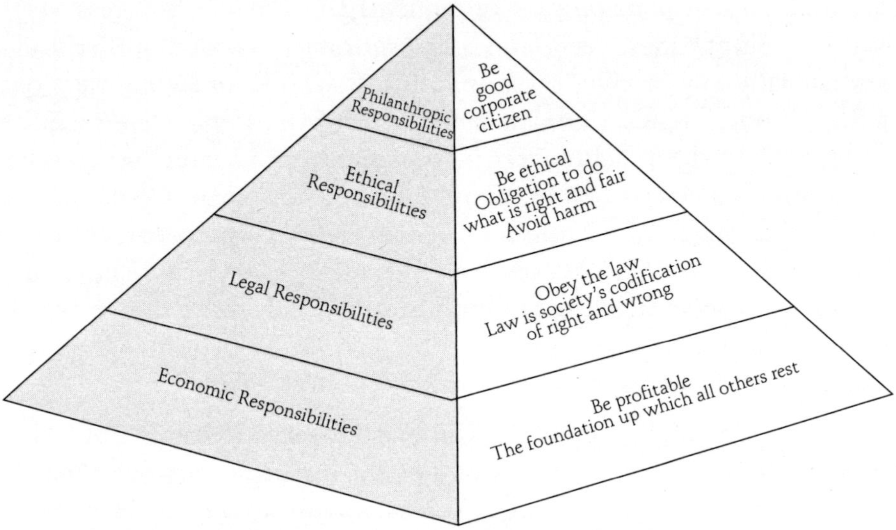

Wood 1991 Conceptualisation

Wartick and Cochran (1985) and Wood (1991) developed a complete model of corporate social performance (CSP) which was built upon the issues of CSR and included corporate social responsiveness as a measurement. Wood (1991) brought significant alterations his the model to examine issues relating to the principles motivating responsible behaviour, the processes of responsiveness and the outcomes of performance (Jamali and Mirshak, 2007).

Figure 15.2

Corporate Social Performance Model

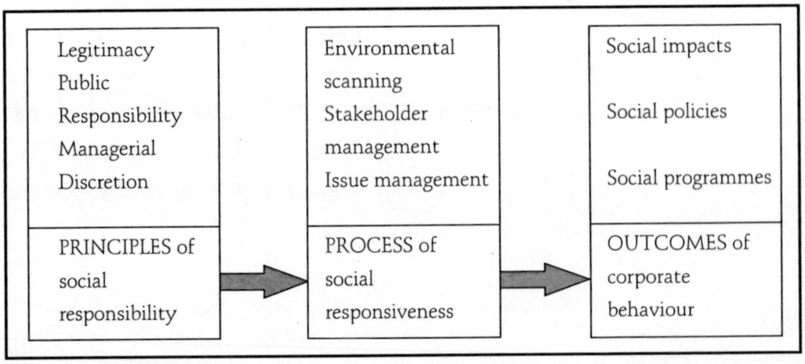

Wood (1991) highlighted that the principle of legitimacy (institutional level) motivates a firm's social responsibility with an objective to maintain credibility and be a responsible societal actor. Referred to as the actions needed to complement the normative and motivational component of social responsibility, responsiveness is comprised of environmental assessment, stakeholder management, and issues management. Stakeholder management deals with devising and monitoring responses related to social issues.

According to the CSP model, outcomes of corporate behaviour consists of social impacts which sees the programmes of companies used to implement responsibility followed by the policies developed by the companies to handle social issues and stakeholder interests. In short, concepts of CSR revealed that businesses are also accountable for the areas related to responsibility and performance. By accomplishing these areas, firms are more enable to allocate their resources and act appropriately so that they can achieve the society's required or desired expectations as well as being profitable and achieving their objectives as well.

Research Methodology

The purpose of this study is to assess the CSR practices of companies listed on the SEM and non-listed banks. The study also attempts to identify and assess the involvement of stakeholders in the CSR initiatives. In addition, this research tries to explore on the reasons motivating non-listed banks and companies listed on the SEM to engage themselves in CSR, how they benefit from these activities as well as investigating whether there are differences in the CSR practices and to assess the impact of CSR as well as identifying the focus areas of CSR in Mauritius.

The targeted population for this particular study includes companies listed on the SEM comprising of 38 companies as in March 2012 and 17 non-listed banks. This targeted population was chosen because both listed companies and non-listed banks are considered as firms with high turnover and thus a better assessment of the CSR practices would be obtained. For this research, as the sample unit was relatively small, no specific sampling technique was used and thus, the 55 companies represented the sample unit. In line with previous studies, the main research instrument used in gathering primary data was the questionnaire. The questionnaire used for this particular study had been adapted from various reports and studies on CSR and it was duly designed according to the research objectives and the nature of the sample unit [EMIT, 2007; Núñez, 2008; Institute for Corporate Culture Affairs (ICCA), 2005; Pantic and Mesche, 2011]. The questionnaire is divided into four different sections each having a specific purpose which is linked to the initial study objectives.

For the data collection, the questionnaire was administered in various ways. With the objective to be ecological and environmental friendly, the questionnaire was administered online on *www.kwiksurveys.com* as well as in PDF format using Adobe Reader (Version 9.0 Pro).

All the companies were contacted by phone in order to obtain their consent. The questionnaire administered in PDF format was sent to the companies by email accompanied by a covering letter. The respondents were able to fill the questionnaire online and returned it back through emails without the need to print the questionnaire.

From the total sample size, 71 per cent of the respondents were companies listed on the SEM, while on the contrary 29 per cent represented banks. Out of 38 listed companies, only 24 positively responded to the survey while only 10 out of 17 banks responded. The low response rate for commercial banks was due to the confidentiality of information. Even if respondents were reassured that confidentiality would be maintained, they preferred not to fill the questionnaire.

Cohen *et al.* (2007) highlighted that a minimum of 30 responses is needed in order to perform statistical test. Subsequently, as there were 34 responses, the questionnaires were compiled and then input on the Statistical Package for the Social Science (SPSS, version 20.0) to generate results for various tests such as mean score and frequencies, Pearson's Chi-square test and Pearson's correlation test. Barkemeyer (2011) pointed out that non-parametric test are carried out when the size of the sample is relatively small. As a result, the Mann-Whitney U tests and Kruskal-Wallis tests as the non-parametric tests were conducted according to the study objectives.

Results and Discussions

Descriptive

The number of entities represents 28 listed companies since corporations such as ENL Commercial Limited (Ltd.) and ENL Land Ltd. as well as the Mauritius Commercial Bank (MCB) Ltd. and Fincorp Investment Ltd. fall under the ENL Group and MCB Group respectively. In addition, the Caudan Development Ltd. is a subsidiary of Promotion and Development Ltd. Moreover, 74 per cent of the listed companies and 59 per cent of the non-listed banks responded to the survey resulting in an overall response rate of 67 per cent. Hence, companies listed on the SEM were more responsive to the study compared to non-listed banks. A sectorial break down of the response rate shows that the majority with 47 per cent represents the banks, insurance and other financial sector. It is obvious that this particular sector is at the first position, as it comprises of both non-listed banks and some of the companies listed on the official list of the SEM. The industry and commerce sectors represent only 26 per cent followed by investment and sugar sectors with 18 per cent and finally debt, leisure, hotels and transport with only 9 per cent.

For this study, industry was merged to commerce, investments to sugar and leisure and hotels to transport. The sugar and investments sectors were merged together because the sugar industry consists of only two companies namely, ENL Land Ltd. and Omnicane Ltd. ENL Land Ltd. operates under the ENL Group and the latter operates under the investments sector as well. In addition, the leisure and hotels sector has been merged to debt, as Lux Island Resorts Ltd. operates under both sectors and to transport which consists of Air Mauritius Ltd. only. The leisure and hotels sector and the transport sector are more or less dependent on each other, as Air Mauritius Ltd. offers the carrier to bring tourists in the country, while on the other hand hotels accommodate these tourists. Thus, these two sectors are inter-related.

From the respondents, 38 per cent of the companies surveyed are CSR leaders signifying companies which have first initiated and implemented CSR and also known as the front-runners of the market. In addition, 32 per cent represent companies which are CSR adopters that is they adopt the CSR strategies which have been initiated by other companies. Finally, CSR newcomers hold 30 per cent of the sample surveyed and these corporations are especially those which are new comers on the market or they have just adopted CSR initiatives when contribution to the CSR fund was made mandatory. However, there is not a significant difference between the different groups. The CSR group is also dependent on the number of years the companies have been operating on the market as well as their objectives and strategies. Moreover, the CSR group also illustrates the level of investment in CSR by companies. Usually, the CSR leaders invest extensively in CSR activities compared to CSR adopters whose investment in CSR is at a moderate level. Finally, the level of investment in CSR by newcomers is often low, as the companies have just been engaged in the concept and they contribute only the 2 per cent legally required.

It is also observed that half of the companies surveyed have their own and specific CSR departments or dedicated teams to monitor and implement their CSR activities. On the contrary, for companies which do not have dedicated teams or departments to oversee CSR, the task is assigned to other departments where it is noted that 24 per cent of the companies surveyed monitor CSR under the human resource (HR)/administration department, 23 per cent under the marketing, communications and external affairs department and finally the compliance department holding only 3 per cent. However, the low result from the compliance department shows that only a few companies view CSR as a legal obligation. In addition, 44 per cent of the companies surveyed integrate CSR through communication followed by 41 per cent through corporate positioning, 35 per cent through company's strategy, 21 per cent through marketing and 6 per cent through their product. Hence, it is observed that companies are well involved in CSR as most of them do have a CSR department and they integrate CSR within their usual business activities. These findings show that the companies have well-structured CSR strategies and are well engaged in CSR.

Freeman (1984) argued that firms have relationships with many fundamental groups and stakeholders. Thus, it is in the best interest of companies to address their CSR activities towards stakeholders efficiently as these individuals or organisations may affect the company in terms of their existence on the market, access to capital or license to operate. Seventy-nine per cent of the companies surveyed aim at acknowledging their CSR initiatives towards NGOs. In addition, 59 per cent of the respondents address their CSR initiatives towards the local community, 50 per cent towards customers, 47 per cent towards employees, 29 per cent towards shareholders and 21 per cent towards the government. Finally, 12 per cent address their CSR initiatives towards the regulatory bodies and suppliers respectively and only 3 per cent towards competitors.

The relatively high response rates for addressing CSR initiatives towards the local communities and customers are because customers are from the local communities and they are significant determinants of firms' turnover. Addressing CSR initiatives towards employees demonstrates that companies do consider their workforce since staffs represent the assets of these companies. If the labour force is motivated, the efficiency as well as the output of firms will increase resulting in high productivity and returns. Moreover, NGOs (mean 4.12; median 4.5) are much involved in the planning and implementation process of CSR in the organisations compared to employees and shareholders having the same involvement with a mean score of 3.59. The result is obvious because the Mauritian government has initiated a list of approved NGOs and these organisations are well placed to allocate the CSR fund in needy and approved areas. Most NGOs have well-established plans and strategies and they are 'charitable' organisations closer to the individuals or groups who need assistance. Further it is observed that employees are also involved in decision making related to CSR, but on the contrary, shareholders and the other stakeholders are not too involved with a mean score close to 3.

While addressing CSR initiatives towards the different stakeholders, firms have their own perspective and objectives towards these acknowledged stakeholders as they do play an important role towards the organisations. It is revealed that 71 per cent of the companies surveyed have established their objective towards the societal and environmental impact whereas only 41 per cent clarified their needs and expectations. In addition, 38 per cent and 35 per cent set their objectives to be social care of workers and attracting/retaining HR respectively despite the fact that only 29 per cent and 9 per cent set their objectives to be internal business improvement and benchmarking respectively. Besides the above-mentioned objectives, some firms also advance that their objectives is to enable NGOs and local communities to meet their objectives by sponsoring specific projects that address the needs of their beneficiaries.

While investing in portfolios or activities, any individual or firm expects to obtain returns and the same applies for companies which invested in CSR. It is observed that 74 per cent of the companies surveyed gained from CSR activities through the enhancement of their image and reputation. Consequently, 68 per cent, 47 per cent and 32 per cent recognised that they have a better public relationships, motivated employees and better relationship with clients respectively. However, only a minority of 9 per cent stated that they benefited in terms of better access to capital. Responding firms also added that through CSR, there are more opportunities for the staff of different departments or companies of the group to meet during the community days organised by their CSR foundation, thus creating better relationships and a stronger team. The above results are in line with Santos (2011) where it was empirically found that one of the main direct benefits of CSR is better reputation. Even Dolphin's (2004) study supported that a sound reputation does contribute to a winning competitive advantage. In addition, Santos (2011) also recognised that another benefit of CSR results in increasing employees' satisfaction and according to the Deliotte Report (2008), increasing employees' satisfaction leads to a motivated workforce. Simultaneously, Santos (2011) empirically reported that satisfaction and motivation of employees have direct implications on performance, quality and internal productivity. Ruschak (2012) argued that the benefits of CSR cannot be measured directly in a financial way, as CSR activities have both direct and indirect advantages to an organisation.

In Mauritius, the focus of companies listed on the SEM and non-listed banks towards CSR can be categorised in various key areas. From the companies surveyed, it is observed that the main focus of companies is towards education (19%), followed by poverty (17%), community/livelihood development (16%), and health and safety (15%). Furthermore, it is noted that the focus of both listed companies and non-listed banks on disaster relief, environment and arts and culture are 12 per cent, 11 per cent and 10 per cent respectively. In addition to these areas, some firms also focus on leisure and sports. The results coincide with Ragodoo's (2009) findings where it was mentioned that "...health and the local community have higher ranking on the CSR agenda of Mauritian business organisations." As the one of the main focuses identified in the findings is education, the impact on this initiative is expected to benefit both the organisations and the country as a whole. The literacy rate will increase, as more students will have access to education resulting in an increase in qualified and skilled labour force. Thus, the GDP (gross domestic product) of the country will increase thereafter increasing the standard of living.

On the other hand, the main obstacles which companies face while integrating CSR in their business operations are lack of funds and time (24%), followed by lack of HR (18%), lack of know-how (15%), and lack of employees' motivation (12%). In addition, 6 per cent found that there are no expected benefits from CSR, while 3 per cent point out that unavailability of technology is the biggest obstacle to integrate CSR in their operations. Some of the companies also added that lack of management's commitment is one of the biggest obstacles. However, the results are quite obvious as companies tend to invest in activities or projects that will generate more cash flows for their survival and meeting their economic responsibilities. As CSR is a relatively new field in Mauritius, many firms do not have the necessary knowledge and competencies to deal with the topic.

Analysis to Test Differences in Stakeholder's Involvement

The Mann-Whitney Test is used to test the null hypothesis (H0) of two independent samples drawn from the same population, and under this study, the test is used to investigate whether there are differences in stakeholder's involvement between companies listed on the SEM and non-listed banks in adopting CSR initiatives.

H0: There are no differences in stakeholders' involvement between companies listed on the SEM and non-listed banks in adopting CSR initiatives.

H1: There are differences in stakeholders' involvement between companies listed on the SEM and non-listed banks in adopting CSR initiatives.

When looking at the probabilities, it is observed that most of them are less than the level of significance that is the P-value is less than 0.05. Thus there is a significant difference in the involvement of stakeholders between companies listed on the SEM and non-listed banks while adopting CSR initiatives. Therefore, H0 is rejected in favour of H1 for stakeholders such as employees, shareholders, suppliers, business partners, and customers as their probabilities are 0.019, 0.07, 0.029 and 0.01 respectively.

Considering the mean ranks of employees, shareholders, suppliers and business partners as well as customers, they are higher for non-listed banks compared to companies listed on the SEM. The findings clearly explain that non-listed banks associate their stakeholders while adopting CSR initiatives instead of taking decisions wholly according to management. When employees are involved in decision-making, they feel that they are important to the organisation which will in turn increase their satisfaction and commitment towards the organistions. As such, the finding is consistent with Santos (2011) who identified that CSR increases employee satisfaction, while Skudiene and Auruskeviciene (2012) reported that CSR has a positive impact on employees' commitment, satisfaction, trust, loyalty and motivated workforce for companies involved in CSR.

In addition, the involvement of customers is highly significant that is there is a significant difference in the involvement of CSR between non-listed banks and listed companies. While comparing their mean ranks, it is observed that the level of customers' involvement in non-listed banks is higher than in listed companies with a mean value of 26.05 and 13.94 respectively. The result is practical because the normal activities of banks depend largely on customers. Banks use the funds deposited by the customers (depositors) and lend the funds as loan to other customers (borrowers). In both ways, different customers are linked to the activities of the banks and it is therefore important for banks to involve customers in their CSR activities.

On the contrary, H1 is rejected in favour of H0 for the involvement of the local community and NGOs as their P-values are 0.407 and 0.513 respectively. It clearly means that both groups involve these stakeholders while adopting their CSR initiatives. This is because the local community have a relationship with these companies irrespective of whether they are private limited companies or public limited companies. Furthermore, the results is also obvious for NGOs because the Mauritian Government has initiated an approved list of NGOs and many companies associate themselves to these organisations while adopting CSR strategies.

Analysis to Test Differences in the Motives to Engage in CSR Activities

Thc Mann-Whitney U test, a non-parametric test, was used to compare two unpaired groups within the sample. The latter has been used as a statistical hypothesis to determine whether there are differences in the motives of engaging in CSR between the two groups namely the companies listed on the SEM and the non-listed banks.

Referring to Carroll's CSR Pyramid, firms have different responsibilities to fulfil. As a result, these responsibilities can also act as the motives for engaging in CSR. Consequently, for the analysis, the motives of engaging in CSR have been segregated into the economic responsibilities, legal responsibilities, ethical responsibilities and philanthropic responsibilities.

Economic Responsibilities

H0: There are no differences between companies listed on the SEM and non-listed banks in the motives to engage in CSR activities to fulfil their economic responsibilities.

H1: There are differences between companies listed on the SEM and non-listed banks in the motives to engage in CSR activities to fulfil their economic responsibilities.

The findings reveal that all the probabilities are insignificant that is the asymptotic significance (P-value) is greater than 0.05. Hence, H1 is rejected in favour of the null hypothesis. The results signify that there are no differences between listed companies and non-listed banks in their motives in engaging in CSR to fulfil their economic responsibilities. In line with Idowu and Filho (2009), economic responsibilities deal with the primary objective of firms which is to create profit and wealth of owners. The findings are obvious because both the listed companies and non-listed banks operate with the objective to maximise profit as they are private companies.

However, it is observed that companies listed on the SEM with a mean rank of 17.54 are more engaged in CSR in order to attract potential investors and customers compared to non-listed banks with a lower mean rank of 17.40. This is theoretically sound since listed companies issue shares to investors and the success of these organisations depends on the potential investors. Normally, these individuals inject their funds where they will have maximum returns. The findings are in line with the literature review as Hillman and Keim (2001) emphasised that investors are more enthusiastic to invest in businesses that have better reputation due to less risks associated.

Legal Responsibilities

H0: There are no differences between companies listed on the SEM and non-listed banks in the motives to engage in CSR activities to fulfil their legal responsibilities.

H1: accepted: There are differences between companies listed on the SEM and non-listed banks in the motives to engage in CSR activities to fulfil their legal responsibilities.

It is observed that the P-value exceeds the 5 per cent level significance meaning that there are no differences between the two groups. Hence, H0 is accepted. The findings are obvious because in Mauritius, organisations irrespective of the sector in which they operate are bound to contribute 2 per cent of their book profit towards CSR that is both listed companies and non-listed banks have to contribute towards CSR.

Ethical Responsibilities

H0: There are no differences between companies listed on the SEM and non-listed banks in the motives to engage in CSR activities to fulfil their ethical responsibilities.

H1: There are differences between companies listed on the SEM and non-listed banks in the motives to engage in CSR activities to fulfil their ethical responsibilities.

The probabilities are statistically insignificant as the P-value is greater than level of significance 0.05. Thus, H1 is rejected in favour of H0 meaning that there are no significant differences between firms listed on the SEM and non-listed banks in the motives to engage in CSR to fulfil ethical responsibilities.

As ethical responsibilities is referred to do what is right, just and fair, companies have to operate according to the expectations of the society as well as other stakeholders and avoid prohibited actions. The above findings reveal that both groups are engaged in CSR in order to fulfil their ethical responsibilities. It is also noted that both groups are motivated to engage in CSR due to third parties' pressure, community's pressure as well as the retention and attraction of employees as their probabilities are 0.221, 0.222 and

0.294 respectively, while the probability of social concerns relating products and services is 0.729.

Philanthropic Responsibilities

H0: There are no differences between companies listed on the SEM and non-listed banks in the motives to engage in CSR activities to fulfil their philanthropic responsibilities.

H1: There are differences between companies listed on the SEM and non-listed banks in the motives to engage in CSR activities to fulfil their philanthropic responsibilities

Based on the P-value, H0 is accepted. Even if the probabilities are insignificant, most listed companies engage themselves in CSR to support NGOs compared to non-listed banks as their mean ranks are 19.33 and 13.10 respectively, while on the other hand more non-listed banks are engaged in CSR due to philanthropy. In addition, the findings are obvious because both groups are motivated to engage in CSR with the objective to fulfil their philanthropic responsibilities that is to be good citizens.

Analysis to Test Differences on the Impact of CSR

The Kruskal-Wallis Test is a non-parametric test for testing whether samples originate from the same distribution and it is used for comparing more than two samples that are independent or not related and it was used in order to investigate whether there are differences in the impact of CSR on companies operating in the different sectors. In line with the literature review, Brejning (2012) pointed out that the impact of CSR is dominated advantages and disadvantages of CSR to businesses, and the advantages analysed were identified by Santos (2011), Porter and Kramer (2006) and Schiebel and Pöchtrager (2003).

H0: There are no sectorial differences in the impact of CSR.

H1: There are sectorial differences in the impact of CSR.

The reported statistics confirm that there are no sectorial differences in the impact of CSR. Irrespective of the sector in which the companies are operating, the impact of CSR is more or less the same for all of them. The overall impact of CSR in terms of operational costs is more or less the same for all the sectors. However, it is observed that CSR has a greater impact on companies operating in the debt, leisure, hotels and transport sectors (20.50) than the others.

Also, it is noted that all companies are benefiting from CSR. The results are obvious as they are in line with the findings of Skudiene and Auruskeviciene (2012) who advanced that CSR has a positive impact on employees' commitment, satisfaction, trust, loyalty and motivated workforce, while Santos (2011) found that satisfaction and motivation of employees have direct implications on performance, quality and internal productivity. Furthermore, the studies of Berrone *et al.* (2007) showed that CSR enhances the performance of firms as it creates intangible assets such as image and reputation, while Kraisornsuthasinee and Swierczek (2009) reported that CSR enhances the brand image and allows the companies to differentiate, gain a price premium and build the brand based on CSR values and sustainability actions.

Carroll and Buchholtz (2009) pointed out that CSR enables firms to engage in new opportunities in order to understand and enhance the market place so as to be competitive and innovation also helps companies to improve their position in the industry. Broomhill (2007) also highlighted that doing the right thing enables firms to offset risk. The benefits of CSR are also interconnected that is one benefit leads to another benefit. In addition to these benefits, companies also benefit in terms of better profitability as CSR has an indirect positive impact on companies' financial performance.

To determine the relationship between the number of years engaged in CSR and the level of investment in CSR, the Pearson Chi-square test along with Phi and Cramer's V were used.

H0: There is no relationship between the numbers of years engaged in CSR and the level of investment in CSR.

H1: There is a relationship between the numbers of years engaged in CSR and the level of investment in CSR.

Based on the Pearson Chi-square value and the significance level (.002), H0 is rejected in favour of H1 . Therefore, the results indicate that the level of investment in CSR largely depends on the number of years companies are engaged in CSR. It is observed that as the number of years increases, the companies move from CSR newcomers towards CSR leaders. For example, since CSR became mandatory in 2009, 60 per cent of the companies surveyed are newcomers which mean that their level of investment in CSR activities is low while only 7.7 per cent are CSR leader with extensive levels of investment in CSR. On the other hand, 38.5 per cent are CSR leaders, which are engaged in CSR for more than 20 years, while there no companies with low level of investments for the same number of years.

Factors Encouraging Listed Companies and Non-listed Banks to Engage in CSR

Factor analysis has been used to regroup different variables in specific categories and followed by the principal components used as predictor or criterion variables in subsequent analyses. Respondents were asked to rate on a 5-point Likert scale the factors that encouraged them to engage in CSR. The different statements were grouped into four components namely benefits, concerns, external pressures and legal using the principal component analysis (PCA) techniques as shown in Table 15.1.

Following the Kaiser-Meyer-Olkin (KMO) and Bartlett's test, it was found that the KMO value is 0.712 and a value close to 1 indicates that the patterns of correlations are relatively compact and so the factor analysis should yield distinct and reliable factors. Correspondingly, the value is good as it falls into the range and thus the factor analysis is appropriate to the variables under the study. Cronbach's Alpha is greater than 0.5 apart from the legal component which is 0.398. It is deduced that reliability of the benefit component (0.851) is good, concerns component (0.78) is acceptable while for external pressures (0.563) and legal (0.398) components are poor.

Table 15.1

Factors Encouraging Companies to Engage in CSR

	Component				*Communalities H*
	Benefits	*Concerns*	*External Pressures*	*Legal*	
Legal Obligation				0.788	0.683
Pressure of Third Parties			0.699		0.741
Government Financial Incentives				0.706	0.752
Success of Organisation		0.727			0.795
Improvement in Turnover & Customer Loyalty	0.67				0.626
Community Pressure	0.836				0.787
Differentiation Opportunities	0.659				0.631
Social Concerns relating to products and services		0.717			0.618
Attracting Potential Investors/ and Customers	0.693				0.753
Support NGOs		0.530			0.588
Retaining and Attracting Employees	0.795				0.764
Stakeholder Requirements			0.871		0.855
Environmental Concerns relating to products and services		0.806			0.688
Philanthropy		0.735			0.609
Eigenvalues (%)	4.772	2.488	1.483	1.147	
Per cent of variance explained	23.981	23.238	12.332	11.088	
Cronbach's Alpha	0.851	0.78	0.563	0.398	
Total of per cent of variance explained	70.64				
KMO of Sampling Adequacy	0.712				
	Approx. Chi-Square				202.752
Bartlett's Test of Sphericity	Df				91
	Significance				.000

Extraction Method: Principal Component Analysis.

Rotation Method: Varimax with Kaiser Normalisation.

In addition, Bartlett's test of Sphericity tests the null hypothesis and is an indicator of the strength of relationship among variables. For the above variables, the Bartlett's test was 202.752 with a significance level of 0.000. As the KMO is highly significant, the strength of relationship among variable is strong, and therefore we can proceed with a factor analysis for the data and it means that the correlation matrix is not an identity matrix. The final factor solution reduce the variables captured through 14 statements into four distinct components and the factor groupings with loading lesser than .40 were suppressed. Table 15.1 shows the results of the PCA with an octagonal rotation for the 14 variables used in determining the factors that encouraged firms to engage in CSR.

The eigenvalue which represents the proportion of variance attributed to a factor is used to determine the number of factors that should be retained from the factor analysis. Prior to the rotation, the first factor accounted for 34.08 per cent of total variance compared to the other three factors which were 17.77 per cent, 10.59 per cent and 8.19 per cent. However, after extraction, it accounted for 23.98 per cent compared to 23.24 per cent, 12.33 per cent and 11.09 per cent.

Conclusion

Under this study, a broad understanding of the concept of CSR was reviewed. As such, the findings revealed significant facts related to the CSR practices of companies listed on the SEM and non-listed banks. Stakeholders are one of the most influential factors towards an organisation, and this study tried to identify and assess the involvement of stakeholders between non-listed banks and companies listed on the SEM. It was also noted that companies involve the different stakeholders in the planning and implementation process of CSR. However, it was found that there are sectorial differences in the involvement of stakeholders.

Furthermore, the study pointed out that there are no differences in the reasons that motivated listed companies and non-listed banks to engage in CSR in order to fulfil their economic, legal, ethical and philanthropic responsibilities. The factors that encouraged firms to engage in CSR were also regrouped in four different components namely benefits, concerns, external pressures and legal. The results also revealed that there is a relationship between the number of years engaged in CSR and the level of investment in CSR, and the level of sales is positively correlated to the level of investment in CSR.

It was also noted that half of the companies surveyed have their own CSR departments or dedicated teams to address CSR and the concept is integrated in a formal and structured way. Among the different companies surveyed, it was found that funds are the major resources allocated towards CSR as all companies are bound to contribute 2 per cent of their book profit towards CSR, and the concept proved that it is much beneficial to companies as it enhanced the image and reputation of the company as well as better public relationship. Furthermore, the study also highlighted that there are no sectorial differences in the impact of CSR on different issues related to the organisations. However, while integrating CSR within the organisation, the main obstacles were lack of funds and lack of time.

This study revealed that there are significant differences in the involvement of stakeholders such as employees, shareholders and customers in the planning and implementation process of CSR in organisations and it was also observed that listed companies involve these stakeholder lesser than banks. Therefore, it is important for companies listed on the SEM to increase the involvement of stakeholders in their decision-making relating to CSR. While involving them in the decision-making process, employees' motivation is increased leading to high productivity. Employees can be involved by organising seminars and workshops where employees can share their ideas. In this dynamic environment, nearly everyone has access to the Internet. Customers also can be involved in decision making by posting polls on the web and requiring customers to respond to them or even give their suggestions through mails or suggestion boxes. This will enhance the reputation as well as the image of the company. Shareholders' involvement can be achieved at the annual general meeting (AGM); shareholders along with management can debate on the future;

CSR activities where new and innovative ideas can be generated in favour of the organisation.

In addition, it was also highlighted that the main focus of the CSR initiatives of companies addresses mainly education, health and safety, environment, poverty, arts and culture, disaster relief, and community or livelihood development. However, it was noted that only a minority focuses on leisure and sports. Therefore, it is important for firms to review their focus related to their CSR initiatives and integrate leisure and sports appropriately as the need for sports is becoming more and more important in Mauritius as the island is the third country in the world which has the highest percentage of diabetics.

Additionally, as revealed in the study, another obstacle in integrating CSR is lack of know-how. As CSR is a new concept in Mauritius, firms, especially newly established one, do not have the necessary expertise about the concept to integrate it in the organisation effectively and efficiently. Thus, it is important for the government as well as the NEF to organise seminars and workshops which will educate companies on issues pertaining to CSR activities.

This study sets out to explore the CSR practices for companies listed on the SEM and non-listed banks. The groups surveyed are companies with high turnover and are considered to be large organisations. It might be complex to generalise the findings for all companies in Mauritius. As a result, future study can analyse the CSR practices of small and medium enterprises (SMEs) given the growing importance of SMEs to the Mauritian economy. In addition, most studies related to CSR practices have focused on developed countries, investigating the relationships between control variables and motivators such as firms' size and profitability to CSR. There are only a few studies on CSR for the case of Mauritius and most of them are specific to issues such as poverty alleviation. Therefore, it is important to carry out future research to complement and validate this research while going more in depth to issues pertaining to the resources allocated towards CSR. Another focus could be studies to examine the link between firm's performance and CSR activities.

References

Andriof, J. and S. Waddock (2002). *Unfolding Stakeholder Thinking: Theory, Responsibility and Engagement*. UK: Greenleaf Publishing Limited.

Banhegyi, S., B. Bates, K. Booysen, A. Bosch, M. Botha, S. Botha, P. Cunningham, S. Goodman, W. Ladzani, O. Lotz, S. Musengi, A. Steward Smith, K. Visser and O. Williams (2008). *Business Management*. South Africa: Pearson.

Barkemeyer, R. (2011). "Corporate Perceptions of Sustainability Challenges in Developed and Developing Countries: Constituting a CSR Divide?", *Social Responsibility Journal* 7(2): 257–81.

Berrone, P., J. Surroca and J.A. Tribó (2007). "Corporate Ethical Identity as a Determinant of Firm Performance: A Test of the Mediating Role of Stakeholder Satisfaction", *Journal of Business Ethics* 76: 35-53.

Bhattacharyya, S.S. (2010). "Exploring the Concept of Strategic Corporate Social Responsibility for an Integrated Perspective", *European Business Review* 22(1): 82-101.

Bhattacharyya, S.S., A. Sahay, A.P. Arora and A. Chaturvedi (2008). "A Toolkit for Designing Firm Level Strategic Corporate Social Responsibility (CSR) Initiatives", *Social Responsibility Journal* 4(3): 265–82.

Brejning, J. (2012). *Corporate Social Responsibility and the Welfare State*. England: Ashgate Publishing Limited.

Broomhill, R. (2007). "Corporate Social Responsibility: Key Issues and Debates", *Dunstan Paper*. Vol 1, from: *http://firgoa.usc.es/drupal/files/Ray_Broomhill.pdf* (accessed 10 February 2012)

Budget Speech 2008/09, from: *http://www.gov.mu/portal/goc/mof/files/bud0809.pdf* (accessed 30 March 2012).

Buciuniene, I. and R. Kazlauskaite (2012). "The Linkage between HRM, CSR and Performance Outcomes", *Baltic Journal of Management* 7(1): 5–24.

Carroll, A.B. (1979). "Three-Dimensional Conceptual Model of Corporate Performance", *The Academy of Management Review* 4(4): 497-505.

———. (1991). "The Pyramid of Corporate Social Responsibility: Toward the Moral Management of Organisational Stakeholders", *Business Horizons* 34(4): 39-48.

Carroll, A.B. and A.K. Buchholtz (2009). *Business and Society: Ethics and Stakeholder Management*, 7th edition. USA: Cengage Learning.

———. (2011). *Business & Society: Ethics, Sustainability and Stakeholder Management*. USA: Cengage Learning.

Chatterjee, D.K. (2011). *Encyclopedia of Global Justice*. London: Springer.

Chen, H. and X. Wang (2011). "Corporate Social Responsibility and Corporate Financial Performance in China: An Empirical Research from Chinese Firms", *Corporate Governance* 11(4): 361–370.

Cohen, L., L. Manion, K. Morrison, R.B. Keith and K.R.B. Morrison (2007). *Research Methods in Education*. Oxon: Routledge.

Crisóstomo, V.L., F.S. Freire and F.C. Vasconcellos (2011). "Corporate Social Responsibility, Firm Value and Financial Performance in Brazil", *Social Responsibility Journal* 7(2): 295–309.

Deliotte Report (2008). *Review of Corporate Social Responsibility Policies and Actions in Mauritius and Rodrigues*, from: *http://winmauritius.net/Userfiles/file/Review_of_CSR_policies_in_mtius.pdf* (accessed 15 March 2012)

Ditlev-Simonsen, C.D. (2010). "From Corporate Social Responsibility Awareness to Action?", *Social Responsibility Journal* 6(3): 452-68.

Dolphin, R.R. (2004). "Corporate Reputation—A Value Creating Strategy", *Corporate Governance* 4(3): 77–92.

Dusuki, A.W. (2008). "What does Islam Say about Corporate Social Responsibility?", *Review of Islamic Economics* 12(1): 5-28.

EMIT (2007) *Training Workshop on Improving Business Performance through Sustainability*, from: *http://www.emitcsr.de/documents/annex3_CSR_Framework%20Questionnaire.pdf* (accessed 10 March 2012)

European Competitiveness Report (2008). *Overview of the links between Corporate Social Responsibility and Competitiveness*, from: *http://ec.europa.eu/enterprise/policies/sustainablebusiness/files/csr/documents/csrreportv002_en.pdf* (accessed 23 February 2012)

Evans, N. and J. Sawyer (2010). "CSR and Stakeholders of Small Businesses in Regional South Australia", *Social Responsibility Journal* 6(3): 433-51.

Freeman, R.E. (1984). *Strategic Management: A Stakeholder Approach*. Boston: Pitman, from: *http://www.zfwu.de/fileadmin/pdf/3_2004/Freeman_HansenBodeMossmeyer*

Friedman, M. (1970). "The Social Responsibility of Business is to Increase its Profits", *The New York Times Magazine*, from: *http://www.umich.edu/~thecore/doc/Friedman.pdf* (accessed 8 February 2012)

Galbreath, J. (2009). "Building Corporate Social Responsibility into Strategy", *European Business Review* 21(2): 109-27.

Gokulsing, R.D. (2011). "CSR Matters in the Development of Mauritius", *Social Responsibility Journal* 7(2): 218-33.

Gupta, M. (2009). *Principles of Management*. New Delhi: PHI Learning Private limited.

Hemphill, T. (2004). "Corporate Citizenship: The Case for a New Corporate Governance Model", *Business & Society Review* 109(3): 1-23.

Hillman, A.J. and G.D. Keim (2001). "Shareholder Value, Stakeholder Management, and Social Issues: What's the Bottom Line?", *Strategic Management Journal* 22(2): 125-39.

Huniche, M. and E.H. Pedersen (2006). *Corporate Citizenship in Developing Countries: New Partnership Perspectives*. Denmark: Copenhagen Business School Press.

ICCA (2005). *CSR Globe*, from: *http://www.csrglobe.com/pdf/Report.pdf* (accessed 20 March 2012)

Idowu, S.O. and W.L. Filho (2009). *Professionals' Perspectives of Corporate Social Responsibility*. New York: Springer.

Jamali, D. and R. Mishak (2007). "Corporate Social Responsibility (CSR): Theory and Practice in a Developing Country Context", *Journal of Business Ethics* 72: 362.

Keinert, C. (2008). *Corporate Social Responsibility as an International Strategy*. Heidelberg: Physica-Verlag.

Khemir, S. and C. Baccouche (2010). "Analysis of the Determinants of Corporate Social Responsibility Disclosure in the Annual Reports of Tunisian Listed Firms", *Research in Accounting in Emerging Economies* 10: 119-44.

Kraisornsuthasinee, S. and F.W. Swierczek (2009). "Doing Well by Doing Good in Thailand", *Social Responsibility Journal* 5(4): 550–65.

Maignan, I. and O.C. Ferrell (2000). "Measuring Corporate Citizenship in Two Countries: The Case of the United States and France", *Journal of Business Ethics* 23: 283-97.

McWilliams, A. and D. Siegel (2001). "Corporate Social Responsibility: A Theory of the Firm Perspective", *The Academy of Management Review* 26(1): 117-27.

Meyer, M.M. and S.E. Fienberg (1992). *Assessing Evaluation Studies: The Case of Bilingual Education Strategies*. Washington: National Press Academy.

Mullerat, R. (2010). *International Corporate Social Responsibility: The Role of Corporations in the Economic Order of the 21st Century*. The Netherlands: Kluwer Law International.

Núñez, G. (2008). *Promoting Corporate Social Responsibility in Small and Medium Enterprises in the Caribbean*, from: *http://www.eclac.org/washington/publicaciones/xml/7/34237/S3EPR-WAS-L2930i-P.pdf*

Pantic, S. and F. Mesche (2011). *Corporate Social Responsibility in European Developing Countries: Exploring the interplay between companies and consumers in Bosnia and Herzegovina*, from: *http://www.iei.liu.se/program/smio/722a31/file-archive/1.273422/SvjetlanaPantic_FranziskaMesche_CorporateSocialResponsibilityInEuropeanDevelopingCountries.pdf* (accessed 15 March 2012)

Porter, M.E. and M.R. Kramer (2006). "Strategy and Society: The Link between Competitive Advantage and Corporate Social Responsibility". *Harvard Business Review* 84(12): 2-17.

Ragodoo, N.J.F. (2009). "CSR as a Tool to Fight against Poverty: The Case of Mauritius", *Social Responsibility Journal* 5(1): 19–33.

Rahman, S. (2011). "Evaluation of Definitions: Ten Dimensions of Corporate Social Responsibility', *World Review of Business Research* 1(1): 166–76.

Roome, N. (2006). "Innovation, Competitiveness and Responsibility—The New Frontier of Corporate Responsibility", *Ethical Corporation*.

Ruschak, K. (2012). "Corporate Social Responsibility and the Theories that it Generates from", Thesis, 177pp.

Santos, M. (2011). "CSR in SMEs: Strategies, Practices, Motivations and Obstacles", *Social Responsibility Journal* 7(3): 490–508.

Schiebel, W. and S. Pöchtrager (2003). "Corporate Ethics as a Factor for Success—The Measurement Instrument of the University of Agricultural Sciences (BOKU), Vienna", *Supply Chain Management: An International Journal* 8(2): 116-21.

Shen, C. and Y. Chang (2009). "Ambition versus Conscience, does Corporate Social Responsibility Pay off? The Application of Matching Methods", *Journal of Business Ethics* 88: 133-53.

Sims, R.R. (2003). *Ethics and Corporate Social Responsibility: Why Giants Fall*. USA: Praeger Publishers.

Skudiene, V. and V. Auruskeviciene (2012). "The Contribution of Corporate Social Responsibility to Internal Employee Motivation", *Baltic Journal of Management* 7(1): 49–67.

Vallabhaneni, D. (2009). *What's Your MBA IQ: A Manager's Career Development Tool*. New Jersey: John Wiley.

Visser, W. (2005). *Revisiting Carroll's CSR Pyramid: An African Perspective*, from: *http://www.waynevisser.com/wpcontent/uploads/2012/04/chapter_wvisser_africa_csr_pyramid.pdf* (accessed 16 January 2012)

Waddock, S.A. and S.B. Graves (1997). "The Corporate Social Performance Financial Performance Link", *Strategic Management Journal* 18(4).

Wartick, S.L. and P.L. Cochran (1985). "The Evolution of the Corporate Social Performance Mode", *Academy of Management Review*: 758-69.

Wood, D.J. (1991). "Corporate Social Performance Revisited", *Academy of Management Review* 16(4): 691-718.

Wright, P. and S. Ferris (1997). "Agency Conflict and Corporate Strategy: The Effect of Divestment on Corporate Value", *Strategic Management Journal* 18: 77-83.

16

P. SHYAM • JIBITESH RATH

Corporate Social Responsibility at NMDC Ltd

Business and Social Vision of NMDC Ltd

National Mineral Development Corporation (NMDC) Ltd is a Central Public Sector Enterprise (CPSE) under the Ministry of Steel, Government of India (GoI), primarily engaged in the business of exploring minerals and developing mines to produce raw material for the industry. Today, NMDC Ltd is the largest iron ore producer in the country with four operating mines in Bailadila (Chhattisgarh) and two in Bellary-Hospet range (Karnataka), and Diamond Mining Project, Panna in Madhya Pradesh among other operations. NMDC is also entering into manufacturing of steel by setting up a green field integrated steel plant at Nagarnar.

However, NMDC has chosen not to rest on its laurels and has spread its wings in the area of corporate social responsibility (CSR). Being a responsible corporate citizen, it has been a pioneer in addressing its responsibility towards society. Its CSR programme is as old as the company itself. NMDC believes that the well-being of society at large is a pre-requisite for the progress of business and prosperity of the organisation.

While pursuing its business vision of expansion in ongoing activities in India and abroad, as also by diversifying into new areas of mineral exploration, NMDC seeks to add value to its CSR effort by aiming for eradication of illiteracy, minimising child and maternal mortality, poverty alleviation and affordable health care in the surrounding villages of its project areas.

Policy on CSR, Including Board-approved Policy

As enunciated earlier, the philosophy underlying the CSR programme in NMDC is the belief that the well-being of society at large is a pre-requisite for the progress of business and prosperity of the organisation. Keeping this in mind, policy makers in NMDC have framed a broad based, well thought out and transparent policy document with respect to its CSR programme. The policy document is widely circulated and is also displayed in the official website of the company.

Objectives

With the aforementioned philosophy and the principle of inclusive growth forming their core thought, the Board of Directors has laid out the following policy objectives of CSR in NMDC keeping the following focus areas in sight:

- Literacy/education/cultural development.
- Safe drinking water/health care and sanitation.
- Skill development for sustainable income generation and livelihood.
- Agriculture and infrastructure development.

Focus areas are:

- Suitable assistance to handicapped and mentally challenged children and underprivileged people in the society.
- Promote awareness programmes against social evils such as alcoholism, AIDS, etc., and to spread the awareness of legal rights and responsibilities.
- Suitable assistance to the victims of natural calamities such as floods, earthquakes, epidemics, etc., in any part of the country.
- Promotion of cultural, social and sports activities.
- Any other area that may need coverage under the CSR policy, depending on the necessity, circumstances with the

approval of CMD and subsequently to be informed to the board.

Budget

NMDC's CSR Policy briefly lays down the following guidelines for allocation and expenditure of CSR Budget:

- The budgetary provision in a financial year towards CSR initiatives shall be at least 2 per cent of the average net profit of the company made during the last three financial years, immediately preceding the year.
- If the allocated budget remains unutilised in any financial year, the board in its report made as specified in the Companies Act shall specify the reasons for the same.
- The unutilised fund will not lapse, instead it will be transferred to a CSR fund, to ensure that the surplus arising out of CSR projects will not form part of the business profit of the company.
- At least 80 per cent of the amount allocated for CSR activities shall have to be spent for implementation of activities in the project area.
- Distribution shall be 80-85 per cent in NMDC project areas/establishments, 5-10 per cent in backward areas identified by Planning Commission for Backward Region Grant Fund, 5 per cent for emergencies like relief assistance during natural calamities, contribution to Prime Minister's Relief Fund, National Disaster Management Authority or any other fund set up by the central government for the welfare of scheduled castes (SCs), scheduled tribes (STs), other backward classes (OBCs), minorities or women.
- Expenditure not exceeding 5 per cent of the CSR Budget on base line surveys needs assessment studies, capacity building exercises, training, seminars, workshops, corporate communication, etc.

Consultative Mechanism

Besides this, NMDC's CSR policy has spawned a unique and widely acclaimed consultative mechanism covering all the stakeholders right from village/community level to district level and extending right upto state government level coordination.

Implementation

Coupled with this consultative mechanism, NMDC has a three pronged approach to CSR programme implementation and these are:

- Directly by NMDC,
- In partnership with state governments by entering into a Memorandum of Understanding (MoU) with the concerned state governments, and
- Through reputed and experienced non-governmental organisations (NGOs)/service providers or fellow public sector enterprises, on nomination basis.

This has given the CSR programme at NMDC immense flexibility and easy operability.

Monitoring

CSR proposals, as well as the corresponding budget proposals, are examined by the CSR and Sustainability Committee of Directors, headed by an independent director, and recommendations of the Committee are finally put up for the approval of the Board. Implementation is monitored through a system of joint inspections with the relevant service providers/NGOs/state government officials, and the monitoring of CSR programmes is done by CSR and Sustainability Committee during its review meetings.

Modalities/Mechanisms for Implementation of CSR in NMDC

As stated *supra*, NMDC follows a three pronged approach on CSR implementation and the relevant guidelines are briefly spelled out here:

- *Directly by NMDC*: Activities that can be implemented either directly by NMDC or by engaging a contractor for infrastructure development shall be taken up directly, periodical activities like medical camps, distribution of school uniforms, etc., donation of ambulance and other medical equipment shall also be taken up by NMDC. The CSR works executed through contractors shall follow the same procedure followed for other NMDC works. To accelerate the pace of development/optimise utilisation of resources, especially in the backward regions, NMDC may join hands/pool resources with other CPSEs among other guidelines.
- *Through NGOs/Voluntary Organisations* (VOs): CSR projects of long duration focusing on overall sustainable development in a given time frame needing a dedicated team and full time attention shall be considered for implementation through NGOs/VOs. NGOs/VOs/service providers are identified based on their credentials, long standing performance in respective fields. NGOs/VOs with proven performance and tax exemption benefits shall be preferred. NGOs approaching with their own proposals shall be examined in terms of the comprehensive nature, specialist area and/or compatibility with the CSR policy objectives of NMDC. All claims/installments of the NGOs for the works completed shall be supported by proper bills and receipts/documents in support of their claim.
- *In Partnership with District/State Government Authorities*: Where it is not possible to take CSR activities directly or through NGOs/VOs/trusts/contractors due to various reasons/constraints, these shall be carried out with the help of respective state/district authorities. The district/state authorities may submit their CSR proposals which shall be funded by NMDC for initiation and implementation, provided these schemes match with that of NMDC's CSR policy and for such CSR works implemented through local bodies/agencies nominated by the district/state authorities

funds shall be released in suitable installments based on progress and utilisation certificate.

- *Through /in Partnership with Other PSUs*: Joint projects with other PSUs may be finalised after thoroughly deliberating on clarity of role, financial outlay, implementing agency, socio-economic gains to the community etc.; the draft proposal shall be further discussed; and recommendations made by a board level committee are put up to the board for approval.

Innovative Practices in CSR

NMDC's CSR has been hailed as a role model by the Department of Public Enterprises, GoI, for other CPSEs to emulate. The novel consultative mechanism adopted by NMDC's CSR programme has, especially, been the object of praise. The inclusiveness of the CSR programme is enhanced by this multilevel consultation process. The involvement of stakeholders starts at the grass-roots community level, followed by district level interaction and culminating in coordination with state governments has ensured conceptual clarity, effective implementation and proper monitoring of the CSR programmes in NMDC. This innovative consultative structure has given NMDC's CSR a distinct edge, as also the variety of initiatives.

CSR Awareness Among Employees

Given the long tradition of CSR in NMDC, it is common belief that each and every employee is aware of the corporation's CSR effort. This awareness is further strengthened by the use of all channels of communication like house magazines, special issues of the in-house magazines, project joint councils, apex joint councils, SC/ST welfare association meetings, as also other welfare association meetings and of course periodical updates on the corporation's website, to name a few.

Details of contribution towards CSR in the last 3 years (including efforts towards social inclusion, health education, skill development, etc.) in given in the following table.

NMDC has been at the forefront of CSR and has been one of the biggest CSR spenders among CPSEs, as is borne out by the statistics for CSR expenditure in the last three financial years given below:

Sl. No.	*Financial Year*	*CSR Expenditure (in ₹ lakhs)*
01	2011-12	8671.75
02	2012-13	10110.04
03	2013-14	13141.96

Some of the Major CSR Undertaken by the Company

Literacy and Education

Scope

Recognising education as an integral and critical aspect of human development and a powerful instrument of emancipation, NMDC's focus is increasingly on improving the literacy levels and quality of education.

Framework

Literacy and educational activities are carried on within the framework of provision of infrastructure (like school buildings, hostels, transport facilities, etc.), improving quality of education, provision of educational aids, education of girl child, running of technical education facilities, scholarships, etc.

Sphere of Activities

Residential School at Nagarnar

A residential school has been established in the year 2010-11 with 194 tribal boys and girls mostly drawn from the interior and remotest villages of Bastar District. This school will be expanded gradually up to 10+2 level. At present, the school and residential facility are fully functional in a *pucca*, semi-permanent building. Construction of a full-fledged school and residential complex is under progress. Present strength is 431 students in classes I to VI.

Industrial Training Institutes (ITIs)

An ITI, initially with Welder and Mason trades, has started functioning from 2010-11 for the benefit of the tribal students of Bastar District mainly focusing on the surrounding villages of Nagarnar, where NMDC is setting up an integrated steel plant. Every year, 28 students are admitted in this ITI. NMDC has established one ITI at Bhansi in South Bastar District, Dantewada. There are five trades in this ITI and every year, 76 students are admitted to various trades. All the tribal students are imparted free education in this ITI.

Polytechnic College at Dantewada

In its endeavour to bring technical education to the doorsteps of the tribal youth of Bastar, a polytechnic has been established at Dantewada, south Bastar District in the year 2010-11. The present intake is 126 (63 in each mechanical and electrical disciplines) each year. Lateral entry in second year: 10 in each discipline. Plans are being drawn to start two new trades from the ensuing year of 2015-16. The Chhattisgarh Government has allotted about 8 acres for the polytechnic. Construction of permanent building and establishment of a full-fledged campus at an estimated expenditure of ₹3,194.80 lakh is in progress. An amount of ₹859.83 lakh has been spent and the building is expected to be ready by the end of this year. This is the only polytechnic college in Chhattisgarh which is totally operated by a public sector undertaking (PSU) without any contribution from the Government of Chhattisgarh.

NMDC management has approved the establishment of another polytechnic college near Nagarnar, Bastar District, and the tendering process for award of work of construction is in progress.

Siksha Sahayog Yojana

NMDC Siksha Sahayog Yojana, a unique scheme granting scholarships to the poor tribal and SC students of seven districts of Bastar region, Chhattisgarh, and eight villages surrounding Donimalai Project, Karnataka, has been extended to about 18,000 students to continue academic pursuit beyond 8th class up to graduation in engineering/medicine. Under this scheme, scholarship is granted from class IX onwards till graduation and the amount is paid through their individual accounts in post offices/banks.

A survey has brought out that this initiative has been widely accepted and has started positively impacting the students and also their families. During 2010-11, the scheme has been enriched with innovative value added activities like debate competitions, sports events, study tours, science exhibitions, etc., relating to personality development.

Education Improvement Programme

NMDC has implemented an education improvement programme in 84 government primary schools in Dantewada block of south Bastar District, aimed at reducing dropout rate, improving education standards, etc., through special initiatives. A total of 4,200 students, mostly tribals, have benefited from this programme.

Balika Siksha Yojana

NMDC has introduced a focused initiative called 'Balika Siksha Yojana' for the benefit of the tribal girl students of Bastar region. Under this scheme, girl students are being sponsored for professional courses in nursing (both GNM and B.Sc. Nursing). The entire expenditure is met by NMDC.

In the first year of 2011-12, 25 tribal girls from Bastar region have been admitted to nursing courses in M/s Apollo Hospitals, Hyderabad. During the academic years 2012-13, 2013-14 and 2014-15, 40 tribal girls in each year were sponsored to these courses in Apollo College & School of Nursing, Hyderabad. Ten more students of Bijapur District, Chhattisgarh, were also sponsored for different nursing courses in 2011-12.

Health Care and Hygiene

Scope

Extending free medical treatment to local tribal/poor people in the project areas and partnering with the state governments and other agencies in providing infrastructure.

Framework

Health care activities are carried on within the framework of provision of free treatment in project hospitals, development of infrastructure, operating mobile medical vans in remote villages, etc.

Sphere of Activities

Free Medical Treatment at Project Hospitals in Karnataka and Chhattisgarh

NMDC is extending free medical facilities to the local tribal/poor people in its project hospitals at Kirandul, Bacheli, Jagdalpur (Nagarnar), Donimalai and Panna. Both indoor and outdoor treatment facilities, including X-rays, pathological tests, medicines, diet to inpatients are provided free of cost. Annually, more than 90,000 outdoor and 9,000 indoor patients are provided free treatment in these hospitals. Ambulance services are provided to interior villages to bring serious patients for treatment in project hospitals.

Hospital on Wheels

In addition, NMDC is also operating 'Hospitals on Wheels,' the mobile medical vans with latest equipment, doctors and para-medical staff, in 37 tribal villages around its project areas in Bastar division providing free medical treatment at the doorsteps of more than 40,000 tribal people.

Construction of a Hospital Partnering Red Cross Society, Hyderabad

NMDC has extended a financial assistance of ₹50.00 lakh for construction of a hospital in partnership mode with Red Cross Society, Hyderabad, for treatment in all five systems of medicine *viz.*, Ayurveda, Yoga and Naturopathy, Unani, Siddha, and Homeopathy along with a research centre under one roof.

Financial Support for Establishing a Medical College at Jagdalpur

NMDC has contributed an amount of ₹50.00 crore to the Government of Chhattisgarh to establish a medical college at Jagdalpur in Bastar region considering the immense benefits to the poor tribal people. As per the MoU signed between NMDC and Government of Chhattisgarh, five seats have been allocated to the wards of NMDC employees apart from preferential treatment to the villagers of eight affected villages of NISP and other residents of villages within 10 km radius of NISP.

Medical Camps in Chhattisgarh and Karnataka

Every year, free eye camps are organised for the benefit of the tribal people suffering from cataract. Further, free orthopaedic, gynaecology, ENT, dermatology, etc., camps are also organised in different surrounding villages in which super specialist doctors participate. Besides these camps, NMDC extends financial and material assistance for conducting special camps on AIDS awareness, family welfare, Pulse Polio Immunisation programmes, etc.

Infrastructure

Roads and Bridges

Construction of Bijapur-Gangalur road of 23.4 km length, including a vented causeway on Cherpal Nallah was taken up in partnership with the Government of Chhattisgarh during the year 2007-08 at a cost of ₹1,108.80 lakh. The work was completed during 2009-10.

Construction of Palnar-Sameli-Aranpur road in south Bastar (Dantewada) District in partnership with the Government of Chhattisgarh at a cost of ₹1,931.31 lakh during the year 2012-13. Expenditure till date is ₹1,992.54 lakh. The work is expected to be completed during 2014-15. The length of the road is 19.6 km.

Construction of a high level bridge over river Dankini at Dantewada has been taken up in partnership with the Government of Chhattisgarh at a cost of ₹525.96 lakh during the year 2010-11. Expenditure till date is ₹525.96 lakh. It is expected to be completed during 2014-15.

Construction of bypass for Jagdalpur: It is NMDC is partnering with the Government of Chhattisgarh for the construction of bypass road for Jagdalpur from Marenga to Adwal over a distance of 19.4 km at a cost of ₹3,586.20 lakh during the year 2011-12. Expenditure till date is ₹2,000.00 lakh. It is expected to be completed during 2014-15.

Construction of Gaurav Path at Dantewada: NMDC has partnered with the Government of Chhattisgarh for construction of Gaurav Path—four way lane at Dantewada over a stretch of 5.6 km at a cost of ₹1,300.00 lakh. Expenditure till date is ₹1,025.00 lakh. It is expected to be completed during 2014-15.

Reconstruction of bypass road from Bhejapadar to Jagdalpur at a cost of ₹198.49 lakh. MoU was signed in December 2011. The work is in progress. Expenditure till date is ₹100.00 lakh.

Construction of cement concrete (CC) road in Dantewada at a cost of ₹25.65 lakh. Expenditure till date is ₹10.26 lakh. MoU was signed in September 2012. It is expected to be completed in 2014-15.

Construction of Dharmashala at Dantewada at a cost of ₹25.87 lakh. Expenditure till date is ₹10.35 lakh. MoU was signed in September 2012. It is expected to be completed in 2014-15.

Farmers development scheme to provide fencing to farmers lands, digging bore wells and installation of pumps at a cost of ₹1,200.00 lakh has been taken up in 2013-14.

Provision of Drinking Water

In order to provide potable drinking water, NMDC has installed about 400 hand pumps/bore-wells and open wells in Chhattisgarh. In addition, regular repair and maintenance works are carried out. A good number of water storage tanks were also constructed by NMDC in different villages. Drinking water facility has been provided in 42 *ashrams* in Bastar region.

NMDC is taking up water and soil conservation works in association with the Forest Department of Chhattisgarh to improve the water table in the villages around the Bailadila Projects.

NMDC has partnered with the Government of Karnataka for providing drinking water facility in seven villages of Bangalore rural districts at a cost of 78.34 lakh. The total number of beneficiaries is 9,480. Work is expected to be completed in 2014-15. NMDC has taken up water supply works through pipeline in the villages around its Panna Project, in Madhya Pradesh (MP).

Skill Development for Sustainable Income Generation in Chhattisgarh

Traditional crafts training: The tribal youth have been imparted basic and advanced training in terracotta, sisal, bell metal and bamboo crafts besides regular tailoring classes which has helped them in income generation by selling the products made by them.

Kaushal Vikas Karyakram: A Kaushal Vikas Karyakram for the 8th pass tribal boys to improve their competitive capabilities is a continuous initiative in Bailadila Projects.

Employable skills in construction activities: Sixty-four tribal youth drawn from the villages around Nagarnar have been sponsored for acquiring employable skills relating to construction industry at the National Academy of Construction, Hyderabad.

Skill development training programme in bamboo, bell metal and tumba art: NMDC has launched Skill Development Programme in bamboo, bell metal and tumba art to provide livelihood generation training to 460 unemployed tribal youth in Bastar District in Chhattisgarh at a cost of ₹181.78 lakh. An amount of ₹31.60 lakh has been spent in 2013-14.

Plans are on the anvil to conduct another training programme for self-employment in Narayanpur District in Chhattisgarh at a total expenditure of ₹175.00 lakh. The details of the programme are being worked out. This is also to be implemented during the year of 2014-15.

NMDC has launched another livelihood skill training programme for 1,260 unemployed youth of Bastar during the year 2013-14. The cost of training programme is ₹59.92 lakh.

Livelihood-linked Learning Programmes

NMDC has implemented two Livelihood-linked Learning Diploma programmes in Air Conditioning & Refrigeration and Automobile Repairs & Service at Raipur by engaging a specialised NGO. All the expenditure on training, boarding and lodging facilities for 80 tribal students of Bastar region was borne by NMDC. All the trainees have completed their training and have been placed successfully.

Another livelihood-linked programme leading to employment in retail, business process outsource (BPO) and hospitality sectors was launched in partnership with Youth4Jobs Foundation at Hyderabad. Under this programme, 14 tribal youth from Bastar region were trained and placed during 2012-13

Integrated Village Development

NMDC has identified 58 tribal villages around its Bailadila Projects in south Bastar (Dantewada) District.

Developmental activities in the areas of education, agriculture, health care and awareness, income generation through acquisition of income-earning skills, formation of self-help groups (SHGs), lift irrigation and modern tools and techniques of cultivation have been undertaken in eight villages. Requisite tools and equipment are also provided to the beneficiaries. This has been extended to additional 10 villages around Kirandul Project, thereby bringing the total number of villages for integrated development to 18.

During the year 2013-14, the total area covered for vegetable cultivation is 19 acres and the total number of beneficiary tribal farmers is 130.

In order to bring scientific cultivation to the tribal areas, paddy seeds were distributed to 349 farmers and the total area covered is 189 acres. The income generated on this account has been to the tune of ₹20.50 lakh. Thus the average increase in production is 3.5 times.

The agriculture-related initiatives have brought out the innate skills of the tribals and their willingness to experiment with latest techniques and tools. Now, they are used to growing vegetables, paddy, maize, etc., using the learning they had during training sessions and also demonstrations. This has also helped them in increasing their income levels. The paddy yield prior to use of modern techniques was 2 quintals per acre and this has gone up to 35 quintals per acre.

Twelve water storage tanks were constructed and 19,226 mts. of PVC pipeline has been laid for distribution of water for irrigation purpose. Fourteen feeder tanks and pump houses have been constructed in five villages. A total of 35 pumps have been installed and 18 ponds were excavated benefiting six villages.

Environment Management

Over the years, NMDC has taken keen interest in tree plantation in and around all its project areas in Chhattisgarh and Karnataka towards a cleaner environment. Several thousand saplings are planted each year with a very good survival rate.

In addition, de-silting works have been sanctioned as part of environment protection measures in Bailadila and Donimalai. Effluent treatment plants are set up to reduce the adverse impact on environment and towards clean energy.

The volume of expenditure and the number of CSR projects funded are not the only barometers for measuring the effectiveness of CSR in NMDC, it is the contribution made in terms of improvement in Human Development Index (HDI) that NMDC does a reality check and an extract of its findings are as follows:

Reduction in Infant Mortality Rate (IMR) (IMR: number of deaths per 1,000 live births).

Reduced Infant Mortality Rate in Dantewada to a low of 58 against Chhattisgarh average of 73 by making available free treatment facilities to local tribals at project hospitals and medical camps.

IMR of Dantewada is better than 'Korba' which has the best HDI among the districts of Chhattisgarh.

Reduction in Maternal Mortality Rate

The use of maternity facilities at project hospitals by the tribals has increased. Although figures are not available, there has been marked improvement in maternal mortality rates (MMRs) which is analogous to use of maternity facilities at hospital and reduced IMRs is vouched by the tribals.

High Per Capita Income

High per capita income of ₹12,060 calculates to an Income Index Value of 0.396.

Infrastructural development works taken up by NMDC *viz.*, roads, bridges, culverts, etc., have contributed to the well-being of the locals by connecting them to the mainstream and providing them opportunities for higher income.

High Income Index Value of 0.396 was achieved against Chhattisgarh state average of 0.310.

Per capita income of Dantewada is next only to 'Korba' which has the best Income Index Value among the districts of Chhattisgarh.

Human Development Index

Substantial Improvement in HDI

Only the developed areas of Chhattisgarh *viz.*, Korba, Raipur, Rajnandgaon, Dhamtari, Durg and Bilaspur which are on the main line of road/rail connectivity have better HDI than Dantewada.

HDI of Dantewada has been improved and is higher than other comparable areas of Chhattisgarh

Human Development Indices

Dantewada	-	0.441
Raigarh	-	0.430
Surguja	-	0.418
Kanker	-	0.397
Koriya	-	0.391
Rajnandgaon	-	0.374
Kabirdham	-	0.326
Bastar	-	0.264

Intangible/Unquantifiable Effects of CSR

Not all benefits of CSR activities are tangible or quantifiable. The intangible/non-quantifiable benefits of CSR are much higher and NMDC is thriving on these.

Land acquisition for setting up the NDMC Iron and Steel Plant (NISP): The only successful land acquisition for a green field project in the last decade of Indian Corporate History facilitated mainly by sincere CSR efforts of NMDC over the years.

Paradigm Shift in CSR Initiatives in Current and Forthcoming Years

As in business strategies, so in CSR programmes, NMDC believes in change as a way to growth and improvement. Towards this end, NMDC has embarked on focused CSR initiatives in the area of education, health and sustainable income generation by partnering with specialist NGOs/VOs/service providers to improve the quality of life for the economically and socially disadvantaged people living around its projects. The proposed initiatives are likely to transform NMDC's CSR programme into a mission-oriented programme rather than a project-oriented one. The objective of the programme is directed towards achieving human development targets and building of lasting and self-sustaining social infrastructure.

Conclusion

NMDC Ltd has over the years silently contributed to the socio-economic development of the Bastar region, besides being a major contributor of revenue to the state and central governments by way of taxes and levies.

17

ANUPAM ANAND
RAJENDER SINGH SAJWAN

Making Corporate Social Responsibility Mandatory: Where are We Heading Towards?

An Empirical Study

Introduction

Essentially corporate social responsibility (CSR) is the deliberate inclusion of society's concern into corporate decisions. The principle of social responsibility revolves around sustainability and accountability. The scope of CSR is quite unlimited and can cover any number of activities related to community development, environment protection, animal welfare, labour security, human rights, disaster relief and so on. It is most productive when adopted to solve community's problems using company's expertise.

The term 'corporate social responsibility' is new but the concept has been in existence since the very concept of business came into being. It is variously referred to as corporate conscience, corporate citizenship or corporate sustainability in various forums.

Proponents argue that corporations increase long-term profits by operating with a CSR perspective, while critics argue that CSR distracts from business' economic role. Business dictionary defines CSR as "A company's sense of responsibility towards the community and environment (both ecological and social) in which it operates. Companies express this citizenship through their waste and pollution reduction processes, by contributing educational and social programmes and by earning adequate returns on the employed resources. In the 1800s, the US government could take away a firm's licence if it acted irresponsibly. Corporations were viewed as "creatures of the state" under the law. On 16 December 2008, the Danish parliament adopted a bill making it mandatory for the 1100 largest Danish companies, investors and state-owned companies to include CSR information in their financial reports. The reporting requirements became effective on 1 January 2009. The required information included:

- CSR/SRI (socially responsible investing) policies.
- How such policies are implemented in practice?
- Results and management expectations.

CSR/SRI is voluntary in Denmark, but if a company has no policy on this, it must state its positioning on CSR in financial reports.

In 2014, India became the world's first country to enact a mandatory minimum CSR spending law. Under Companies Act, 2013, any company having a net worth of 500 crore or more or a turnover of 1,000 crore or more or a net profit of ₹5 crore or more during any financial year shall ensure that the company spends, in every financial year, at least 2 per cent of the average net profits of the company made during the three immediately preceding financial years in pursuance of its CSR policy. The Companies (Corporate Social Responsibility Policy) Rules, 2014, came into effect from 1 April 2014. According to industry estimates, around 8,000 companies will fall into the ambit of the CSR provisions and this would translate into an estimated CSR spend of $1.95 billion to $2.44 billion. With higher economic growth and increase in company's profits, this mandatory spending will go up. But with the above development, a debate has started amongst the experts whether CSR should be mandatory and what shape it should take in the future. This has aroused interest and skepticism in equal measure.

CSR in Hindustan Copper Limited: A Glimpse

HCL: An Overview

Hindustan Copper Limited (HCL), a Mini Ratna Central Public Sector Undertaking, was incorporated in November 1967. It is the only integrated primary copper producer in the country holding all the operating mine leases in India. Its copper mines are spread over three well-known copper deposits in the country, *viz.*, Malanjkhand in Madhya Pradesh (MP), Khetri in Rajasthan and Ghatsila in Jharkhand.

The main activities of the company include mining of copper ore and production of refined copper as well as downstream products like continuous cast copper wire rod. HCL has four operating units, i.e., at Khetri (Rajasthan), Malanjkhand (MP), Ghatsila (Jharkhand) and Taloja (Maharashtra).

HCL CSR&S Policy Statement

For the company, CSR and sustainability (CSR&S) initiative is a planned set of activities, taking into consideration the company's capabilities, expectations of the communities living in and around the areas of its operation, targeted to have significant positive impact in the long term.

The objective of HCL is to play a catalytic role in the sustainable socio-economic development in the region, where the industry is located, attempting to create an enabling working environment for HCL, as well as income generation opportunities for the community, aiming at a sustainable regional development.

Methodology Adopted

Since 2007-08, HCL has been implementing various social developmental activities under CSR, based on the recommendations of the Base Line Survey Report conducted by M/s Informatics. Re-aligning its CSR approach as per the Department of Public Enterprises (DPE) guidelines in 2010, HCL engaged National Institute of Rural Development (NIRD), Hyderabad, which conducted a fresh Need Assessment Survey during 2010-11 and identified CSR projects within an area of 15–20 kms around the three mining units through Participatory Rural Appraisal (PRA) exercises among the communities. Earlier, as per the DPE guidelines, HCL has been allocating minimum 2 per cent of previous year net profit for CSR activities. In FY 2014-15, it has allocated budget as per the Companies Act, 2013. The Company's CSR activities were implemented at selected 19 villages located in the periphery of each of its three major units *viz.*, Indian Copper Complex (ICC) at Ghatsila (Jharkhand), Khetri Copper Complex (KCC) at Khetri (Rajasthan) and Malanjkhand Copper Project (MCP) at Malanjkhand (MP) through non-governmental organisations (NGOs).

HCL conducted a third party impact assessment study by an external agency, MDI, Gurgaon, during December 2011 to January 2012. The overall impact of the initiatives was assessed as positive. The livelihood promotion project of Systematic Rice Intensification (SRI), implemented in villages around Indian Copper Complex, Ghatsila, District-East Singhbhum in collaboration with JHARCRAFT, was considered a great success. Similarly, irrigation through sprinkler system and self-help group (SHG) for women empowerment implemented in villages around Khetri Copper Complex, District-Jhunjhunu in collaboration with Gramin Vikas Trust (GVT) was greatly appreciated by the community. The Third Party Evaluation of CSR&S activities for FY 2012-13 and FY 2013-14 was carried out by M/s Dexter Consultancy Private Limited, and were assessed as positive.

The CSR&S expenditure during the last three financial years and the major projects undertaken are given in Tables 17.1 and 17.2 respectively.

Table 17.1

Expenditure on CSR&S During Last Three Financial Years

Financial Year (FY)	*Budget (₹ crore)*	*Expenditure on CSR&S (₹ crore)*
2011-12	3.00	1.62
2012-13	7.11	5.13
2013-14	7.11	7.78

Table 17.2

Major Projects

Activities undertaken for CSR during the Current Year in HCL

Sl. No.	*Intervention*
1	Livelihood promotion
2	Women Empowerment
3	Conservation/ Recharge of groundwater
4	Drinking Water
5	Health and Sanitation
6	Animal Husbandry
7	Plantation and Agricultural Development
8	Skill/Vocational Training and Education
9	Rural Energy Supply
10	Infrastructure Projects

Highlights of the Projects Undertaken during Last Three Years

Livelihood promotion: Schemes included vermicompost production, SRI, systematic Wheat Intensification (SWI), dona pattal making, handloom weaving unit, tassar spinning unit, jute items, mushroom cultivation.

Women Empowerment: Integrated group activities like strengthening and capacity building of community-based organisations through SHG, exposure visits of progressive farmers/ women to different development institutions, etc.

Water (Conservation/Recharge of Groundwater and drinking Water): Programmes pertaining to water harvesting, deepening of existing ponds with inlet and outlets, construction of rainwater harvesting structure through Central Institute of Mining and Fuel Research (CIMFR), Dhanbad, supply of water filter at *anganwadi* centre for safe drinking water, construction of prototype safe water drinking (borewell with motor fitting), construction of new borewell with installation of hand pump were undertaken.

Health and Sanitation: Focal areas included construction/ support for household sanitation (in collaboration with State Sanitation Programme/Total Sanitation Programme), provisioning for Individual Toilets, health camps with use of existing mobile unit and eye/dental camps.

Plantation/Agriculture/Animal Husbandry: Plantation at Surda mines and river side area, turmeric and ginger cultivation and veterinary camps at KCC and MCP.

Skill/Vocational Training and Education: Reading Skill Improvement Programme for girl child, skill training at National Academy of Construction, Hyderabad, vocational training on plumbing and sanitation including skill certification.

Village Infrastructure/Rural Energy supply: Construction of community centre and installation of solar streetlights.

CSR: An Overview

The corporate world has embraced CSR, with companies like Shell adopting the 'people, profit, planet' approach to sustainable growth. Ever since, some companies have been disclosing social and environmental performance with financial results which was alien to Indian business.

Crises have encouraged the adoption of CSR. The CERES principles were adopted following the 1989 Exxon Valdez incident. Other examples include the lead paint used by toy maker Mattel, which required the recall of millions of toys and caused the company to initiate new risk management and quality control processes. Companies must integrate CSR in business models. The Netherlands has been building infrastructure to support sustainable projects like recapturing used materials from the waste stream to recycle them.

Companies all over the world are under increasing pressure to show that they are responsible citizens, with about 70 per cent of large companies in Europe and the Americas reporting on their CSR initiatives. Despite this, the very concept of CSR remains controversial and has attracted strong opinions on both sides from academics, executives, social activists and NGO officials. One point of controversy is whether companies should be legally required to report on their CSR activities. There already are mandatory CSR reporting requirements in several countries, including Sweden, Norway, the Netherlands, Denmark, France and Australia.

India is not new to corporate philanthropy. Our business houses and entrepreneurs have practised philanthropy for centuries. Whether through building temples or setting up *dharamshalas*, a social connect was always established by the wealthy i.e., by Tatas and Birlas. Sir Ratan Tata Trust, established in 1919, is one of India's oldest philanthropic organisations. Recently, the Azim Premji foundation received $2 billion from its founder, the single-largest philanthropic gift in India.

Mandatory CSR

Earlier, three countries stood out in terms of CSR regulations. The first was Denmark, the first western country to mandate CSR information in companies' annual financial reports. The second was Indonesia that has taken a global lead by passing a law requiring all public companies to issue CSR reports and, third, perhaps the biggest impetus for CSR reporting, came in January 2010, when the US' Securities Exchange Commission asked all US-based public companies to regularly disclose climate-related risks in their annual reports. The new Companies Act, 2013, that came into effect from 1 April 2014 replaced six-decade old legislation Companies Act 1956. CSR has been made mandatory under the new regulation.

Section 135 of the new Companies Act, 2013, states that every company having net worth of ₹500 crore or more, or turnover of ₹1,000 crore or more or a net profit of ₹5 crore or more during any financial year shall constitute a CSR committee of the board consisting of three or more directors, out of which at least one director shall be an independent director. Further, the CSR committee shall formulate and recommend to the board, a CSR policy which shall indicate the activities to be undertaken by the company, recommend the amount of expenditure to be incurred on the activities, and the board of every company shall ensure that the company spends, in every financial year, at least 2 per cent of the average net profits of the company made during the three immediately preceding financial years, in pursuance of its CSR policy. Provided further that if the company fails to spend such amount, the board shall, in its report made under clause (o) of sub-section (3) of section 134, specify the reasons for not spending the amount.

Schedule VII of the Companies Act, 2013, as amended on 27 February 2014 prescribes the following activities which may be included by companies in their CSR policies.

- Eradicating hunger, poverty and malnutrition, promoting preventive health care and sanitation and making available safe drinking water.
- Promotion of education, including special education and employment enhancing vocation skills especially among children, women, elderly and the differently abled and livelihood enhancement projects.
- Promoting gender equality, empowering women, setting up homes and hostels for women and orphans; setting up old age homes, day care centres and such other facilities for senior citizens; and measures for reducing inequalities faced by socially and economically backward groups.
- Ensuring environmental sustainability, ecological balance, protection of flora and fauna, animal welfare, agroforestry, conservation of natural resources and maintaining quality of soil, water and air.
- Protection of national heritage, art and culture including restoration of buildings and sites of historical importance and works of art; setting up public libraries; promotion and development of traditional arts and handicrafts.
- Measures for the benefit of armed forces veterans, war widows and their dependants.
- Training to promote rural sports, nationally recognised sports, Paralympic sports and Olympic sports.

- Contribution to the Prime Minister's National Relief Fund or any other fund set up by the central government for socio-economic development and relief and welfare of the scheduled castes (SCs), the scheduled tribes (STs), other backward classes (OBC), minorities and women.
- Contributions or funds provided to technology incubators located within academic institutions which are approved by the central government.
- Rural development projects.

The above has been further amended on 24 October 2014 as follows:

- In item (i), after the words "and sanitation," the words "including contribution to the Swach Bharat Kosh set-up by the Central Government for the promotion of sanitation" shall be inserted.
- In item (iv), after the words "and water," the words "including contribution to the Clean Ganga Fund set-up by the Central Government for rejuvenation of river Ganga" shall be inserted.

Ernst and Young, the audit and advisory company, estimates that the law would cover about 3,000 companies in India and about $2 billion of expenditures on CSR activities.

Views of Corporate India

Sidharth Birla, president of industry body Federation of Indian Chambers of Commerce and Industry (FICCI), said the businesses by and large welcome the new legislation. However, some issues continue to trouble that need to be addressed by the regulator. This is an evolutionary concept and will gradually evolve over a period of time. Industry is therefore anxious on the implementation of this new provision. Unless the Income Tax law is also changed simultaneously, this could lead to years of protracted litigation and disputes.

Corporate India did not wanted government intervention in voluntary social activity. For years, Indian companies have chosen CSR initiatives in areas where family passions lie. CSR initiatives were directed to national issues only recently. One of the biggest issues in the Companies Act, 2013, will be to monitor the compliance of companies with provisions of the law. Auditing firms can monitor this, providing more credibility to CSR activities.

Corporate India cannot be blamed for having diverse views on the idea of compulsorily investing in CSR. India's many leakages and red tape make it significantly difficult for any aid to reach intended targets. But the CSR model is designed towards creating a robust delivery model.

Some professionals in the CSR field felt that because of the reasons detailed below, the recent law is a really bad idea.

1. Many experts believe that Mandatory CSR is inherently contradictory. Their view is that CSR is fundamentally an inspirational exercise, and it is very difficult to legislate aspirations. Laws only set minimum standards; they do not create any impetus for positive action. For example, it would be difficult to mandate that companies 'build excellent schools.'

They attacked it on the basis of pragmatism as ineffective. According to them, it does not even discuss, let alone define, an enforcement mechanism or penalties for non-compliance. The Act would be an enforcement nightmare, exacerbating an already bad situation where many laws are poorly enforced in India and further undermining respect for law. Curiously, the proposal even includes a loophole. If the company fails to spend such amount, the board shall, in its report made under clause (o) of sub-section (3) of section 134, shall simply specify the reasons for not spending the amount.

2. A mandatory expenditure is a tax. The legislation essentially imposes an additional 2 per cent tax on companies covered by the bill. This is a back-door way to increase corporate taxes without a transparent political debate. The corporate tax rate in India is 32.45 per cent—already one of the highest, compared to a global average of 24.09 per cent according to KPMG. Increasing the corporate tax rate will certainly not lead to making India a more 'attractive investment destination.' Given the emphasis on

economic liberalisation and economic growth, it is unlikely that the Indian polity desires an increase in the corporate tax rate.

3. While India has experienced rapid economic growth, the benefits of this growth have not been distributed equitably. Inequality, which was already high, has increased even more. India's Gini coefficient, the official measure of income inequality, has gone up from 0.32 to 0.38 in the last two decades. For example, about 50 per cent of children in India are malnourished due to pervasive poverty. Trickle-down economics are not working. The act does not go far enough in reducing inequality and helping the disadvantaged. Without a coercive enforcement mechanism, it is unlikely that the law will result in widespread compliance. In other words, 'mandatory' CSR will remain largely voluntary.

4. Many activities that companies undertake are both profitable and good for society. Companies would undertake these activities regardless of the law, since they are profitable activities. Under the new law, they will be able to classify these activities as CSR with no real change in social welfare. Would a corporate training programme qualify as 'promotion of education'? Would making a profitable investment in an energy-efficient machine qualify as 'ensuring environmental sustainability,' even if the firm made that investment on purely financial grounds? This is what is often derisively referred to as 'green washing.' The proposed law would likely increase green washing with no real increase in green activities.

Even to the extent that there would be a real increase in socially beneficial activities, the spending would not go to democratically determined priorities, but rather to whatever the companies prefer to emphasise. It is the government's responsibility to determine high-priority needs of society and target public expenditures in these areas. With the recent law, the government is abdicating one of its primary functions. As per them, it would have been preferable for the government to impose a tax on companies and use the additional funds to provide public goods and reduce inequality in a systematic and democratic manner.

Businesses should address social problems through profitable business models rather than through mandatory CSR activities, said Michael E. Porter, professor at Harvard Business School and a leading expert on competitiveness strategy. Porter also said businesses, through their strategic thinking and value creation, will be critical to India's economic progress in the coming years. Mandatory CSR activities may not create an impact, as businesses may just look at allocating money for such activities rather than seeking optimal ways for addressing social issues, Porter said. The most powerful way a business can have an impact on society is with a business model in which social issues like nutrition and poverty can be addressed and societal needs met while creating profit, he said. "That's the only way to create impact. Meeting the needs and meeting those needs at a profit is crucial," he said. Businesses are facing increasing pressure to play a role in solving India's societal problems. Companies are being made to donate for social causes, but there is no evidence that it is creating any difference, he said. "Organisations just sprinkle money around, but there is no social impact and no solution arises from this approach," Porter said. Businesses will have to actively involve themselves in addressing the country's social and environmental problems, he said.

Experts says that companies constantly face a trade-off while making choices and will need to look at what not to do in order to be successful in their ventures. "We are constantly faced with trade-offs and these are the things that have pretty big impact on organisations. You need to have guiding principles to go through these trade-offs," said B.K. Sethuram, Vice President, Dow Coatings and Construction, Dow India. "Having clear values, clear strategy and set of goals and clear view of current reality is important to make trade-offs and choices.... You need to have constant eyes on what's happening around you, out there, because strategy is based on assumptions," he added.

Why Mandatory CSR is a Good Idea

Institutionalised philanthropy will not depend on individual preferences and a prescriptive model will be better than a voluntary one. CSR investments should be compulsory, through a structure that integrates social, financial and environmental goals. Education, health care, women's welfare, environment, energy and water conservation are areas where companies can play a role.

Apart from development, CSR can address social imbalances. Social divides are increasing and segments of society are seething with resentment. It is evident that the Naxalite movement had taken roots in large parts of the country. It makes sense to be more inclusive. It shall not be prudent to let time fly by as we debate the pros and cons of a statutory CSR spend. It is best to pull the trigger and get everyone fall in line by ensuring the spending of 2 per cent-of-net-profit target.

Conclusion

CSR is best represented by the contributions undertaken by companies to society through its business activities and its social investment. Companies especially in India need to know the fact that in the environment of modern economic development, the corporate sector can no longer function in isolation. Corporations must behave and function as responsible members of the society, just like any other individual. Companies desiring to build and sustain brand equity will do well to remember that discharging social commitments is essential to generating an image in the minds of the people.

At the end of the day, how well an organisation integrates community interests into its core values will be one of the determining factors that will spell its success or failure. A social investment strategy is a must for any progressive organisation's secure future.

Mandatory CSR is a very good move in favour of country and corporate leaders need to take up the responsibility of providing 2 per cent of their net profits and deploying across with the same rigor and review as they strategise and plan their business outcomes. Therefore, with regard to CSR, one can only borrow the tag line from a popular brand .... Just do it!

References

Dadrawala, N. (2013). *Mandatory CSR for Companies: Advantages and Repercussions*. Available at: *http://www.indiacsr.in/en/mandatory-csr-for-companies-advantages-and-repercussions-by-noshir-dadrawala/*(accessed on 24 October, 2014).

Goenka, H. (2012). Why it is a Good Idea to Mandate Corporate Social Responsibility. Available at: *http://www.indiacsr.in/en/why-it-is-a-good-idea-to-mandate-corporate-social responsibility -by-harsh-goenka/*(accessed on 24 October, 2014).

Karnani, A. (2013). *Stanford Social Innovation Review*, 20 May, 2013. Available at: *http://www.ssireview.org/blog/entry/mandatory_csr_in_india_a_bad_proposal?utm_source=Enews&utm_medium=email&utm_content=1&utm_campaign=From* (accessed on 23 October 2014).

Porter, M. (2013). *Mandatory CSR may not Create Impact*. Available at: *http://www.livemint.com/Politics/Nf56hLBZSiXJ2tw71SOUNN/Mandatory-CSR-may-not-create-impact-Michael-E-Porter.html (*accessed on 3 October 2014).

Vijayaraghavan, A. (2013). *Making CSR Mandatory in India*. Available at: *http://www.csrwire.com/*(accessed on 23 September 2014).

ANNEXURE

Best Practices in Corporate Social Responsibility*

I

Neyveli Lignite Corporation (NLC) Limited: CSR Initiatives

NLC a Navratna Public Sector Enterprise was incorporated in 1956, and over five decades, it has been a reliable source of power for Indian industries and households. The company produces energy at low cost by economically mining the lignite reserves. NLC aims at the production and supply of electricity at low cost with minimum impact on the environment. NLC through its environmentally responsible behaviour and economically driven operation has helped to eliminate poverty, simulate social and economic development in the region.

NLC's strategy for sustainability is evolved to achieve the most positive impacts on PEOPLE—for harmonious relationship, PLANET—for preservation of nature and PROFITS—for prosperity and growth. 'Simple Local Solutions' is the CSR Mantra. NLC through its environmentally responsible behaviour and economically driven operation has helped to eliminate poverty, simulate social and economic development in the region.

- *Vision*: To emerge as a leading mining and power company, continue to be a socially responsible company and strive for operational excellence in mining and exploration.

*: Compiled by Shulagna Sarkar and Punam Singh.

- *Mission*: To play an active role in the society and be sensitive to emerging environmental issues.
- *Approach*: A systematic and positive approach to enhance on all the three facets, *viz.*, profit, people and planet in such a manner to deliver value addition to all stakeholders.

NLC has been taking up various CSR projects/activities for the benefits of inhabitants of neighbouring villages right from its inception and had adopted a full-fledged CSR policy in the year 2009-10, for the welfare of the neighbouring society at large. Major thrust areas are: economic performance, social performance embracing education, peripheral development, employability and entrepreneurial development, employability of engineering and management students, health and environmental performance.

CSR Plan

Ideologically, energy from NLC can eliminate poverty, stimulate social benefits and economic development in an environmentally sustainable manner. The value systems of NLC have its base on the Principles of BEST Environmental Management and Business Governance. The CSR process in NLC is 'Methodologically' targeted at attaining the objectives of: (a) striking win-win solutions in all situations involving the interest of the stakeholders, (b) establishing a harmonious relationship of NLC with the local public (c) inclusive growth with appropriate value shared with all the stakeholders and (d) environment protection and up-gradation for the future.

To facilitate the accomplishment, the CSR activities/projects of NLC are 'Geographically' targeted towards the region of about 10 to 15 km radius surrounding the core activity zone. However, CSR projects/activities in locations beyond this limit will be considered on need basis. At the grass-roots level, CSR activities/projects are 'Individually' targeted to benefit the village in terms of creation of or value additions to the Common Resource Properties (CRP).

Impact of Innovative CSR Practices

Peripheral Development

The CSR of NLC is participatory in nature. As regards the Peripheral Development Scheme (PDS) works, rapid baseline survey is being conducted in the locality for the purpose of analysing the needs of the local society and prioritising the needs identified. Moreover, the local village/town *panchayats*, *panchayat* unions and district administration are consulted to dovetail/synergise their efforts in developing the region and to avoid duplication of works/projects. NLC has been making a regular annual fund allocation exclusively for PDS works.

This allocation has been enhanced from ₹1 crore to ₹2 crore per annum (100% increase) from March 2008. The neighbourhood covered within 10 km radius from the core project area is taken for development. To commemorate the occasion of Golden Jubilee of NLC in 2006, a special fund of ₹10 crore was sanctioned for PDS as a good will gesture and a token of expressing NLC's concern for the surrounding community of the society co-created in this manner since 1998.

Support Services to the Vulnerable

- NLC patronises 'Neyveli Health Promotion and Social Welfare Society' which serves by training the physically challenged, widows and destitute, and manufacturing and providing artificial limbs/calipers to the needy. Shravanee, a special school for the hearing impaired and a computer training institute is run by this society.
- NLC provides all assistance including infrastructure and grant for running the Sneha Opportunity School, a day care centre for the mentally disabled children which adopts a holistic approach to make them self-reliant and fit to earn their livelihood by training them in various crafts, arts, weaving, carpentry, gardening, screen-printing, doll making, etc. A garden restaurant Sneha Poushtika at Neyveli main bazar is patronised for the benefit of these children by gainfully employing the alumnus of this school.

Relief operations

- *Tsunami*: When the administration of the worst affected district Nagappatinam was finding it difficult to cope up with the situation after the Tsunami, NLC deputed a strong team of 193 members of various disciplines led by a general Manager to clear debris and dispose of the dead bodies. The team was very well equipped with lorries, jeeps, trench cutters, hydraulic shovels, water lorries and food material. NLC employees contributed 4 crore to the Tsunami relief fund.
- *Flood:* In times of heavy floods, food from NLC canteen is supplied to the victims and NLC schools provide temporary shelter to the needy.
- *Drought*: NLC supplied a billion liters of water by rail and road to Chennai City, 200 km away.

Education

NLC aids the comprehensive human development in the locality through its CSR activities. Enrolment in the schools in Neyveli Township is open to the students from the surrounding area also. Education to the children of local society is provided along with the wards of NLC employees/contract workers in the NLC's primary, middle and higher secondary schools in Neyveli Township. Although the schools under NLC management are getting aid from state government by way of salary grants, other requirements like land, buildings, quarters for teachers, certain special benefits like training, bonus, quarterly incentives, uniforms, shoes, house building advance, conveyance advance, conveyance expenses reimbursement, medical facilities including referral treatment at corporate hospitals at Chennai, promotions, etc., are given by NLC Ltd. from its funds. Besides, grant and infrastructure is being provided by NLC to other educational societies in Neyveli Township to run schools. 13 Aided Schools under NLCs' management and 11 other schools run by educational societies with NLC-provided infrastructures are functioning in Neyveli Township. The student's strength is 10,500 in NLC schools and over 25,000 in private schools.

At least, 40 per cent of them are from peripheral area; 80 per cent of students of NLC schools are from non-NLC employee background. NLC bus passes are provided to Neyveli Township school students at a very highly subsidised rate (₹15 per month). Annual Book Fair at Neyveli adds to the intellectual flair of the local population. Special bus service is arranged on the occasion of Annual Book Fair. NLC is sparing the services of the Education Department of NLC headed by its Secretary at the level of Dy. General Manager with Senior Manager/personnel and staff, and additional facilities like jeep, school buses for daily trips, permanent buses of Education Department for excursions, etc. Numbers of students from Neyveli Schools have reached great heights in their career/occupation.

Training/Employability

The training facilities at NLC's training complex is also utilised for conducting regular training programmes targeted on students and teachers of the locality. Students' guidance programme such as 'Jaithu Kattuvom' (meaning 'we will show success') and training to teachers at NLC training complex like 'Counseling Techniques', 'Total Quality Teaching,' 'Innovative Teaching Techniques,' etc., are the regular activities. NLC grooms hundreds of engineering/management whiz kids from across the country through its training facilities. At least, 1,000 students from various professional courses such as engineering, Master of Computer Applications (MCA), Master of Business Administration (MBA), Human Resource Management (HRM), etc., undergo in-plant training as well as carry out project works every year under guidance of NLC executives. Besides, a number of institutes come in batches for industrial visits for one or two days. If requested, they are provided with formal lecture by our executives, career guidance, mock interview sessions, etc., in NLC's training complex. Beneficiaries in 2009-10 are:

- focused guidance for students (23 programmes): 7,871,
- special training for teachers: 146,
- in-plant training: 3,615,
- project work guidance: 1,868,
- the total beneficiaries: 13,500.

Health

A fully equipped general hospital of 10 departments and 5 peripheral dispensaries including Ayurvedic dispensary with Yoga centre provides comprehensive health care to the residents of Neyveli and peripheral villages. A permanent Well Baby Clinic is functioning in NLC Hospital for the health of the children. Programmes since 2009-10 are:

- Specialised medical camps were conducted with free distribution of medicines in 7 villages (10 camps),
- Pulse Polio immunisation for 12,472 children.
- Filarial Control programme has been taken up in the entire Neyveli township,
- Diabetic Retinopathy Screening for 750 persons
- Extended support to elderly in association with the HelpAge India.

Sports and Culture

Hundred students showing promise in sports are offered free accommodation and education in NLC schools up to 12th standard with expert coaching under the Sports Control Board of NLC. NLC preserves heritage structures like temples, churches and mosques.

Access to Facilities of Neyveli Township

NLC provides subsidised transport services to provide common access to all the township facilities to the public, along with its employees. The service connects state highway roads and covers the residential area, NLC offices, schools/college, training complex, parks, places of worships, banks, *bazaar*, daily market, post offices, BSNL office/exchange, Tuesday, Thursday and Sunday Shan dies, LIC, court, police stations, government offices, etc., in Neyveli Township. Special bus service is being arranged on the occasion of local festivals and Neyveli Book Fair. NLC's bus service transports a minimum of 20,000 everyday, out of which at least 50 per cent are public.

Water Management

Surface and groundwater management: Water table management is vital at Neyveli region, given the proximity to the sea. In order to maintain a safe surface water balance and ensure proper hydrological balance in subterranean system, NLC is minimising the pumping from the confined aquifer by allowing a slight positive pressure upon the lignite seam and consciously substituting storm water for pumped water wherever possible. 'Artificial Recharge' of demarcated recharge area is carried out with rainwater run-off to compensate for the water drawn from the confined aquifer by NLC for safe mining and by others in the surroundings for various reasons. A series of check dams, percolation wells in percolation pond and recharge wells in deep water table·zone built by NLC ensures this. Check dams and recharge wells have been constructed at the cost of ₹32.63 lakh in two villages Nadiapattu and Maligampattu situated in the recharge area. Mine water is continuously supplied for irrigating 23,000 acres of lands in the surrounding villages.

A unique proactive study on infiltration measures into groundwater through injection wells with technical expertise from Germany has been taken up. Indian Institute of Technology (IIT), Chennai, is also an associate of NLC in the Artificial Recharge of Ground into the Neyveli deep-seated aquifer. Widespread rainwater harvesting contributes to the effectiveness of total water management. Eight thousand GPM of Mine-I sump water is being treated in the water treatment plant (cost of ₹1489.30 lakh) and supplied to the residents of NLC Township for drinking purpose from May 2005 onwards to reduce groundwater consumption; 15,000 GPM of treated storm water from Mine-II sump will soon be catering to the needs of power stations. Arrangements made in the Neyveli Township in harvesting the hefty storm water run-off from over 35 sq km, 12 check dams, 12 soak pits and one pond of 34,000 M3 capacity with 3 infiltration wells built at a total cost of ₹25 lakh aid in elevating the water table. This project benefits the nearby villagers who source the water for irrigation and domestic needs by means of bore wells and open wells. Five observation wells along the drains, two dug wells near pond area and one dug well at a downstream location of a drain are there to monitor subsurface water table.

Swachh Bharat Mission

Shri B. Surender Mohan, Chairman-cum-Managing Director (CMD), NLC, after launching the 'Swachh Bharat (clean India) Mission, has highlighted that this noble mission being the mass movement can be achieved by involving all employees of NLC and schools of peripheral villages, NLC schools, Jawahar Science College, township administration and general hospital and in general all employees of NLC. NLC has committed to constructing toilet blocks in the schools at an estimate of ₹1.3 crore (around Neyveli projects) under 'Swachh Vidyalay Abhiyan' Movement.

II

Bharat Petroleum Corporation Limited

Bharat Petroleum Corporation Limited (BPCL) is a fortune 500 oil refining, exploration and marketing PSU with Navratna status. Following nationalisation in 1976, BPCL changed its gears and embarked upon a rapid growth path. Turnover, profitability and financial reserves grew by leaps and bounds. Over the years, BPCL continues to meet the challenges of the rapidly changing environment, leading to changes in the marketing of products and services. In all these changes, only one factor has remained constant and has been the source of BPCL's strength and inspiration for any future innovations i.e., BPCL's People. The feeling of ownership has facilitated all employees to understand the complexity of the market and needs of the customers, and to respond to these needs with innovative initiatives and offerings.

CSR Vision

- We are a Model Corporate Entity with Social Responsibility.
- Build a Powerful Partnership with Society for 'Sustainable Development.'
- Building Sustainable Communities—to have a positive impact on the communities in which we operate.

Figure A-1

The CSR Building Blocks

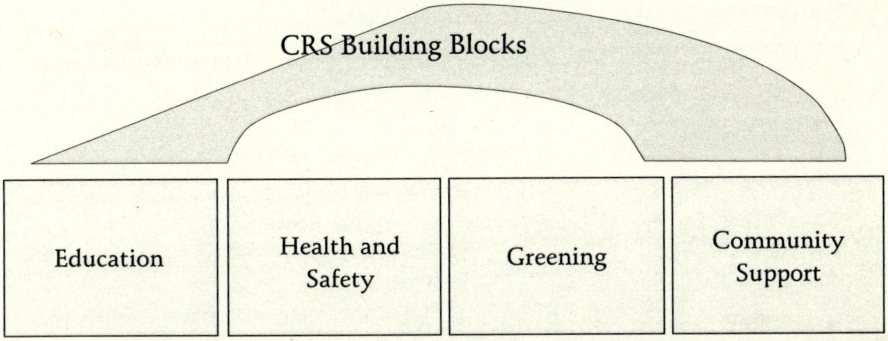

- Health and Safety—to ensure the health and safety of our workforce and communities.
- Environment—to minimise adverse impacts while taking steps to protect and enhance the natural environment.
- Employees—train tomorrow's leaders in teamwork skills and running socially responsible business.

Figure A-2

Implementation Model

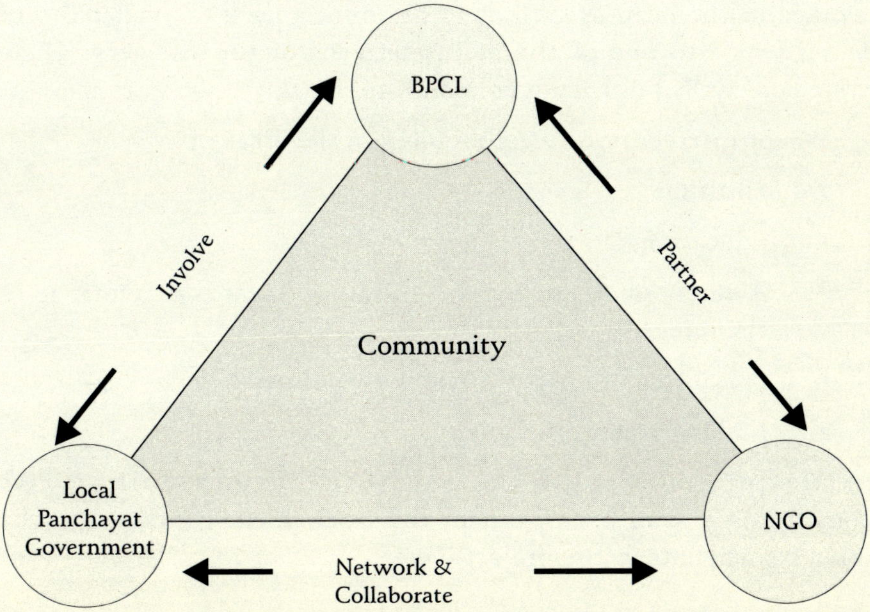

Thematic Areas of CSR: Health, Education, Infrastructure, Income Generation, Vocational Guidance, Livelihood and Environment Conservation

Case Study: Community Development at village 'Ramthenga,' Jajpur District, Orissa.

Objectives of the Project

- To help the village become socially conscious.
- To improve the general health of the villagers.
- To improve community participation.
- To help them become self-reliant.

This village is dominated by the tribal population—'Santhal Tribe.' Their socio-economic status was highly impoverished. Most of the villagers worked in the neighbouring mines. Due to prolonged and non-conducive working environment, they had developed severe respiratory/skin infections.

The children did not attend any school and the nutrition status of the children was very poor. There was also a severe problem of alcohol abuse amongst the men. The women were suppressed and worked in the farm as well as in the mines. Lack of availability of water was also one of the main concerns of the villagers. There were bore wells but they were non-functional.

Major interventions were required in the areas of:

- Health.
- Education.
- Awareness about health/sanitation/hazards of working in the mines.
- Precautions to prevent respiratory illness.
- Making water available.

Having understood the need of the community, BPCL constituted a team to implement the work in the community. The main participants in the project were:

- Villagers.
- Non-governmental organisation (NGO) partner—Research Analysis Consultants.
- BPCL LPG Team based in Bhuvaneshwar and Khurda headed by TM Khurda.
- BPCL HR Team at Kolkata headed by HR Chief and CSR co-ordinator.
- BPCL Corporate CSR Team headed by GM (Admin).

Strategy and Execution

A plethora of activities were undertaken in the village. However, depending upon the need at that particular time, the activities were phased out. The activity matrix developed was very strategically planned and executed.

Phase 1

A visit was made to the village by BPCL Kurda Team. There was lot of inhibition among the villagers to discuss and participate. However with repeated visits, the villagers began to open up.

Since there was a need to execute the project very professionally, the BPCL Khurda Team identified an NGO with its main office in Bhuvaneshwar. The NGO had extensive experience of having worked in the mentioned areas and implemented community development projects.

The NGO did a need assessment of the village with complete village participation. Assistance for providing health services and primary education emerged as one of the main needs.

Also what emerged from the need assessment was to enable the formation of self-help groups (SHGs). The general participation level among the villagers was very high.

Phase 2

BPCL supported the project through NGO Regional Activity Centre (RAC) by:

Providing the Services of a Doctor (from Neighbouring Area)

The homeopathic doctor would check the patients for free thrice in a week. Since the medicines were sweet, there was less resistance among the villagers and children to eat the same. Moreover for the problems that they were more succumbing to, like respiratory illness, skin infections, homeopathic medicines were much more effective.

Initiating a *Balwadi* (pre-primary) for Children within the Village

This put the children into the habit of attending school especially when their parents would go to work in the mine. The teacher for the village was identified from within the village. She was subsequently trained about innovative methods in teaching and needs of pre-primary children. She was also the main force in convincing the parents to put the children in main school after their pre-primary.

Phase 3

Once the basic trust level amongst the villagers was attained, then:

Awareness was Created about Precautions for Working in the Mines

Awareness was created amongst the villagers about the precautions they need to take while working in the mines nearby. The modes of communication were through street plays, skits during village festivals and drawing competitions for children. The homeopathic doctor played a vital role in creating this awareness. A lot of awareness was also created about alcohol abuse.

Deepening of Village Pond and Encouraging Fishery

There was a pond in the village, which had to be cleaned. With support from RAC, the villagers engaged in cleaning the pond and also dredging the same. With the help of Central Institute of Fresh Acqua Culture, Bhuvaneshwar, the villagers were trained of fishery management. It was a community pond, and the fishes caught were shared by the villagers. This activity was more favoured by villagers during monsoon, when there is ample of water in the pond.

Need for Formation of Self-help Groups (SHGs)

The fishery management activity established the need for the formation of SHGs—a group which would be trained in activities that can generate income. Meetings were held in the village for the formation of SHGs.

Repair and Maintenance of Bore Wells

Availability of water was an area of concern for the villagers. There were bore wells in the village, but they were non-functional. With the help of volunteers from the village, the bore wells were repaired and the villagers were also trained to maintain the same. Now there is ample water to sustain throughout the year.

Phase 4

The first batch of SHG was formed comprising of mainly women.

Formation of First SHG in the Village

The group comprised mainly of women. They had mutually agreed to learn stitching and appliqué work (a form of embroidery famous in eastern India). BPCL supported by way of providing teacher from the nearby village and also four sewing machines. Initially the women used to learn stitching work, etc., in the spare time they got after working in the mines.

Subsequently when the first batch finished the course, simultaneously a course was conducted on marketing the stitched products. A group of women were trained to market the stitched products in the local haats (local bazaar). The course included:

- Communication skills.
- Perceiving the market requirements.

- Quality of stitched products.
- Pricing the clothes stitched.
- Co-ordination within SHG.
- Roles and responsibilities.

The group slowly began to generate income through stitching and that made a breakthrough in the village. The women from the SHG were able to, though in very small way, substitute the family income which came mainly from mining and agriculture. More and more women began to learn stitching and discontinued the mining job.

Promoting Mushroom Cultivation

The NGO assisted the villagers through the SHG to initiate mushroom cultivation. The SHG would purchase mushroom sponge at ₹17 a packet from Orissa Institute of Agriculture and Technology, Bhuvaneshwar. Each packet of sponge would generate approximately 1.5 kg of mushroom. This mushroom when sold generates ₹80 from the ₹17 per packet. The villagers who had very poor health, especially the children were encouraged to include mushroom in their diet and the extra ones were sold in the local market. This activity also generated income for the SHG.

Phase 5

There were two well-functioning SHGs in the village. The success of the women's SHG was instrumental in the formation of the second group, which was a mixed group of men and women. The good work done by SHGs in this village was duly recognised by the Block Development Officer (BDO), who in turn has rewarded them with the 'Best SHG Award' in the district. As an incentive, they were given a sum of ₹2 lakh. With this, the SHG has bought a stone-cutting machine, which is in turn fetching the SHG ₹15,000 to 20,000 per month.

Where working in the mines, the villagers use to earn a meager amount of ₹50 per day, and were employed hardly for 10 to 12 days

bottlers combine concentrate or beverage bases as the case may be with sweetener (depending on the product), water or carbonated water to produce finished beverages. These finished beverages are packaged in authorised containers bearing the company's trademarks—such as cans, refillable glass bottles, non-refillable PET bottles and tetra packs, and are then sold to wholesalers or retailers. In India, additionally, the company also sells certain powdered beverage mixes such as Vitingo.

Sustainability: Their global Sustainability framework 'Me We World' was developed with a vision for the global company. It recognised the need for a directive focus on sustainability across the organisation, and the ability of local entities to use their knowledge of local conditions and priorities to further elaborate their sustainability objectives.

The company aspire to help people lead active, healthy lives by producing a wide variety of beverages; providing nutrition information and consumer health education; and supporting physical activity programmes.

Thematic Areas of CSR: health, environment, education, livelihood.

According to Atul Singh, President and CEO, Coca-Cola India,

> We at Coca-Cola are committed to refresh the lives of communities on an everyday, all-day basis. As part of the same strategy sustainable water management remains our top priority. We will continue to find innovative solutions in all areas of water management through our integrated 4 R strategy. Starting in 2000, over the last 7 years, we have taken the lead in improving water use efficiency by nearly 30 percent in our operations across India.

They identify partners primarily on the basis of the need of a specific project, understand their experience and expertise in specific fields; their ability to deal/engage with the community; their working relationships with other stakeholders such as the government at state/local or district level; their commitment to make the project sustainable; manage crisis as and when they arise, etc. They form a group comprising of experts from (within the system) departments such as technical, public affairs and communications, regional bottling units and the implementing agency; visit the project sites; interact with the community frequently; understand the progress and impact of the project. So far, the company's water initiatives have improved the lives of more than 140,000 Indians and made millions more aware of the crucial importance of water conservation. The company's aim is to return whatever water it has been drawing from the ground by 2009 through water conservation projects.

To this effect, they have taken the lead in improving water use efficiency by nearly 30 per cent in their operations across India and have returned 85 per cent of the total water that we have returned approximately 85 per cent of the water that they have drawn from the ground.

Their key activities include:

a) Rainwater Harvesting

Working alongside local NGOs and communities, Coca-Cola India has been installing rooftop rainwater harvesting (RWH) projects at all of its bottling plants in India besides other communities and has also been installing check dams, recharge shafts, etc., in rural areas. In Delhi alone, the existing RWH structures have the potential to harvest over 100 million liters of rainwater. Other key water sustainability projects that have run alongside the rainwater harvesting programmes are the construction of check dams.

b) Check dams

In Andhra Pradesh (AP), in partnership with the Hyderabad Urban Development Agency, local village committees and NGOs, Coca-Cola India has helped 16,000 villagers of Saroor Nayar in restoring existing 'check dam' water catchment areas. The project involved removing silt, recreating the pond and making the check dam with strengthened stone in order to stop the decline in groundwater levels. In Bangalore, Karnataka, the company recently dedicated a check dam at Kurubarakarena Halli.

With a capacity to harvest 1,080 kilo liters (10,80,000 litres) of rainwater per annum, this check dam with a catchment area of 2 sq km will benefit 3,000 people in the villages around. The system helps in recharging (improving water levels) of 30 bore wells around the check dam area.

c) Recharge Shafts

Also in Rajasthan, in its many arid open areas, the company has undertaken the construction of more than 100 recharge shafts where rainwater collects but does not percolate into the ground due to the nature of the soil.

Today, nearly 15,000 villagers are reaping the benefits of a steady or increasing water table without having the need to further deepen their existing bore wells.

The result of the water programmes is an increase in the amount of groundwater available to local residents. Studies of the Rajasthan State Groundwater Board, for example, show the 2005 Kaladera groundwater level was 21.85 metres below the ground, up from 22.23 metres in 2004.

d) Restoring Old Water Bodies

In Rajasthan, one of the driest states of India, Coca-Cola has aided the restoration of a series of ancient and historic *bawari*, or step well, water catchment systems.

The 400-year-old Sarai Bawari and Kala Hanuman ki Bawari, both located on the Delhi-Jaipur highway in Jaipur, both have been completed, and residents in the nearby communities are now able to draw drinking water from them.

The restoration project of Kale Hanuman ki Bawari witnessed active community involvement in the selection of the project site, design, source of supply for labour and material, implementation and creation of awareness for the project.

The actual restoration work included the removal of silt, rubble and algae, repairs to the infrastructure in the traditional 'Jaipuri' style, and re-opening of the facility for use.

Today, thousands of gallons of water flow into the step wells from underground pores or streams, and the storage and recharge capacity has reached more than 8 m liters of water.

More than 3,000 villagers near each of the *bawaris* now have a sustained source of clean water. In addition, both step wells are now fully restored heritage sites and tourist attractions.

Facilitating Water Access

In its aim to provide access to clean drinking for the underprivileged in and around Chennai and in northern parts of Tamil Nadu covering the districts of Thiruvannamalai, Vellore, Kanchipuram and Chengelpet, the company has launched Elixir of Life, which is a convergence of the vision of the two partners—Rotary International (RI) and Coca-Cola India, and is an extension of the Rotary's 'Schools into Smiles' project that envisages betterment of the quality of lives of students. Elixir of Life is enhancing the quality of life of students in these schools as unsafe water is the root cause for most of the health hazards and fatal diseases affecting young children, and in particular those from the underprivileged sections in the country.

These children are more susceptible to the water-borne diseases and the project is helping to realise one of their distant dreams by making clean drinking water available to them.

The unique aspect of the Elixir of Life project includes a pioneering initiative to maintain the system for the next 3 years. In addition to this, a comprehensive maintenance and servicing protocol has been prepared for ensuring the ongoing success of this project.

This includes fortnightly inspection, cleaning of raw and treated water tanks, rinsing and flushing of micron filters, apart from emergency breakdown and repair service.

When Rotary celebrated the 100th year during 2004-05, RI District 3230 planned to execute a landmark project to commemorate the centenary year. The team surveyed 1,200 schools in five northern districts of Tamil Nadu and selected the 100 worst schools.

Thereafter, these schools were adopted through different Rotary Clubs which reconstructed the schools and added new class rooms, compound walls, good toilet/water facilities, besides providing noon meal kitchens, desks and benches. The Schools into Smiles project is being continued this year by adding more schools but, at the same time, in order to improve the existing schools which have already been renovated, the Elixir of Life project has been launched with the support of Coca-Cola India so that every child gets access to potable water. As of now, the project has been completed in 20 schools impacting the lives of around 10,000 children.

Creating Awareness

Besides the quantitative results, Coca-Cola's water initiatives in India have ushered in a new wave of water consciousness. Millions of Indians are being made aware of the importance of water management through the company's marketing activities and other different fora in partnership with key institutions across the country: Seminars/Workshops; Jal Yatra; Jaidhara Karavan; Jal Bima Abhiyan; Jal Sanchay Abhiyan; Film on Water Conservation, Community Mobilisation Programme, India celebrations on Water Day and World Environment Day, key events with Assocham, CII, FICCI, Rotary, etc.

Playing the Role of a Mentor

The company would be happy to play the role of a mentor in setting up water conservation projects on which it has developed core expertise.

IV

Dr Reddy's Laboratories

At Dr Reddy's, the company strives every day to do what matters most to patients: accelerating access to affordable medicines and finding solutions for unmet needs.Their generics products bring expensive medicines within reach of patients by helping reduce the cost of therapy. Their portfolio consists of all dose forms in multiple therapeutic areas as well as biologic drugs.

CSR Overview

Our CSR initiatives are undertaken by Dr Reddy's Foundation (DRF) and Dr Reddy's Foundation for Health Education (DRFHE). In the reporting year, 106 Labs were operating across 18 states and 2 union territories in India, and DRF had helped create more than 280,000 of livelihoods up to that time. The total number of beneficiaries through DRFHE reached 118,288, with 3,568 programmes organised to date. The majority of these initiatives were carried out in India, although high-impact programmes have also been conducted abroad. Nine pillars of sustainable operations include: people; safety; quality; availability; environment; community; productivity; engineering excellence; and continuous improvement.

Thematic Areas: microfinance, education, health, environment, livelihood and social entrepreneurship

Dr Reddy's purpose is to help people lead healthier lives. This, combined with a clear commitment to their values and ethical practices forms the foundation of sustainability or CSR. Being a pharmaceutical company they are deeply sensitive to the needs of accessibility and affordability of medicines in developing and developed countries. They define their strategy and determine their impact. In an era when increasing demands are being made on health care services, generic medicines provide a major benefit to society by ensuring patient access to quality, safe and effective medicines while reducing the cost of health care. Generic medicines cost a fraction of the original products, which is good news for patients and means greater access for more people.

Their active pharmaceutical ingredients (API) and generics businesses focus on affordability by providing lower cost alternatives. They are addressing access needs by investing in innovation with emphasis on New Chemical Entity (NCE) Research and Differentiated Product Development that address unmet and poorly met medical needs.

Their product development effort with biosimilars is an example of innovation in making medicines affordable and accessible. In addition, the triple bottom line approach enables us to deliver sustained value with equal emphasis on people, planet and profits through environmentally friendly and socially responsible operations.

Their CSR efforts encompass sustainable business practices, safety, health and environment (SHE) systems, patient assistance programmes, community development, people practices and citizenship. Dr Reddy's was one of the earliest in establishing a zero liquid discharge facility to ensure 100 per cent effluent recycling. They have significant improvements in process development with growing emphasis on green chemistry. Energy saving initiatives and awareness communication on climate change are being accelerated in the company.

Programmes like Sparsh, betaCare and Sarathi deliver assistance to doctors, pharmacists and patients by improving access to medicines and patient education. These efforts complement our commitment to product responsibility addressing quality and safety of our products.

Dr Reddy's Execution Excellence Model (DREEM) has spawned focus action in lean manufacturing ("doing more with less") in both finished dosage and active pharmaceuticals. Organisational redesign of teams has increased throughput, provided higher quality, lower cost and integration of intellectual property in product development.

The community development efforts are evident in places where we live and work, with specific focus on manufacturing locations, implemented by CSR teams in each facility. With a combination of approaches, communities in the neighbourhood are being assisted to access health care, improved education opportunities and sustainable livelihoods. They encourage employee giving in association with Naandi foundation, an organisation co-founded by Dr Reddy's 6,000, employees contribute to The Power of Ten, the employee giving programme.

Employees are encouraged to volunteer by forming specific interest groups and also join volunteering programmes with Dr Reddy's Foundation. The Foundation, set-up by the company, demonstrates their citizenship work in the area of poverty alleviation, with specific emphasis on quality in education and sustainable livelihoods.

Over 100,000 sustainable livelihoods with Livelihood Advancement Business School (LABS) programme and outreach to over 34,000 children in government run schools through School Community Partnerships in Education (SCOPE). Sustainability involves almost every aspect of a company. This ranges from purpose and values, marketplace and innovation, workplace safety, people practices, environment management, human rights to community contribution.

Dr Reddy's embraces the principles of sustainability to drive responsibility and to create the capacity to re-invent, sustain and thrive through changing generations of technology, managers, shareholders and society. Dr Reddy's is the only Indian pharmaceutical company to publish a sustainability report and among the few Indian companies to do so. The report is prepared according to guidelines recommended by Global Reporting Initiatives.

V

Apollo Tyres Limited

Apollo Tyres Ltd. (ATL), with its corporate headquarters in Gurgaon, India, is in the business of manufacture and sale of tyres since its inception in 1972. Over the years, the company has grown manifold, establishing its footprint across the globe. The company offers a comprehensive product portfolio spread across passenger car, light truck, truck-bus, off highway and bicycle tyres, retreading material and retreaded tyres.

CSR Overview

ATL's CSR philosophy stems from its vision statement of "... continuously enhancing stakeholder value." The overall aim is to add value to the lives of stakeholders, through not-for-profit initiatives, with the objective of ensuring that all programmes and initiatives remain sustainable and relevant. The company believes that if undertaken in the right spirit and process, social initiatives can be a long-term risk mitigator and help manage key business and operational challenges. This framework clearly revolves around the principle of 3 I's i.e., Involve, Influence and Impact stakeholders. Apollo Tyres Foundation is the body which works dedicatedly towards achievement of these goals.

Apollo Tyres Ltd.: A Case Study of HIV-AIDS Programme

Background

Apollo started its fight against human immunodeficiency virus-acquired immuno deficiency syndrome (HIV-AIDS) in a project called Healthy Highways. The project was in partnership with Department of International Development (DFID) and started in Sanjay Gandhi Transport Nagar in the year 2000.

Today Apollo has a comprehensive programme on HIV-AIDS focusing on its employees, customers and supply chain. The programme focus is on building awareness and prevention aspect of the epidemic. The approach is to forge strategic tie-ups with organisations, which bring the technical skills and capacity building aspects into the partnership.

Apollo Tyres Health Care Centres

Apollo Tyres Health Care Centres are targeted interventions for truckers. The location for clinics is identified on the HIV prevalence, density of trucking and mobile population, and the current level of work being done by other organisations in the area.

Currently, the company has seven clinics running in north, west and south of India. All clinics are strategically located in transport nagars.

They are positioned as general health clinics to avoid stigma attached to HIV-AIDS, however the focus of the services provided is on HIV-AIDS.

The main components of the programme are:

- Behaviour Change Communication (BCC): The communication is directed at increasing awareness regarding the basics of HIV/AIDS. The communication adresses the modes of transmission, myths regarding HIV, connection between sexually transmitted diseases and HIV through one-to-one and one-to-group interactions.

- Peer Educators: Building an effective peer educator network is the most important link of the entire programme. The peer educators become imperative given the geographical spread of the transport nagars and the mobile nature of the population.
- Condom Promotion: Condom promotion takes place through free distribution as well as social marketing of condoms. These condoms are available at various outlets and strategic points within the transport nagars.

Sexually Transmitted Diseases and Infection Identification and Treatment

The outreach workers and the peer educators are trained in the identification of sexually transmitted diseases and infections. There is a strong referral system in place and patients are guided by the outreach workers and peer educators to the clinic.

The clinics provide treatment for sexually transmitted diseases and infections only. In case the doctor or the counsellors are not satisfied, they refer the patient for voluntary testing at the government hospitals. The pre-and post test counseling is available at all Apollo Tyres Health Care Centres.

Workplace Programme

In June 2006, a workplace sensitisation programme was rolled out in partnership with International Labour Organisation (ILO). The programme targets 7,500 employees across all locations of the company. The programme started with a half day sensitisation of the top management of Apollo. A steering committee was formed post the sensitisation of the top management. About 26 ambassadors were identified and trained as master trainers in a two day workshop and simultaneously a survey to gauge the existing knowledge in the company was undertaken.

So far over 5,000 employees have been covered under the programme. The next level of this programme is targeting contract workers.

Integration with Supply Chain

Extension of the HIV programme into the supply chain was a natural progression for ATL. Under this, Apollo has taken the prevention and awareness programme across its supply chain.

The model is similar to the employee engagement programme wherein a peer educator network is trained by Apollo's master trainers. The objective is to create a chain which has a multiplier effect in carrying the message on prevention forward.

Monitoring, Reporting and Evaluation

- The reporting system is standardised and a common format is available with all clinics to file a monthly report. The reports capture all details of BCC, STI (sexually transmitted infection) and counseling at the centres. The reports provide both quantitative and qualitative aspect.
- A monthly report is filed by the master trainers for the workplace programme as per ILO's format.
- A monthly report is received from supply chain partners and also by Apollo.
- A six monthly detailed report is filed to steering committee on the entire committee.
- A study on an annual basis is undertaken to gauge the impact of the programme across the target segments. The first one has been conducted in December 2007.